CONTENTS

INTRODUCTION

If you are finding healthy recipes with healthy cooking method then this book is for you. In this book, we have used an advanced and modern cooking gadget which is the combination of convection and air fryer cooking. Air fryer cooking is one of the healthy methods of cooking your food with less oil or no oil. If you are one of those people who like fried food but worried about extra calories then these cooking gadgets is for you. In this book, we have used a modern cooking appliance popularly known as Breville smart air fryer oven.

Breville smart air fryer oven is equipped with advanced cooking technology. It runs on super convection technology, in which two convection fans to maintain the inner airflow and evenly distribute the heat into the cooking chamber. This is perfect for air frying, roasting and dehydrating your food. Another smart element IQ technique makes your oven really smart. In this technique, 6 independent quartz heating elements are sense and adjust the power where needed most and give you precise and even cooking.

The book contains healthy and delicious recipes from different categories. In this book, you have to find the recipes from breakfast and brunch, poultry, meat, snack and appetizer, fish and seafood, vegetables, dehydrated and desserts. All the recipes written in this book are with their exact preparation and cooking time. The recipes in this book are easily understandable form with their exact nutritional values. I hope you have to enjoy all the recipes in this book. There are lots of books available in the market on this topic thanks for choosing my book.

CHAPTER 1: UNDERSTANDING BREVILLE SMART AIR FRYER OVEN

Breville Smart Air Fryer Oven

Breville smart air fryer oven is one of the smart cooking and air frying kitchen gadget. It looks like a convection oven and also air fry or cooks your food with the convection method. It circulates hot air around the food which is place into the cooking tray. The hot air circulation technology is the same as the convection method. The heating elements are seen at the top side of Brevelle smart air fryer oven with a power full blowing fan. The fan helps to circulate hot air flow equally into the oven; this will help to cook your food fast and evenly from all the sides. It fries your food into very less oil it takes a tablespoon or less than a tablespoon of oil to fry and crisp your food. If you want to fry a bowl of French fries your Brevelle smart air fryer oven just fry your fries within a tablespoon of oil. It makes your French fries nice crisp from outside and tenders from inside.

Breville smart air fryer oven not only used for air frying your food but also roast your favourite chicken, bakes cakes and cookies and also reheat your frozen foods. It comes with 13 smart cooking functions these functions are Toast, bagel, bake, roast, broil, pizza, cookies, reheat, warm, air fry, proof, dehydrate and slow cook. It runs with smart Element IQ system which finds the cold spot and automatically adjusts the temperature with sensing and digital PID temperature control, it gives you even and precise cooking. Smart ovens automatically adjust the wattages of its heating elements to gives you more cooking flexibility. The smart air fryer oven runs with dual-speed convection technology, using this technique you can cook your food faster by reducing the cooking time using convection. Smart air fryer oven comes with a display panel which shows all 11 smart functions as well as temperature and cooking time. The smart air fryer oven also equipped with integrated oven light, you can turn this light any time to see the cooking progress or it may automatically on after completion of the cooking cycle.

The smart air fryer oven is made up of most durable materials; the housing of the oven is made up of reinforced stainless steel. In the smart oven instead of the metal element quartz is used because quartz responds quickly compare to the metal element. It heats up your oven quickly and evenly, the inner parts of the smart oven are coated with non-stick coating which makes your daily cleaning process easier. To prevent any burn the rack of the oven are magnetic auto ejected racks when you open oven door the racks are automatically ejected halfway of the oven.

Breville smart oven air fryer has one of the versatile cooking appliances easily operated by anyone. It is more than the toaster oven it works as an air fryer, convectional cooking, slow cooking and also ability to dehydrate your food. If only air frying is not the main purpose then this is the right choice to your kitchen. This smart oven really works well for heating your food at the correct temperature due to convection technology. It is one of the expensive toaster ovens in this segment, if your priority is more function, good performance and versatility then Breville smart oven air fryer is the best choice for your family.

How to Prepare the Smart Oven Before First Use

It is necessary to run the smart oven empty for 20 minutes before first use to remove any protective substance stick on the elements. Before conducting test first place your oven into the well-ventilated area and follow the instructions given below

1.   First remove the promotional stickers, poly covers or any packaging materials from the oven.

2.   Remove the roasting pan, crumb tray, dehydrate or air fry basket, pizza pan, roasting pan, broiling rack, wire rack from poly packaging and wash them into warm water or soapy water using a soft cloth and dry them.

3.   Take a soft, damp sponge to wipe the interior of the oven and dry it thoroughly.

4.   Place your oven into well-ventilated area make sure minimum 4 to 6 inch of distance space on both the sides of the oven.

5.   Now insert the crumb tray into the oven at its position and plug the power cord into a power socket.

6.   The oven screen will illuminate with alert sound and functions menu will appear and the default indicator is on TOAST menu setting.

7.   Now rotate SELECT/CONFIRM dial until the pointer reaches on PIZZA settings.

8.   Press the START/STOP button. After pressing this button, the button backlight illuminated into red color and the oven digital display screen will be illuminated into orange color with sound alert.

9.   Then the display indicating PREHEATING by blinking. After completion of preheating the oven sound alerts and the timer automatically begin countdowns.

10.   After finishing the cooking cycle oven alert with sound then START/STOP backlight off and the oven LCD display goes white in color. This will indicate that the oven is now ready for first use.

Functions of Smart Oven Air Fryer

Breville smart air fryer oven comes with 13 smart cooking functions these functions are as follows

1.   **TOAST:** This function is used to toast your bread. It makes your bread brown and crisp from outside. It is also used for English muffins and frozen waffles.

2.   **BAGEL:** This function is used to make crisp from inside of your cut bagels and also lightly toast from outside. It also ideal for toasting thick sized specialty bread or crumpets.

3.   **BROIL:** Using this function you can broil poultry, thin cut of meats, fish, vegetable and sausages. It is also ideal for browning the top of the gratins, casseroles and desserts.

4.   **BAKE:** This function is used to bake your favorite cake, muffins and brownies.

5.   **ROAST:** Using this function you can roast your favorite poultry and meats. You can also roast a whole chicken; roasting makes your food tender and juicy from inside.

6.   **WARM:** This function helps to prevent bacterial growth. It maintains your oven temperature 160°C/70°C.

7. **PIZZA:** This function melts cheese toppings and also makes it brown from the top during the crisping pizza cuts.

8. **PROOF:** Using this function you can make the ideal environment for proofing dough's, rolls, bread and pizza.

9. **AIRFRY:** Using these functions you can make your food crispy and brown. This function is ideal for making French fries.

10. **REHEAT:** This function is ideal for reheat your frozen food or leftover foods without browning or drying the food.

11. **COOKIES:** This function is used to bake your favorite cookies and other baked treats.

12. **SLOW COOK:** This function is used to cook your food for a long time at low temperature.

13. **DEHYDRATE:** This function is used to dry out your food without heating or cooking them. It is ideal for dehydrating your favorite fruit slices.

Benefits of Smart Air Fryer Oven

Smart air fryer oven comes with various benefits some of them are as follows

- **Healthy and oil-free meals**

Smart air fryer oven runs on convection technology. It blows hot air into the cooking tray to cook your food quickly and evenly from all the sides. When you air fry your food into smart air fryer oven it takes a tablespoon or less than a tablespoon of oil. a bowl of French fries requires just a tablespoon of oil and makes your French fries crisp from outside and tender from inside. If you are one of those people who like fried food but worried about extra calories then this kitchen appliance is for you.

- **Offers 13 in 1 function**

Brevelle smart air fryer oven offers 13 functions in a single appliance these functions are Toast, Bagel, Broil, Bake, Roast, Warm, Pizza, Proof, Air Fry, Reheat, Cookies, Slow cook and dehydrate. All these are smart programs offers versatile cooking.

- **Safe to use**

The smart air fryer oven is one of the safest cooking appliances compare to a traditional one. While cooking your food the appliance is closed from all sides due to this there is no risk of splatter hot oil on your finger. This is one of the safe methods of frying compare to another traditional deep frying method. A close cooking method gives you a splatter-free cooking experience. The smart element IQ technology makes the appliance safer there are no chances to burn your food. Smart IQ automatically sense and adjust the element temperature as per the recipe needs.

- **Easy to clean**

Brevelle smart air fryer oven is made up of reinforced stainless steel and the inner body is coated with non-stick materials. All the inner accessories are dishwasher safe you can wash it within a dishwasher or also wash it with soapy water. The smart air fryer cooks your food into very less oil, less oil means less mess.

Care and Cleaning

1.   Before start, the cleaning process makes sure the power cord is removed from the power outlet. Allow your oven and accessories to cool down at room temperature before starting the cleaning process.

2.   Wipe out the oven body with the help of soft, damp sponge use cleanser over sponge during the cleaning process. While cleaning the glass door you can use glass cleaner and plastic scouring pad for cleaning. Do not use metal scouring pad it may scratch your oven surface.

3.   The inner body of the oven is made up of non-stick coating. Use a soft damp sponge to clean the interior of the oven. Apply cleanser over sponge do not apply it directly on oven body. You can also use a mild spray solution to avoid stains.

4.   Before cleaning elements make sure oven is cool down at room temperature then gently rub it with soft damp cloth or sponge.

5.   Cleaning crumb tray with the help of a soft, damp sponge. You can use a non-abrasive liquid cleanser. Apply cleanser on a sponge and clean the tray.

6.   To cleaning a baking tray soak it into the warm soapy water and wash it with the help of plastic scouring pad or soft sponge.

7.   Always remember that to dry all the accessories thoroughly before inserting it into the oven. Insert the crumb tray on its position before plugging the oven into its outlet. Now your oven is ready for next use.

CHAPTER 2: BREAKFAST RECIPES

Basil Tomato Frittata

Preparation Time: 10 minutes
Cooking Time: 35 minutes
Serve: 6
Ingredients:
- 12 eggs
- 1/2 cup cheddar cheese, grated
- 1 1/2 cups cherry tomatoes, cut in half
- 1/2 cup fresh basil, chopped
- 1 cup baby spinach, chopped
- 1/2 cup yogurt
- Pepper
- Salt

Directions:
1. Spray a baking dish with cooking spray and set aside.
2. Insert wire rack in rack position 6. Select bake, set temperature 390 F, timer for 35 minutes. Press start to preheat the oven.
3. In a large bowl, whisk eggs and yogurt.
4. Layer spinach, basil, tomatoes, and cheese in prepared baking dish. Pour egg mixture over spinach mixture. Season with pepper and salt.
5. Bake in the oven for 35 minutes.
6. Serve and enjoy.

Nutritional Value (Amount per Serving):
- Calories 188
- Fat 12.2 g
- Carbohydrates 4.2 g
- Sugar 3.4 g
- Protein 15.2 g
- Cholesterol 338 mg

Italian Breakfast Frittata

Preparation Time: 10 minutes
Cooking Time: 30 minutes
Serve: 4
Ingredients:
- 8 eggs
- 1 tbsp fresh parsley, chopped
- 3 tbsp parmesan cheese, grated
- 2 small zucchinis, chopped and cooked
- 1/2 cup pancetta, chopped and cooked
- Pepper
- Salt

Directions:
1. Spray a baking dish with cooking spray and set aside.
2. Insert wire rack in rack position 6. Select bake, set temperature 350 F, timer for 20 minutes. Press start to preheat the oven.
3. In a mixing bowl, whisk eggs with pepper and salt. Add parsley, cheese, zucchini, and pancetta and stir well.

4. Pour egg mixture into the prepared baking dish.
5. Bake frittata for 20 minutes.
6. Serve and enjoy.

Nutritional Value (Amount per Serving):
- Calories 327
- Fat 23.2 g
- Carbohydrates 3.5 g
- Sugar 1.7 g
- Protein 26 g
- Cholesterol 367 mg

Healthy Baked Omelette

Preparation Time: 10 minutes
Cooking Time: 45 minutes
Serve: 6
Ingredients:
- 8 eggs
- 1 cup bell pepper, chopped
- 1/2 cup onion, chopped
- 1/2 cup cheddar cheese, shredded
- 6 oz ham, diced and cooked
- 1 cup milk
- Pepper
- Salt

Directions:
1. Spray an 8-inch baking dish with cooking spray and set aside.
2. Insert wire rack in rack position 6. Select bake, set temperature 350 F, timer for 45 minutes. Press start to preheat the oven.
3. In a large bowl, whisk eggs with milk, pepper, and salt. Add remaining ingredients and stir well.
4. Pour egg mixture into the prepared baking dish.
5. Bake omelet for 45 minutes.
6. Slice and serve.

Nutritional Value (Amount per Serving):
- Calories 199
- Fat 12.3 g
- Carbohydrates 6.1 g
- Sugar 3.7 g
- Protein 16.1 g
- Cholesterol 248 mg

Easy Egg Casserole

Preparation Time: 10 minutes
Cooking Time: 55 minutes
Serve: 8
Ingredients:
- 8 eggs
- 1/2 tsp garlic powder
- 2 cups cheddar cheese, shredded
- 1 cup milk

- 24 oz frozen hash browns, thawed
- 1/2 onion, diced
- 1 red pepper, diced
- 4 bacon slices, diced
- 1/2 lb turkey breakfast sausage
- Pepper
- Salt

Directions:
1. Spray a 9*13-inch baking dish with cooking spray and set aside.
2. Insert wire rack in rack position 6. Select bake, set temperature 350 F, timer for 50 minutes. Press start to preheat the oven.
3. Cook breakfast sausage in a pan over medium heat until cooked through. Drain well and set aside.
4. Cook bacon in the same pan. Drain well and set aside.
5. In a mixing bowl, whisk eggs with milk, garlic powder, pepper, and salt. Add 1 cup cheese, hash browns, onion, red pepper, bacon, and sausage and stir well.
6. Pour the entire egg mixture into the baking dish. Sprinkle remaining cheese on top.
7. Cover dish with foil and bake for 50 minutes. Remove foil and bake for 5 minutes more.
8. Serve and enjoy.

Nutritional Value (Amount per Serving):
- Calories 479
- Fat 29.1 g
- Carbohydrates 34.1 g
- Sugar 4.2 g
- Protein 20.2 g
- Cholesterol 207 mg

Flavor Packed Breakfast Casserole

Preparation Time: 10 minutes
Cooking Time: 40 minutes
Serve: 8
Ingredients:
- 12 eggs
- 1/2 cup cheddar cheese, shredded
- 1 tsp garlic powder
- 1 cup milk
- 1/4 cup onion, diced
- 2 bell pepper, cubed
- 4 small potatoes, cubed
- 2 cups sausage, cooked and diced
- Pepper
- Salt

Directions:
1. Spray a 9*13-inch baking dish with cooking spray and set aside.
2. Insert wire rack in rack position 6. Select bake, set temperature 350 F, timer for 40 minutes. Press start to preheat the oven.
3. In a large bowl, whisk eggs with milk, garlic powder, pepper, and salt.

4. Add sausage, bell peppers, and potatoes into the baking dish. Pour egg mixture over sausage mixture. Sprinkle with cheese and onion.
5. Bake casserole for 40 minutes.
6. Slice and serve.

Nutritional Value (Amount per Serving):
- Calories 232
- Fat 11.6 g
- Carbohydrates 18.3 g
- Sugar 4.6 g
- Protein 14.2 g
- Cholesterol 261 mg

Vegetable Sausage Egg Bake

Preparation Time: 10 minutes
Cooking Time: 35 minutes
Serve: 4
Ingredients:
- 10 eggs
- 1 cup spinach, diced
- 1 cup onion, diced
- 1 cup pepper, diced
- 1 lb sausage, cut into 1/2-inch pieces
- 1 tsp garlic powder
- 1/2 cup almond milk
- Pepper
- Salt

Directions:
1. Spray an 8*8-inch baking dish with cooking spray and set aside.
2. Insert wire rack in rack position 6. Select bake, set temperature 390 F, timer for 35 minutes. Press start to preheat the oven.
3. In a bowl, whisk eggs with milk and spices. Add vegetables and sausage and stir to combine.
4. Pour egg mixture into the prepared baking dish. Bake for 35 minutes.
5. Slice and serve.

Nutritional Value (Amount per Serving):
- Calories 653
- Fat 50.6 g
- Carbohydrates 12.6 g
- Sugar 3.3 g
- Protein 38.3 g
- Cholesterol 504 mg

Ham Egg Brunch Bake

Preparation Time: 10 minutes
Cooking Time: 60 minutes
Serve: 6
Ingredients:
- 4 eggs
- 20 oz hash browns
- 1 onion, chopped
- 2 cups ham, chopped
- 3 cups cheddar cheese, shredded
- 1 cup sour cream
- 1 cup milk
- Pepper

- Salt

Directions:

1. Spray a 9*13-inch baking dish with cooking spray and set aside.
2. Insert wire rack in rack position 6. Select bake, set temperature 375 F, timer for 35 minutes. Press start to preheat the oven.
3. In a large mixing bowl, whisk eggs with sour cream, milk, pepper, and salt. Add 2 cups cheese and stir well.
4. Cook onion and ham in a medium pan until onion is softened.
5. Add hash brown to the pan and cook for 5 minutes.
6. Add onion ham mixture into the egg mixture and mix well.
7. Pour egg mixture into the prepared baking dish. Cover dish with foil and bake for 35 minutes.
8. Remove foil and bake for 25 minutes more.
9. Slice and serve.

Nutritional Value (Amount per Serving):

- Calories 703
- Fat 46.2 g
- Carbohydrates 41.2 g
- Sugar 4.6 g
- Protein 30.8 g
- Cholesterol 214 mg

Cheese Broccoli Bake

Preparation Time: 10 minutes
Cooking Time: 30 minutes
Serve: 12

Ingredients:

- 12 eggs
- 1 1/2 cup cheddar cheese, shredded
- 2 cups broccoli florets, chopped
- 1 small onion, diced
- 1 cup milk
- Pepper
- Salt

Directions:

1. Spray a 9*13-inch baking dish with cooking spray and set aside.
2. Insert wire rack in rack position 6. Select bake, set temperature 390 F, timer for 30 minutes. Press start to preheat the oven.
3. In a large bowl, whisk eggs with milk, pepper, and salt. Add cheese, broccoli, and onion and stir well.
4. Pour egg mixture into the prepared baking dish and bake for 30 minutes.
5. Slice and serve.

Nutritional Value (Amount per Serving):

- Calories 138
- Fat 9.5 g
- Carbohydrates 3.1 g
- Sugar 1.8 g
- Protein 10.2 g
- Cholesterol 180 mg

Cheese Ham Omelette

Preparation Time: 10 minutes
Cooking Time: 25 minutes
Serve: 6

Ingredients:

- 8 eggs
- 1 cup ham, chopped
- 1 cup cheddar cheese, shredded
- 1/3 cup milk
- Pepper
- Salt

Directions:

1. Spray a 9*9-inch baking dish with cooking spray and set aside.
2. Insert wire rack in rack position 6. Select bake, set temperature 390 F, timer for 25 minutes. Press start to preheat the oven.
3. In a large bowl, whisk eggs with milk, pepper, and salt. Stir in ham and cheese.
4. Pour egg mixture into the prepared baking dish and bake for 25 minutes.
5. Slice and serve.

Nutritional Value (Amount per Serving):

- Calories 203
- Fat 14.3 g
- Carbohydrates 2.2 g
- Sugar 1.2 g
- Protein 16.3 g
- Cholesterol 252 mg

Sweet Potato Frittata

Preparation Time: 10 minutes
Cooking Time: 30 minutes
Serve: 6

Ingredients:

- 10 eggs
- 1/4 cup goat cheese, crumbled
- 1 onion, diced
- 1 sweet potato, diced
- 2 cups broccoli, chopped
- 1 tbsp olive oil
- Pepper
- Salt

Directions:

1. Spray a baking dish with cooking spray and set aside.
2. Insert wire rack in rack position 6. Select bake, set temperature 390 F, timer for 20 minutes. Press start to preheat the oven.
3. Heat oil in a pan over medium heat. Add sweet potato, broccoli, and onion and cook for 10-15 minutes or until sweet potato is tender.
4. In a large mixing bowl, whisk eggs with pepper and salt.
5. Transfer cooked vegetables into the baking dish. Pour egg mixture over vegetables. Sprinkle with goat cheese and bake for 15-20 minutes.
6. Slice and serve.

Nutritional Value (Amount per Serving):

- Calories 201
- Fat 13 g
- Carbohydrates 8.4 g
- Sugar 3.3 g
- Protein 13.5 g
- Cholesterol 282 mg

Squash Oat Muffins

Preparation Time: 10 minutes
Cooking Time: 20 minutes
Serve: 12
Ingredients:
- 2 eggs
- 1 tbsp pumpkin pie spice
- 2 tsp baking powder
- 1 cup oats
- 1 cup all-purpose flour
- 1 tsp vanilla
- 1/3 cup olive oil
- 1/2 cup yogurt
- 1/2 cup maple syrup
- 1 cup butternut squash puree
- 1/2 tsp sea salt

Directions:
1. Line 12 cups muffin pan with cupcake liners.
2. Insert wire rack in rack position 6. Select bake, set temperature 390 F, timer for 20 minutes. Press start to preheat the oven.
3. In a large bowl, whisk together eggs, vanilla, oil, yogurt, maple syrup, and squash puree.
4. In a small bowl, mix together flour, pumpkin pie spice, baking powder, oats, and salt.
5. Add flour mixture into the wet mixture and stir to combine.
6. Scoop the batter to the prepared muffin pan and bake for 20 minutes.
7. Serve and enjoy.

Nutritional Value (Amount per Serving):
- Calories 171
- Fat 7.1 g
- Carbohydrates 23.8 g
- Sugar 9.4 g
- Protein 3.6 g
- Cholesterol 28 mg

Hashbrown Casserole

Preparation Time: 10 minutes
Cooking Time: 60 minutes
Serve: 10
Ingredients:
- 32 oz frozen hash browns with onions and peppers
- 2 cups cheddar cheese, shredded
- 15 eggs, lightly beaten
- 5 bacon slices, cooked and chopped
- Pepper
- Salt

Directions:

1. Spray 9*13-inch casserole dish with cooking spray and set aside.
2. Insert wire rack in rack position 6. Select bake, set temperature 350 F, timer for 60 minutes. Press start to preheat the oven.
3. In a large mixing bowl, whisk eggs with pepper and salt. Add 1 cup cheese, bacon, and hash browns and mix well.
4. Pour egg mixture into the prepared casserole dish and sprinkle with remaining cheese.
5. Bake for 60 minutes or until the top is golden brown.
6. Slice and serve.

Nutritional Value (Amount per Serving):
- Calories 403
- Fat 27.1 g
- Carbohydrates 23.6 g
- Sugar 0.6 g
- Protein 19 g
- Cholesterol 280 mg

Mexican Breakfast Frittata

Preparation Time: 10 minutes
Cooking Time: 25 minutes
Serve: 6
Ingredients:
- 8 eggs, scrambled
- 1/2 cup cheddar cheese, grated
- 3 scallions, chopped
- 1/3 lb tomatoes, sliced
- 1 green pepper, chopped
- 1/2 cup salsa
- 2 tsp taco seasoning
- 1 tbsp olive oil
- 1/2 lb ground beef
- Pepper
- Salt

Directions:
1. Spray a baking dish with cooking spray and set aside.
2. Insert wire rack in rack position 6. Select bake, set temperature 375 F, timer for 25 minutes. Press start to preheat the oven.
3. Heat oil in a pan over medium heat. Add ground beef in a pan and cook until brown.
4. Add salsa, taco seasoning, scallions, and green pepper into the pan and stir well.
5. Transfer meat into the prepared baking dish. Arrange tomato slices on top of meat mixture.
6. In a bowl, whisk eggs with cheese, pepper, and salt. Pour egg mixture over meat mixture and bake for 25 minutes.
7. Serve and enjoy.

Nutritional Value (Amount per Serving):
- Calories 231
- Fat 13.9 g
- Carbohydrates 4.5 g
- Sugar 2.5 g
- Protein 22.2 g

- Cholesterol 262 mg

Perfect Brunch Baked Eggs

Preparation Time: 10 minutes
Cooking Time: 20 minutes
Serve: 4

Ingredients:
- 4 eggs
- 1/2 cup parmesan cheese, grated
- 2 cups marinara sauce
- Pepper
- Salt

Directions:
1. Spray 4 shallow baking dishes with cooking spray and set aside.
2. Insert wire rack in rack position 6. Select bake, set temperature 390 F, timer for 20 minutes. Press start to preheat the oven.
3. Divide marinara sauce into four baking dishes.
4. Break the egg into each baking dish. Sprinkle cheese, pepper, and salt on top of eggs and bake for 20 minutes.
5. Serve and enjoy.

Nutritional Value (Amount per Serving):
- Calories 208
- Fat 10.1 g
- Carbohydrates 18 g
- Sugar 11.4 g
- Protein 11.4 g
- Cholesterol 174 mg

Green Chile Cheese Egg Casserole

Preparation Time: 10 minutes
Cooking Time: 40 minutes
Serve: 12

Ingredients:
- 12 eggs
- 8 oz can green chilies, diced
- 6 tbsp butter, melted
- 3 cups cheddar cheese, shredded
- 2 cups curd cottage cheese
- 1 tsp baking powder
- 1/2 cup flour
- Pepper
- Salt

Directions:
1. Spray a 9*13-inch baking dish with cooking spray and set aside.
2. Insert wire rack in rack position 6. Select bake, set temperature 350 F, timer for 40 minutes. Press start to preheat the oven.
3. In a large mixing bowl, beat eggs until fluffy. Add baking powder, flour, pepper, and salt.
4. Stir in green chilies, butter, cheddar cheese, and cottage cheese.
5. Pour egg mixture into the prepared baking dish and bake for 40 minutes.
6. Slice and serve.

Nutritional Value (Amount per Serving):
- Calories 284
- Fat 21.3 g
- Carbohydrates 7.4 g
- Sugar 1.8 g
- Protein 17 g
- Cholesterol 217 mg

Kale Zucchini Bake

Preparation Time: 10 minutes
Cooking Time: 30 minutes
Serve: 4

Ingredients:
- 6 eggs
- 1 cup cheddar cheese, shredded
- 1 cup kale, chopped
- 1 onion, chopped
- 1 cup zucchini, shredded and squeezed out all liquid
- 1/2 tsp dill
- 1/2 tsp oregano
- 1/2 tsp basil
- 1/2 tsp baking powder
- 1/2 cup almond flour
- 1/2 cup milk
- 1/4 tsp salt

Directions:
1. Spray a 9*9-inch baking dish with cooking spray and set aside.
2. Insert wire rack in rack position 6. Select bake, set temperature 375 F, timer for 35 minutes. Press start to preheat the oven.
3. In a large mixing bowl, whisk eggs with milk. Add remaining ingredients and stir until well combined.
4. Pour egg mixture into the prepared baking dish and bake for 35 minutes.
5. Slice and serve.

Nutritional Value (Amount per Serving):
- Calories 333
- Fat 23.3 g
- Carbohydrates 11.1 g
- Sugar 3.7 g
- Protein 20.5 g
- Cholesterol 278 mg

Cheesy Breakfast Casserole

Preparation Time: 10 minutes
Cooking Time: 60 minutes
Serve: 6

Ingredients:
- 4 eggs
- 2 cups of milk
- 1 1/2 cup cheddar cheese, shredded
- 5 bread slices, cut into cubes
- Pepper
- Salt

Directions:

1.   Spray 1 1/2-quart baking dish with cooking spray and set aside.
2.   Layer bread cubes and shredded cheese alternately in prepared baking dish.
3.   In a bowl, whisk eggs with milk, pepper, and salt and pour over bread mixture. Place a baking dish in the refrigerator overnight.
4.   Insert wire rack in rack position 6. Select bake, set temperature 350 F, timer for 60 minutes. Press start to preheat the oven.
5.   Remove baking dish from the oven. Bake for 60 minutes.
6.   Slice and serve.

Nutritional Value (Amount per Serving):
- Calories 216
- Fat 14.2 g
- Carbohydrates 8.4 g
- Sugar 4.4 g
- Protein 14 g
- Cholesterol 145 mg

Easy Hash Brown Breakfast Bake

Preparation Time: 10 minutes
Cooking Time: 45 minutes
Serve: 8
Ingredients:
- 8 eggs
- 30 oz frozen cubed hash brown potatoes, thawed
- 2 cups of milk
- 1 cup cheddar cheese, shredded
- 1 lb bacon slices, cooked and crumbled
- Pepper
- Salt

Directions:
1.   Spray a 13*9-inch baking dish with cooking spray and set aside.
2.   Insert wire rack in rack position 6. Select bake, set temperature 350 F, timer for 45 minutes. Press start to preheat the oven.
3.   Add hash brown, bacon, and 1/2 cup cheese into the prepared baking dish.
4.   In a bowl, whisk eggs with milk, pepper, and salt and pour over hash brown mixture. Sprinkle with remaining cheese and bake for 45 minutes.
5.   Slice and serve.

Nutritional Value (Amount per Serving):
- Calories 442
- Fat 24.5 g
- Carbohydrates 40.9 g
- Sugar 4.7 g
- Protein 14.9 g
- Cholesterol 185 mg

Mexican Chiles Breakfast Bake

Preparation Time: 10 minutes
Cooking Time: 40 minutes
Serve: 15
Ingredients:

- 6 eggs
- 20 oz hash brown potatoes, shredded
- 1/4 tsp ground cumin
- 1/2 cup milk
- 2 cups Mexican cheese, shredded
- 1 lb pork sausage, cooked and crumbled
- 1 cup chunky salsa
- 28 oz can whole green chiles
- Pepper
- Salt

Directions:
1.   Spray a 13*9-inch baking dish with cooking spray and set aside.
2.   Insert wire rack in rack position 6. Select bake, set temperature 350 F, timer for 40 minutes. Press start to preheat the oven.
3.   Layer half potatoes, chilis, salsa, half sausage, and half cheese into the prepared baking dish. Cover with remaining sausage, potatoes, and cheese.
4.   In a bowl, whisk eggs with milk, cumin, pepper, and salt and pour over potato mixture and bake for 40 minutes.
5.   Serve and enjoy.

Nutritional Value (Amount per Serving):
- Calories 300
- Fat 19.6 g
- Carbohydrates 103 g
- Sugar 1.6 g
- Protein 12.6 g
- Cholesterol 103 mg

Delicious Amish Baked Oatmeal

Preparation Time: 10 minutes
Cooking Time: 30 minutes
Serve: 8
Ingredients:
- 2 eggs
- 3 cups rolled oats
- 1 tsp cinnamon
- 1 1/2 tsp vanilla
- 1 1/2 tsp baking powder
- 1/4 cup butter, melted
- 1/2 cup maple syrup
- 1 1/2 cups milk
- 1/4 tsp salt

Directions:
1.   Spray an 8*8-inch baking dish with cooking spray and set aside.
2.   Insert wire rack in rack position 6. Select bake, set temperature 350 F, timer for 30 minutes. Press start to preheat the oven.
3.   In a large bowl, whisk eggs with milk, cinnamon, vanilla, baking powder, butter, maple syrup, and salt. Add oats and mix well.
4.   Pour mixture into the baking dish and bake for 30 minutes.
5.   Slice and serve with warm milk and fruits.

Nutritional Value (Amount per Serving):

- Calories 261
- Fat 9.8 g
- Carbohydrates 37.1 g
- Sugar 14.3 g
- Protein 7 g
- Cholesterol 60 mg

Chewy Breakfast Brownies

Preparation Time: 10 minutes
Cooking Time: 30 minutes
Serve: 9
Ingredients:
- 1 egg
- 2 tbsp cocoa powder
- 1 tsp vanilla
- 1 1/4 cup milk
- 1/2 cup applesauce
- 1/4 cup brown sugar
- 2 1/4 cup quick oats

Directions:
1. Spray a 9*9-inch baking dish with cooking spray and set aside.
2. Insert wire rack in rack position 6. Select bake, set temperature 350 F, timer for 30 minutes. Press start to preheat the oven.
3. In a large bowl, mix together brown sugar, cocoa powder, and oats.
4. Add wet ingredients and mix until well combined.
5. Pour mixture into the baking dish and spread well.
6. Cover baking dish with foil and bake for 15 minutes. Remove cover after 15 minutes and bake for 15 minutes more.
7. Serve and enjoy.

Nutritional Value (Amount per Serving):
- Calories 127
- Fat 2.7 g
- Carbohydrates 21.8 g
- Sugar 7.1 g
- Protein 4.7 g
- Cholesterol 21 mg

Peach Banana Baked Oatmeal

Preparation Time: 10 minutes
Cooking Time: 35 minutes
Serve: 5
Ingredients:
- 2 eggs
- 1 tsp vanilla
- 1 1/2 cups milk
- 1/2 tsp cinnamon
- 3/4 tsp baking powder
- 1/4 cup ground flax seed
- 2 1/2 cups steel-cut oats
- 2 bananas, sliced
- 1 peach, sliced
- 1/2 tsp salt

Directions:

1. Spray an 8*8-inch baking dish with cooking spray and set aside.
2. Insert wire rack in rack position 6. Select bake, set temperature 350 F, timer for 35 minutes. Press start to preheat the oven.
3. Add all ingredients except one banana into the mixing bowl and mix until well combined.
4. Pour mixture into the baking dish and spread well. Spread the remaining 1 banana slices on top and bake for 35 minutes.
5. Serve and enjoy.

Nutritional Value (Amount per Serving):
- Calories 304
- Fat 7.9 g
- Carbohydrates 47.3 g
- Sugar 12.6 g
- Protein 11.8 g
- Cholesterol 71 mg

Healthy Poppyseed Baked Oatmeal

Preparation Time: 10 minutes
Cooking Time: 25 minutes
Serve: 8
Ingredients:
- 3 eggs
- 1 tbsp poppy seeds
- 1 tsp baking powder
- 1 tsp vanilla
- 1 tsp lemon zest
- 1/4 cup lemon juice
- 1/4 cup honey
- 2 cups almond milk
- 3 cups rolled oats
- 1/4 tsp salt

Directions:
1. Spray a baking dish with cooking spray and set aside.
2. Insert wire rack in rack position 6. Select bake, set temperature 350 F, timer for 25 minutes. Press start to preheat the oven.
3. In a large bowl, mix together all ingredients until well combined.
4. Pour mixture into the baking dish and spread well and bake for 25 minutes.
5. Serve and enjoy.

Nutritional Value (Amount per Serving):
- Calories 320
- Fat 18.5 g
- Carbohydrates 33.8 g
- Sugar 11.5 g
- Protein 7.8 g
- Cholesterol 61 mg

Healthy Berry Baked Oatmeal

Preparation Time: 10 minutes
Cooking Time: 20 minutes
Serve: 4
Ingredients:
- 1 egg

- 1 cup blueberries
- 1/2 cup blackberries
- 1/2 cup strawberries, sliced
- 1/4 cup maple syrup
- 1 1/2 cups milk
- 1 1/2 tsp baking powder
- 2 cups old fashioned oats
- 1/2 tsp salt

Directions:

1. Spray a baking dish with cooking spray and set aside.
2. Insert wire rack in rack position 6. Select bake, set temperature 375 F, timer for 20 minutes. Press start to preheat the oven.
3. In a mixing bowl, mix together oats, salt, and baking powder. Add vanilla, egg, maple syrup, and milk and stir well.
4. Add berries and stir well. Pour mixture into the baking dish and bake for 20 minutes.
5. Serve and enjoy.

Nutritional Value (Amount per Serving):

- Calories 461
- Fat 8.4 g
- Carbohydrates 80.7 g
- Sugar 23.4 g
- Protein 15 g
- Cholesterol 48 mg

Apple Oatmeal Bars

Preparation Time: 10 minutes
Cooking Time: 25 minutes
Serve: 12

Ingredients:

- 2 eggs
- 2 tbsp butter
- 1/2 cup honey
- 1 tbsp vanilla
- 1 cup milk
- 1 tbsp cinnamon
- 2 tsp baking powder
- 2 cups apple, chopped
- 3 cups old fashioned oats
- Pinch of salt

Directions:

1. Spray a 9*13-inch baking dish with cooking spray and set aside.
2. Insert wire rack in rack position 6. Select bake, set temperature 375 F, timer for 25 minutes. Press start to preheat the oven.
3. In a mixing bowl, mix together dry ingredients.
4. In a separate bowl, whisk together wet ingredients. Pour wet ingredient mixture into the dry mixture and mix well.
5. Pour mixture into the baking dish and bake for 25 minutes.
6. Slice and serve.

Nutritional Value (Amount per Serving):

- Calories 261

- Fat 5.7 g
- Carbohydrates 44.7 g
- Sugar 17.7 g
- Protein 6.8 g
- Cholesterol 34 mg

Walnut Banana Bread

Preparation Time: 10 minutes
Cooking Time: 50 minutes
Serve: 10

Ingredients:

- 3 eggs
- 1 tsp baking soda
- 4 tbsp olive oil
- 1/2 cup walnuts, chopped
- 2 cups almond flour
- 3 bananas

Directions:

1. Grease loaf pan with butter and set aside.
2. Insert wire rack in rack position 6. Select bake, set temperature 350 F, timer for 50 minutes. Press start to preheat the oven.
3. Add all ingredients into the food processor and process until combined.
4. Pour batter into the prepared loaf pan and bake for 50 minutes.
5. Slices and serve.

Nutritional Value (Amount per Serving):

- Calories 271
- Fat 21.4 g
- Carbohydrates 13.6 g
- Sugar 4.5 g
- Protein 8.4 g
- Cholesterol 49 mg

Cinnamon Zucchini Bread

Preparation Time: 10 minutes
Cooking Time: 60 minutes
Serve: 12

Ingredients:

- 3 eggs
- 1/2 tsp nutmeg
- 1 1/2 tsp baking powder
- 1 1/2 tsp erythritol
- 2 1/2 cups almond flour
- 1 tsp vanilla
- 1/2 cup walnuts, chopped
- 1 cup zucchini, grated & squeeze out all liquid
- 1/4 tsp ground ginger
- 1 tsp cinnamon
- 1/2 cup olive oil
- 1/2 tsp salt

Directions:

1. Grease loaf pan with butter and set aside.
2. Insert wire rack in rack position 6. Select bake, set temperature 350 F, timer for 60 minutes. Press start to preheat the oven.

3.	In a bowl, whisk eggs, vanilla, and oil. Set aside.
4.	In a separate bowl, mix together almond flour, ginger, cinnamon, nutmeg, baking powder, salt, and sweetener. Set aside.
5.	Add grated zucchini into the egg mixture and stir well.
6.	Add dry ingredients into the egg mixture and stir to combine.
7.	Pour batter into the loaf pan and bake for 60 minutes.
8.	Slices and serve.

Nutritional Value (Amount per Serving):
- Calories 264
- Fat 23.7 g
- Carbohydrates 7.1 g
- Sugar 1 g
- Protein 7.8 g
- Cholesterol 41 mg

Italian Breakfast Bread

Preparation Time: 10 minutes
Cooking Time: 50 minutes
Serve: 10
Ingredients:
- 5 egg whites
- 2 egg yolks
- 1/2 cup black olives, chopped
- 5 sun-dried tomatoes, chopped
- 2 tbsp psyllium husk powder
- 2 tbsp apple cider vinegar
- 1 tbsp baking powder
- 1/2 cup boiling water
- 1 tbsp thyme, dried
- 1 tbsp oregano, dried
- 2 1/2 oz feta cheese
- 4 tbsp coconut oil
- 2 cups flaxseed flour
- 1/2 tsp salt

Directions:
1.	Grease loaf pan with butter and set aside.
2.	Insert wire rack in rack position 6. Select bake, set temperature 350 F, timer for 50 minutes. Press start to preheat the oven.
3.	In a bowl, mix together psyllium husk powder, baking powder, and flaxseed.
4.	Add oil and eggs and stir to combine. Add vinegar and stir well.
5.	Add boiling water and stir to combine.
6.	Add tomatoes, olives, and feta cheese. Mix well.
7.	Pour batter into the loaf pan and bake for 50 minutes.
8.	Sliced and serve.

Nutritional Value (Amount per Serving):
- Calories 258
- Fat 21.6 g
- Carbohydrates 17.3 g
- Sugar 2.1 g

- Protein 10.4 g
- Cholesterol 48 mg

Coconut Zucchini Bread

Preparation Time: 10 minutes
Cooking Time: 45 minutes
Serve: 12
Ingredients:
- 4 eggs
- 1/2 cup coconut flour
- 1 tbsp coconut oil
- 1 banana, mashed
- 1 tsp stevia
- 1 cup zucchini, shredded and squeeze out all liquid
- 1/2 cup walnuts, chopped
- 1 tsp apple cider vinegar
- 1/2 tsp nutmeg
- 1 tbsp cinnamon
- 3/4 tsp baking soda
- 1/2 tsp salt

Directions:
1.	Grease loaf pan with butter and set aside.
2.	Insert wire rack in rack position 6. Select bake, set temperature 350 F, timer for 45 minutes. Press start to preheat the oven.
3.	In a large bowl, whisk together egg, banana, oil, and stevia.
4.	Add all dry ingredients, vinegar, and zucchini and stir well. Add walnuts and stir.
5.	Pour batter into the loaf pan and bake for 45 minutes.
6.	Sliced and serve.

Nutritional Value (Amount per Serving):
- Calories 95
- Fat 6.3 g
- Carbohydrates 7 g
- Sugar 1.6 g
- Protein 4 g
- Cholesterol 55 mg

Protein Banana Bread

Preparation Time: 10 minutes
Cooking Time: 1 hour 10 minutes
Serve: 16
Ingredients:
- 3 eggs
- 1/3 cup coconut flour
- 1/2 cup Swerve
- 2 cups almond flour
- 1/2 cup ground chia seed
- 1/2 tsp vanilla extract
- 4 tbsp butter, melted
- 3/4 cup almond milk
- 1 tbsp baking powder
- 1/3 cup protein powder
- 1/2 cup water
- 1/2 tsp salt

Directions:

1. Grease loaf pan with butter and set aside.
2. Insert wire rack in rack position 6. Select bake, set temperature 325 F, timer for 1 hour 10 minutes. Press start to preheat the oven.
3. In a small bowl, whisk together chia seed and 1/2 cup water. Set aside.
4. In a large bowl, mix together almond flour, baking powder, protein powder, coconut flour, sweetener, and salt.
5. Stir in eggs, milk, chia seed mixture, vanilla extract, and butter until well combined.
6. Pour batter into the prepared loaf pan and bake for 1 hour 10 minutes.
7. Sliced and serve.

Nutritional Value (Amount per Serving):

- Calories 162
- Fat 13.4 g
- Carbohydrates 6 g
- Sugar 0.5 g
- Protein 5.2 g
- Cholesterol 40 mg

Cheese Soufflés

Preparation Time: 10 minutes
Cooking Time: 25 minutes
Serve: 8

Ingredients:

- 6 eggs, separated
- 3/4 cup heavy cream
- 1/4 tsp cayenne pepper
- 1/2 tsp xanthan gum
- 1/2 tsp pepper
- 1/4 tsp cream of tartar
- 1/4 cup chives, chopped
- 2 cups cheddar cheese, shredded
- 1 tsp ground mustard
- 1 tsp salt

Directions:

1. Spray 8 ramekins with cooking spray and place on a baking sheet.
2. Insert wire rack in rack position 6. Select bake, set temperature 350 F, timer for 25 minutes. Press start to preheat the oven.
3. In a large bowl, mix together almond flour, cayenne pepper, pepper, mustard, salt, and xanthan gum.
4. Add heavy cream and stir to combine.
5. Whisk in egg yolks, chives, and cheese until combined.
6. In a mixing bowl, add egg whites and cream of tartar and beat until stiff peaks form.
7. Fold egg white mixture into the almond flour mixture until combined.
8. Pour mixture into the ramekins and bake for 25 minutes.
9. Serve and enjoy.

Nutritional Value (Amount per Serving):

- Calories 204

- Fat 16.9 g
- Carbohydrates 2.3 g
- Sugar 0.5 g
- Protein 11.7 g
- Cholesterol 168 mg

Easy Kale Muffins

Preparation Time: 10 minutes
Cooking Time: 30 minutes
Serve: 8

Ingredients:

- 6 eggs
- 1/2 cup milk
- 1/4 cup chives, chopped
- 1 cup kale, chopped
- Pepper
- Salt

Directions:

1. Spray 8 cups muffin pan with cooking spray and set aside.
2. Insert wire rack in rack position 6. Select bake, set temperature 350 F, timer for 30 minutes. Press start to preheat the oven.
3. Add all ingredients into the mixing bowl and whisk well.
4. Pour mixture into the prepared muffin pan and bake for 30 minutes.
5. Serve and enjoy.

Nutritional Value (Amount per Serving):

- Calories 59
- Fat 3.6 g
- Carbohydrates 2 g
- Sugar 1 g
- Protein 5 g
- Cholesterol 124 mg

Mozzarella Spinach Quiche

Preparation Time: 10 minutes
Cooking Time: 45 minutes
Serve: 6

Ingredients:

- 4 eggs
- 10 oz frozen spinach, thawed
- 1/2 cup mozzarella cheese, shredded
- 1/4 cup parmesan cheese, grated
- 8 oz mushrooms, sliced
- 2 oz feta cheese, crumbled
- 1 cup almond milk
- 1 garlic clove, minced
- Pepper
- Salt

Directions:

1. Spray a pie dish with cooking spray and set aside.
2. Insert wire rack in rack position 6. Select bake, set temperature 350 F, timer for 45 minutes. Press start to preheat the oven.
3. Spray medium pan with cooking spray and heat over medium heat.

4.	Add garlic, mushrooms, pepper, and salt in a pan and sauté for 5 minutes.
5.	Add spinach in pie dish then add sautéed mushroom on top of spinach.
6.	Sprinkle feta cheese over spinach and mushroom.
7.	In a bowl, whisk eggs, parmesan cheese, and almond milk.
8.	Pour egg mixture over spinach and mushroom then sprinkle shredded mozzarella cheese and bake for 45 minutes.
9.	Sliced and serve.

Nutritional Value (Amount per Serving):
- Calories 197
- Fat 16 g
- Carbohydrates 6.2 g
- Sugar 2.8 g
- Protein 10.4 g
- Cholesterol 121 mg

Cheesy Zucchini Quiche

Preparation Time: 10 minutes
Cooking Time: 60 minutes
Serve: 8

Ingredients:
- 2 eggs
- 2 cups cheddar cheese, shredded
- 2 lbs zucchini, sliced
- 1 1/2 cup almond milk
- Pepper
- Salt

Directions:
1.	Grease quiche pan with cooking spray and set aside.
2.	Insert wire rack in rack position 6. Select bake, set temperature 375 F, timer for 60 minutes. Press start to preheat the oven.
3.	Season zucchini with pepper and salt and set aside for 30 minutes.
4.	In a large bowl, whisk eggs with almond milk, pepper, and salt.
5.	Add shredded cheddar cheese and stir well.
6.	Arrange zucchini slices in quiche pan.
7.	Pour egg mixture over zucchini slices then sprinkle with shredded cheese.
8.	Bake for 60 minutes.
9.	Serve and enjoy.

Nutritional Value (Amount per Serving):
- Calories 251
- Fat 21.4 g
- Carbohydrates 6.7 g
- Sugar 3.7 g
- Protein 10.8 g
- Cholesterol 71 mg

Healthy Asparagus Quiche

Preparation Time: 10 minutes
Cooking Time: 60 minutes
Serve: 6

Ingredients:
- 5 eggs, beaten
- 1 cup almond milk
- 15 asparagus spears, cut ends then cut asparagus in half
- 1 cup Swiss cheese, shredded
- 1/4 tsp thyme
- 1/4 tsp white pepper
- 1/4 tsp salt

Directions:
1.	Grease quiche pan with cooking spray and set aside.
2.	Insert wire rack in rack position 6. Select bake, set temperature 350 F, timer for 60 minutes. Press start to preheat the oven.
3.	In a bowl, whisk together eggs, thyme, white pepper, almond milk, and salt.
4.	Arrange asparagus in quiche pan then pour egg mixture over asparagus. Sprinkle with shredded cheese.
5.	Bake for 60 minutes.
6.	Sliced and serve.

Nutritional Value (Amount per Serving):
- Calories 225
- Fat 18.3 g
- Carbohydrates 5.9 g
- Sugar 3 g
- Protein 11.7 g
- Cholesterol 153 mg

Mini Veggie Quiche Cups

Preparation Time: 10 minutes
Cooking Time: 20 minutes
Serve: 12

Ingredients:
- 8 eggs
- 3/4 cup cheddar cheese, shredded
- 10 oz frozen spinach, chopped
- 1/4 cup onion, chopped
- 1/4 cup mushroom, diced
- 1/4 cup bell pepper, diced

Directions:
1.	Spray 12 cups muffin pan with cooking spray and set aside.
2.	Insert wire rack in rack position 6. Select bake, set temperature 375 F, timer for 20 minutes. Press start to preheat the oven.
3.	Add all ingredients into the mixing bowl and beat until combine.
4.	Pour egg mixture into the prepared muffin pan and bake for 20 minutes.
5.	Serve and enjoy.

Nutritional Value (Amount per Serving):
- Calories 78
- Fat 5.4 g
- Carbohydrates 1.6 g
- Sugar 0.6 g
- Protein 6.2 g
- Cholesterol 117 mg

Lemon Blueberry Muffins

Preparation Time: 10 minutes
Cooking Time: 25 minutes
Serve: 12
Ingredients:
- 2 eggs
- 1 tsp baking powder
- 5 drops stevia
- 1/4 cup butter, melted
- 1 cup heavy whipping cream
- 2 cups almond flour
- 1/4 tsp lemon zest
- 1/2 tsp lemon extract
- 1/2 cup fresh blueberries

Directions:
1. Spray 12 cups muffin pan with cooking spray and set aside.
2. Insert wire rack in rack position 6. Select bake, set temperature 350 F, timer for 25 minutes. Press start to preheat the oven.
3. In a mixing bowl, whisk eggs.
4. Add remaining ingredients to the eggs and mix until well combined.
5. Pour batter into the prepared muffin pan and bake for 25 minutes.
6. Serve and enjoy.

Nutritional Value (Amount per Serving):
- Calories 195
- Fat 17.2 g
- Carbohydrates 5.4 g
- Sugar 0.7 g
- Protein 5.2 g
- Cholesterol 51 mg

Baked Breakfast Donuts

Preparation Time: 10 minutes
Cooking Time: 20 minutes
Serve: 6
Ingredients:
- 4 eggs
- 1/3 cup almond milk
- 1 tbsp liquid stevia
- 3 tbsp cocoa powder
- 1/4 cup coconut oil
- 1/3 cup coconut flour
- 1/2 tsp baking soda
- 1/2 tsp baking powder
- 1/2 tsp instant coffee

Directions:
1. Spray donut pan with cooking spray and set aside.
2. Insert wire rack in rack position 6. Select bake, set temperature 350 F, timer for 20 minutes. Press start to preheat the oven.
3. Add all ingredients into the mixing bowl and mix until well combined.
4. Pour batter into the donut pan and bake for 20 minutes.

5. Serve and enjoy.
Nutritional Value (Amount per Serving):
- Calories 184
- Fat 16.2 g
- Carbohydrates 7.1 g
- Sugar 0.7 g
- Protein 5.4 g
- Cholesterol 109 mg

Blueberry Almond Muffins

Preparation Time: 10 minutes
Cooking Time: 15 minutes
Serve: 8
Ingredients:
- 1 egg
- 3/4 cup heavy cream
- 1/4 cup butter
- 1/4 tsp baking powder
- 2 1/2 cup almond flour
- 1/2 cup fresh blueberries
- 1/2 tsp baking soda
- 5 drops liquid stevia
- 1/4 tsp vanilla extract
- 1/2 tsp salt

Directions:
1. Spray 8 cups muffin pan with cooking spray and set aside.
2. Insert wire rack in rack position 6. Select bake, set temperature 375 F, timer for 15 minutes. Press start to preheat the oven.
3. In a bowl, mix together almond flour, salt, and baking powder.
4. In a large bowl, whisk together egg, butter, vanilla, stevia, baking soda, and heavy cream.
5. Add almond flour mixture into the egg mixture and stir to combine.
6. Pour batter into the muffin pan and bake for 15 minutes.
7. Serve and enjoy.

Nutritional Value (Amount per Serving):
- Calories 313
- Fat 27.1 g
- Carbohydrates 9.3 g
- Sugar 1 g
- Protein 8.6 g
- Cholesterol 51 mg

Feta Broccoli Frittata

Preparation Time: 10 minutes
Cooking Time: 20 minutes
Serve: 4
Ingredients:
- 10 eggs
- 2 oz feta cheese, crumbled
- 2 cups broccoli florets, chopped
- 1 tomato, diced
- 1 tsp black pepper
- 1 tsp salt

Directions:

1.	Grease baking dish with butter and set aside.
2.	Insert wire rack in rack position 6. Select bake, set temperature 390 F, timer for 20 minutes. Press start to preheat the oven.
3.	In a bowl, whisk eggs, pepper, and salt. Add veggies and stir well.
4.	Pour egg mixture into the baking dish and sprinkle with crumbled cheese.
5.	Bake for 20 minutes.
6.	Serve and enjoy.

Nutritional Value (Amount per Serving):
- Calories 214
- Fat 14.2 g
- Carbohydrates 5.4 g
- Sugar 2.6 g
- Protein 17.3 g
- Cholesterol 422 mg

Creamy Spinach Quiche

Preparation Time: 10 minutes
Cooking Time: 35 minutes
Serve: 6
Ingredients:
- 10 eggs
- 1 cup heavy cream
- 1 cup of coconut milk
- 1 tbsp butter
- 1 cup fresh spinach
- 1/4 cup fresh scallions, minced
- 1 cup cheddar cheese, shredded
- 1/4 tsp pepper
- 1/4 tsp salt

Directions:
1.	Spray 9*13-inch baking pan with cooking spray and set aside.
2.	Insert wire rack in rack position 6. Select bake, set temperature 350 F, timer for 35 minutes. Press start to preheat the oven.
3.	In a bowl, whisk eggs, cream, coconut milk, pepper, and salt.
4.	Pour egg mixture into the baking pan and sprinkle with spinach, scallions, and cheese.
5.	Bake for 35 minutes.
6.	Serve and enjoy.

Nutritional Value (Amount per Serving):
- Calories 361
- Fat 32.4 g
- Carbohydrates 4.1 g
- Sugar 2.1 g
- Protein 15.5 g
- Cholesterol 325 mg

Crustleass Cheese Egg Quiche

Preparation Time: 10 minutes
Cooking Time: 45 minutes
Serve: 8
Ingredients:
- 12 eggs

- 8 oz cheddar cheese, grated
- 3/4 cup butter
- 4 oz cream cheese, softened
- Pepper
- Salt

Directions:
1.	Spray 10-inch pie pan with cooking spray and set aside.
2.	Insert wire rack in rack position 6. Select bake, set temperature 375 F, timer for 20 minutes. Press start to preheat the oven.
3.	Add half cup cheese into the pie pan.
4.	Add eggs, cream cheese, and butter into the blender and blend until well combined.
5.	Pour egg mixture in pie pan. Season with pepper and salt.
6.	Sprinkle remaining cheese on top and bake for 45 minutes.
7.	Serve and enjoy.

Nutritional Value (Amount per Serving):
- Calories 411
- Fat 38.2 g
- Carbohydrates 1.3 g
- Sugar 0.7 g
- Protein 16.6 g
- Cholesterol 337 mg

Mushroom Frittata

Preparation Time: 10 minutes
Cooking Time: 20 minutes
Serve: 2
Ingredients:
- 6 eggs
- 2 oz butter
- 2 oz scallions, chopped
- 3 oz fresh spinach
- 5 oz mushrooms, sliced
- 4 oz feta cheese, crumbled
- Pepper
- Salt

Directions:
1.	Spray a baking dish with cooking spray and set aside.
2.	Insert wire rack in rack position 6. Select bake, set temperature 350 F, timer for 20 minutes. Press start to preheat the oven.
3.	In a bowl, whisk eggs, cheese, pepper, and salt.
4.	Melt butter in a pan over medium heat. Add mushrooms and scallions and sauté for 5-10 minutes.
5.	Add spinach and sauté for 2 minutes. Transfer mushroom spinach mixture into the baking dish.
6.	Pour egg mixture over mushroom spinach mixture and bake for 20 minutes.
7.	Serve and enjoy.

Nutritional Value (Amount per Serving):
- Calories 576
- Fat 48.6 g

- Carbohydrates 9.3 g
- Sugar 5.4 g
- Protein 28.9 g
- Cholesterol 602 mg

Lemon Poppy Seed Donuts

Preparation Time: 10 minutes
Time: 15 minutes
Serve: 8
Ingredients:
- 4 eggs
- 2 tsp lemon zest
- 1/4 cup coconut oil, melted
- 1 tsp baking powder
- 1 tbsp poppy seeds
- 1/4 cup Swerve
- 1/2 tsp lemon extract
- 8 tbsp water
- 1/2 cup coconut flour
- 1/4 tsp salt

Directions:
1. Spray donut pan with cooking spray and set aside.
2. Insert wire rack in rack position 6. Select bake, set temperature 350 F, timer for 15 minutes. Press start to preheat the oven.
3. In a mixing bowl, mix together coconut flour, baking powder, poppy seed, sweetener, and salt.
4. Stir in eggs, lemon extract, water, lemon zest, and melted oil until well combined.
5. Pour batter into the donut pan and bake for 15 minutes.
6. Serve and enjoy.

Nutritional Value (Amount per Serving):
- Calories 128
- Fat 10.2 g
- Carbohydrates 5.9 g
- Sugar 0.4 g
- Protein 4 g
- Cholesterol 82 mg

Artichoke Spinach Quiche

Preparation Time: 10 minutes
Cooking Time: 40 minutes
Serve: 4
Ingredients:
- 3 eggs
- 1 cup artichoke hearts, chopped
- 1 cup mushrooms, sliced
- 1 small onion, chopped
- 3 garlic cloves, minced
- 1/2 cup cottage cheese,
- 10 oz spinach, frozen
- 1 tsp olive oil
- Pepper
- Salt

Directions:

1. Spray a pie dish with cooking spray and set aside.
2. Insert wire rack in rack position 6. Select bake, set temperature 350 F, timer for 40 minutes. Press start to preheat the oven.
3. Heat oil in a pan over medium heat. Add onion, mushrooms, garlic, and spinach and sauté for a minute.
4. In a mixing bowl, add cheese, artichoke hearts, eggs, pepper, and salt stir well. Add sautéed vegetables and stir well.
5. Pour egg mixture into the pie dish and bake for 40 minutes.
6. Serve and enjoy.

Nutritional Value (Amount per Serving):
- Calories 128
- Fat 5.4 g
- Carbohydrates 10.2 g
- Sugar 2 g
- Protein 12 g
- Cholesterol 125 mg

Coconut Zucchini Muffins

Preparation Time: 10 minutes
Cooking Time: 25 minutes
Serve: 8
Ingredients:
- 6 eggs
- 1/4 cup Swerve
- 1/3 cup coconut oil, melted
- 1 cup zucchini, grated
- 3/4 cup coconut flour
- 1/4 tsp ground nutmeg
- 1 tsp ground cinnamon
- 1/2 tsp baking soda

Directions:
1. Spray 8 cups muffin pan with cooking spray and set aside.
2. Insert wire rack in rack position 6. Select bake, set temperature 350 F, timer for 25 minutes. Press start to preheat the oven.
3. Add all ingredients except zucchini in a bowl and mix well. Add zucchini and stir well.
4. Pour batter into the muffin pan and bake for 25 minutes.
5. Serve and enjoy.

Nutritional Value (Amount per Serving):
- Calories 174
- Fat 13.5 g
- Carbohydrates 8.5 g
- Sugar 0.5 g
- Protein 5.8 g
- Cholesterol 123 mg

Spicy Jalapeno Muffins

Preparation Time: 10 minutes
Cooking Time: 20 minutes
Serve: 8
Ingredients:

- 5 eggs
- 3 tbsp jalapenos, sliced
- 3 tbsp erythritol
- 2/3 cup coconut flour
- 1/4 cup coconut milk
- 1/3 cup coconut oil, melted
- 2 tsp baking powder
- 3/4 tsp sea salt

Directions:

1. Spray 8 cups muffin pan with cooking spray and set aside.
2. Insert wire rack in rack position 6. Select bake, set temperature 350 F, timer for 20 minutes. Press start to preheat the oven.
3. In a large bowl, mix together coconut flour, baking powder, erythritol, and sea salt.
4. Stir in eggs, jalapenos, milk, and coconut oil until well combined.
5. Pour batter into the muffin pan and bake in for 20 minutes.
6. Serve and enjoy.

Nutritional Value (Amount per Serving):

- Calories 177
- Fat 14.6 g
- Carbohydrates 13.6 g
- Sugar 6.2 g
- Protein 5 g
- Cholesterol 102 mg

Spinach Egg Casserole

Preparation Time: 10 minutes
Cooking Time: 35 minutes
Serve: 6

Ingredients:

- 2 eggs
- 1 cup mushrooms, sliced
- 2 cups frozen spinach, thawed and drained
- 1 1/2 cups egg whites
- 1 1/4 cup cheddar cheese, shredded
- 1/2 red pepper, chopped
- 1/2 green pepper, chopped
- 1/2 onion, chopped
- Pepper
- Salt

Directions:

1. Spray casserole dish with cooking spray and set aside.
2. Insert wire rack in rack position 6. Select bake, set temperature 375 F, timer for 35 minutes. Press start to preheat the oven.
3. Heat medium pan over medium-high heat.
4. Add chopped vegetables except spinach to the pan and sauté until vegetables are softened.
5. Add sauteed vegetables and spinach into the casserole dish.
6. In a bowl, whisk eggs, egg whites, pepper, and salt.
7. Pour egg mixture over the vegetables and sprinkle with shredded cheese.

8. Bake for 35 minutes.
9. Serve and enjoy.

Nutritional Value (Amount per Serving):

- Calories 161
- Fat 9.5 g
- Carbohydrates 3.7 g
- Sugar 2 g
- Protein 15.3 g
- Cholesterol 79 mg

Healthy Spinach Pie

Preparation Time: 10 minutes
Cooking Time: 30 minutes
Serve: 6

Ingredients:

- 5 eggs, beaten
- 10 oz frozen spinach, thawed, squeezed, and drained
- 1/4 tsp garlic powder
- 1 tsp dried onion, minced
- 2 1/2 cup cheddar cheese, grated
- Pepper
- Salt

Directions:

1. Spray a 9-inch pie dish with cooking spray and set aside.
2. Insert wire rack in rack position 6. Select bake, set temperature 375 F, timer for 30 minutes. Press start to preheat the oven.
3. Add all ingredients into the mixing bowl and stir to combine.
4. Pour mixture into the pie dish and bake for 30 minutes.
5. Serve and enjoy.

Nutritional Value (Amount per Serving):

- Calories 254
- Fat 19.4 g
- Carbohydrates 2.8 g
- Sugar 0.8 g
- Protein 17.7 g
- Cholesterol 186 mg

Creamy Spinach Mushroom Quiche

Preparation Time: 10 minutes
Cooking Time: 40 minutes
Serve: 6

Ingredients:

- 6 eggs
- 1/2 tsp garlic powder
- 1 cup mozzarella cheese, shredded
- 1/3 cup parmesan cheese, shredded
- 8 oz can mushroom, sliced
- 10 oz frozen spinach, thawed and drained
- 1/2 cup water
- 1/2 cup heavy cream
- 2 cheese slices
- Pepper
- Salt

Directions:
1. Insert wire rack in rack position 6. Select bake, set temperature 350 F, timer for 40 minutes. Press start to preheat the oven.
2. Spread spinach into a pie pan and spread mushrooms over spinach.
3. In a bowl, whisk eggs with water and heavy cream. Stir in garlic powder, parmesan, pepper, and salt.
4. Pour egg mixture into the pie pan. Top with mozzarella cheese.
5. Bake for 40 minutes.
6. Serve and enjoy.

Nutritional Value (Amount per Serving):
- Calories 184
- Fat 13.2 g
- Carbohydrates 4.2 g
- Sugar 0.7 g
- Protein 13 g
- Cholesterol 193 mg

Almond Butter Muffins

Preparation Time: 10 minutes
Cooking Time: 15 minutes
Serve: 8

Ingredients:
- 2 scoops vanilla protein powder
- 1/2 cup almond flour
- 1/2 cup coconut oil
- 1/2 cup pumpkin puree
- 1/2 cup almond butter
- 1 tbsp cinnamon
- 1 tsp baking powder

Directions:
1. Spray 8 cups muffin pan with cooking spray and set aside.
2. Insert wire rack in rack position 6. Select bake, set temperature 350 F, timer for 15 minutes. Press start to preheat the oven.
3. In a large bowl, combine together all dry ingredients and mix well.
4. Add wet ingredients into the dry ingredients and stir to combine.
5. Pour batter into the muffin pan and bake for 15 minutes.
6. Serve and enjoy.

Nutritional Value (Amount per Serving):
- Calories 201
- Fat 17.6 g
- Carbohydrates 4.1 g
- Sugar 0.7 g
- Protein 8.7 g
- Cholesterol 0 mg

Bacon Egg Muffins

Preparation Time: 10 minutes
Cooking Time: 25 minutes
Serve: 12
Ingredients:

- 12 eggs
- 2 tbsp fresh parsley, chopped
- 1/2 tsp mustard powder
- 1/3 cup heavy cream
- 2 green onion, chopped
- 4 oz cheddar cheese, shredded
- 8 bacon slices, cooked and crumbled
- Pepper
- Salt

Directions:
1. Spray 12 cups muffin pan with cooking spray and set aside.
2. Insert wire rack in rack position 6. Select bake, set temperature 375 F, timer for 25 minutes. Press start to preheat the oven.
3. In a mixing bowl, whisk eggs, mustard powder, heavy cream, pepper, and salt.
4. Divide cheddar cheese, onions, and bacon into the muffin cups then pour egg mixture into the muffin cups.
5. Bake for 25 minutes.
6. Serve and enjoy.

Nutritional Value (Amount per Serving):
- Calories 183
- Fat 14.1 g
- Carbohydrates 1 g
- Sugar 0.5 g
- Protein 12.8 g
- Cholesterol 192 mg

Zucchini Ham Quiche

Preparation Time: 10 minutes
Cooking Time: 40 minutes
Serve: 6

Ingredients:
- 8 eggs
- 1 cup cheddar cheese, shredded
- 1 cup zucchini, shredded and squeezed
- 1 cup ham, cooked and diced
- 1/2 tsp dry mustard
- 1/2 cup heavy cream
- Pepper
- Salt

Directions:
1. Spray a 9-inch pie dish with cooking spray.
2. Insert wire rack in rack position 6. Select bake, set temperature 375 F, timer for 40 minutes. Press start to preheat the oven.
3. Mix ham, cheddar cheese, and zucchini in a pie dish.
4. In a bowl, whisk eggs, heavy cream, and seasoning.
5. Pour egg mixture over ham mixture.
6. Bake for 40 minutes.
7. Serve and enjoy.

Nutritional Value (Amount per Serving):
- Calories 235
- Fat 17.8 g
- Carbohydrates 2.6 g

- Sugar 0.9 g
- Protein 16.3 g
- Cholesterol 256 mg

Breakfast Egg Cups

Preparation Time: 10 minutes
Cooking Time: 25 minutes
Serve: 12

Ingredients:
- 12 eggs
- 4 oz cream cheese
- 12 bacon slices
- 1/4 cup buffalo sauce
- 2/3 cup cheddar cheese, shredded
- Pepper
- Salt

Directions:
1. Spray 12 cups muffin pan with cooking spray and set aside.
2. Insert wire rack in rack position 6. Select bake, set temperature 375 F, timer for 20 minutes. Press start to preheat the oven.
3. Line each muffin cup with one bacon strip.
4. In a bowl, whisk eggs, pepper, and salt.
5. Pour egg mixture into each muffin cup and bake for 10 minutes.
6. In a separate bowl, mix together cheddar cheese and cream cheese and microwave for 30 seconds. Stir well and add buffalo sauce.
7. Remove muffin pan from oven and add 2 tsp cheese mixture in the center of each egg cup and bake for 15 minutes more.
8. Serve and enjoy.

Nutritional Value (Amount per Serving):
- Calories 224
- Fat 17.7 g
- Carbohydrates 1 g
- Sugar 0.4 g
- Protein 14.9 g
- Cholesterol 202 mg

Broccoli Muffins

Preparation Time: 10 minutes
Cooking Time: 30 minutes
Serve: 6

Ingredients:
- 2 eggs
- 2 cups almond flour
- 1 cup broccoli florets, chopped
- 1 tsp baking powder
- 2 tbsp nutritional yeast
- 1 cup almond milk
- 1/2 tsp sea salt

Directions:
1. Spray 6-cups muffin pan with cooking spray and set aside.
2. Insert wire rack in rack position 6. Select bake, set temperature 350 F, timer for 30 minutes. Press start to preheat the oven.

3. Add all ingredients into the large bowl and whisk until well combined.
4. Pour egg mixture into the muffin pan and bake for 30 minutes.
5. Serve and enjoy.

Nutritional Value (Amount per Serving):
- Calories 355
- Fat 29 g
- Carbohydrates 13.3 g
- Sugar 1.7 g
- Protein 12.7 g
- Cholesterol 55 mg

Dijon Zucchini Gratin

Preparation Time: 10 minutes
Cooking Time: 25 minutes
Serve: 4

Ingredients:
- 1 egg, lightly beaten
- 1 1/4 cup unsweetened almond milk
- 3 medium zucchini, sliced
- 1 tbsp Dijon mustard
- 1/2 cup nutritional yeast
- 1 tsp sea salt

Directions:
1. A spray casserole dish with cooking spray.
2. Insert wire rack in rack position 6. Select bake, set temperature 390 F, timer for 25 minutes. Press start to preheat the oven.
3. Arrange zucchini slices in a casserole dish.
4. In a saucepan, heat almond milk over low heat and stir in Dijon mustard, nutritional yeast, and sea salt. Add beaten egg and whisk well.
5. Pour sauce over zucchini slices and bake for 25 minutes.
6. Serve and enjoy.

Nutritional Value (Amount per Serving):
- Calories 125
- Fat 3.7 g
- Carbohydrates 15 g
- Sugar 2.7 g
- Protein 12.8 g
- Cholesterol 41 mg

Sausage Egg Muffins

Preparation Time: 10 minutes
Cooking Time: 25 minutes
Serve: 12

Ingredients:
- 6 eggs
- 1/2 red pepper, diced
- 1 cup egg whites
- 1 lb ground pork sausage
- 1/2 cup mozzarella cheese
- 1 cup cheddar cheese
- 3 tbsp onion, minced

Directions:
1. Spray 12-cups muffin pan with cooking spray and set aside.

2. Insert wire rack in rack position 6. Select bake, set temperature 350 F, timer for 25 minutes. Press start to preheat the oven.
3. Brown sausage in a pan over medium-high heat.
4. Divide red pepper, cheese, cooked sausages, and onion into each muffin cups.
5. In a large bowl, whisk together egg whites, egg, pepper, and salt.
6. Pour egg mixture into each muffin cups and bake for 25 minutes.
7. Serve and enjoy.
Nutritional Value (Amount per Serving):
- Calories 206
- Fat 15.6 g
- Carbohydrates 1.1 g
- Sugar 0.7 g
- Protein 14.4 g
- Cholesterol 126 mg

Cream Cheese Muffins

Preparation Time: 10 minutes
Cooking Time: 20 minutes
Serve: 8
Ingredients:
- 2 eggs
- 1/2 cup erythritol
- 8 oz cream cheese
- 1 tsp ground cinnamon
- 1/2 tsp vanilla

Directions:
1. Spray 8-cups muffin pan with cooking spray and set aside.
2. Insert wire rack in rack position 6. Select bake, set temperature 350 F, timer for 20 minutes. Press start to preheat the oven.
3. In a bowl, mix together cream cheese, vanilla, erythritol, and eggs until soften.
4. Pour batter into the prepared muffin pan and sprinkle cinnamon on the top.
5. Bake for 20 minutes.
6. Serve and enjoy.
Nutritional Value (Amount per Serving):
- Calories 116
- Fat 11 g
- Carbohydrates 16.1 g
- Sugar 15.2 g
- Protein 3.5 g
- Cholesterol 72 mg

Sausage Egg Bake

Preparation Time: 10 minutes
Cooking Time: 25 minutes
Serve: 8
Ingredients:
- 6 eggs, lightly beaten
- 1 small onion, diced
- 1 lb sausage
- 1 cup cheddar cheese, shredded
- 1/2 tsp black pepper
- 1/2 tsp salt

Directions:
1. Insert wire rack in rack position 6. Select bake, set temperature 375 F, timer for 25 minutes. Press start to preheat the oven.
2. Brown onion and sausage in a pan over medium heat.
3. In a bowl, whisk eggs, cheese, pepper, and salt.
4. Add onion and sausage into the baking dish and pour the egg mixture on top.
5. Bake for 25 minutes.
6. Serve and enjoy.
Nutritional Value (Amount per Serving):
- Calories 300
- Fat 24.1 g
- Carbohydrates 1.3 g
- Sugar 0.7 g
- Protein 18.8 g
- Cholesterol 185 mg

Easy Cheese Pie

Preparation Time: 10 minutes
Cooking Time: 25 minutes
Serve: 4
Ingredients:
- 8 eggs
- 1 1/2 cups heavy whipping cream
- 1 lb cheddar cheese, grated
- Pepper
- Salt

Directions:
1. Spray a pie dish with cooking spray and set aside.
2. Insert wire rack in rack position 6. Select bake, set temperature 350 F, timer for 25 minutes. Press start to preheat the oven.
3. In a bowl, whisk eggs, half cheese, heavy cream, pepper, and salt.
4. Sprinkle remaining cheese in prepared dish and bake for 5 minutes.
5. Remove dish from oven and let it cool slightly.
6. Now Pour egg mixture into the dish and bake 15-20 minutes.
7. Serve and enjoy.
Nutritional Value (Amount per Serving):
- Calories 738
- Fat 63 g
- Carbohydrates 3.4 g
- Sugar 1.3 g
- Protein 40.2 g
- Cholesterol 508 mg

CHAPTER 3: POULLTRY RECIPES

Crispy Chicken Thighs

Preparation Time: 10 minutes
Cooking Time: 35 minutes
Serve: 6
Ingredients:
- 6 chicken thighs
- 1 tbsp olive oil
- For rub:
- 1/2 tsp basil
- 1/2 tsp oregano
- 1/2 tsp pepper
- 1 tsp garlic powder
- 1 tsp onion powder
- 1/2 tsp salt

Directions:
1. Insert wire rack in rack position 6. Select bake, set temperature 390 F, timer for 35 minutes. Press start to preheat the oven.
2. Brush chicken thighs with olive oil. In a small bowl, mix together rub ingredients and rub all over the chicken.
3. Arrange chicken on roasting pan and bake for 30-35 minutes.
4. Serve and enjoy.
Nutritional Value (Amount per Serving):
- Calories 49
- Fat 3.4 g
- Carbohydrates 0.9 g
- Sugar 0.3 g
- Protein 4.1 g
- Cholesterol 12 mg

Classic Greek Chicken

Preparation Time: 10 minutes
Cooking Time: 30 minutes
Serve: 4
Ingredients:
- 1 lb chicken breasts, skinless & boneless
- For marinade:
- 1/2 tsp dill
- 1 tsp onion powder
- 1/4 tsp basil
- 1/4 tsp oregano
- 3 garlic cloves, minced
- 1 tbsp lemon juice
- 3 tbsp olive oil
- 1/4 tsp pepper
- 1/2 tsp salt

Directions:
1. Add all marinade ingredients into the mixing bowl and mix well.
2. Add chicken into the marinade and coat well. Cover bowl and place in the refrigerator overnight.
3. Insert wire rack in rack position 6. Select bake, set temperature 390 F, timer for 30 minutes. Press start to preheat the oven.
4. Arrange marinated chicken on roasting pan and bake for 25-30 minutes.
5. Serve and enjoy.
Nutritional Value (Amount per Serving):
- Calories 313
- Fat 19 g
- Carbohydrates 1.5 g
- Sugar 0.3 g
- Protein 33.1 g
- Cholesterol 101 mg

Perfect Juicy Chicken Breast

Preparation Time: 10 minutes
Cooking Time: 15 minutes
Serve: 8
Ingredients:
- 4 chicken breasts, skinless and boneless
- 1 tbsp olive oil
- For rub:
- 1 tsp garlic powder
- 1 tsp onion powder
- 4 tsp brown sugar
- 4 tsp paprika
- 1 tsp black pepper
- 1 tsp salt

Directions:
1. Insert wire rack in rack position 6. Select bake, set temperature 390 F, timer for 30 minutes. Press start to preheat the oven.
2. Brush chicken breasts with olive oil. In a small bowl, mix together rub ingredients and rub all over chicken breasts.
3. Arrange chicken breasts on roasting pan and bake for 12-15 minutes or until internal temperature reaches 165 F.
4. Serve and enjoy.
Nutritional Value (Amount per Serving):
- Calories 165
- Fat 7.3 g
- Carbohydrates 2.7 g
- Sugar 1.8 g
- Protein 21.4 g
- Cholesterol 65 mg

Crispy & Tasty Chicken Breast

Preparation Time: 10 minutes
Cooking Time: 35 minutes
Serve: 4
Ingredients:
- 4 chicken breasts, skinless and boneless
- 1/2 cup butter, cut into pieces
- 1 cup cracker crumbs
- 2 eggs, lightly beaten
- Pepper

- Salt

Directions:
1. Insert wire rack in rack position 6. Select bake, set temperature 375 F, timer for 35 minutes. Press start to preheat the oven.
2. Add cracker crumbs and eggs in 2 separate shallow dishes.
3. Mix cracker crumbs with pepper and salt.
4. Dip chicken in the eggs and then coat with cracker crumb.
5. Arrange coated chicken into the 9*13-inch baking dish.
6. Spread butter pieces on top of the chicken and bake for 30-35 minutes.
7. Serve and enjoy.

Nutritional Value (Amount per Serving):
- Calories 590
- Fat 40 g
- Carbohydrates 9.7 g
- Sugar 0.5 g
- Protein 46.4 g
- Cholesterol 273 mg

Broccoli Bacon Ranch Chicken

Preparation Time: 10 minutes
Cooking Time: 30 minutes
Serve: 4

Ingredients:
- 4 chicken breasts, skinless and boneless
- 1/3 cup mozzarella cheese, shredded
- 1 cup cheddar cheese, shredded
- 1/2 cup ranch dressing
- 5 bacon slices, cooked and chopped
- 2 cups broccoli florets, blanched and chopped

Directions:
1. Insert wire rack in rack position 6. Select bake, set temperature 375 F, timer for 30 minutes. Press start to preheat the oven.
2. Add chicken into the 13*9-inch casserole dish. Top with bacon and broccoli.
3. Pour ranch dressing over chicken and top with shredded mozzarella cheese and cheddar cheese.
4. Bake chicken for 30 minutes.
5. Serve and enjoy.

Nutritional Value (Amount per Serving):
- Calories 551
- Fat 30.8 g
- Carbohydrates 5.4 g
- Sugar 1.7 g
- Protein 60.4 g
- Cholesterol 187 mg

Jerk Chicken Legs

Preparation Time: 10 minutes
Cooking Time: 50 minutes
Serve: 10
Ingredients:

- 10 chicken legs
- 1/2 tsp ground nutmeg
- 1/2 tsp ground cinnamon
- 1 tsp ground allspice
- 1 tsp black pepper
- 1 tbsp fresh thyme
- 1 1/2 tbsp brown sugar
- 1/4 cup soy sauce
- 1/3 cup fresh lime juice
- 1 tbsp ginger, sliced
- 2 habanera peppers, remove the stem
- 4 garlic cloves, peeled and smashed
- 6 green onions, chopped

Directions:
1. Add chicken into the large zip-lock bag.
2. Add remaining ingredients into the food processor and process until coarse.
3. Pour mixture over chicken. Seal bag and shake well to coat the chicken and place it in the refrigerator overnight.
4. Insert wire rack in rack position 6. Select bake, set temperature 375 F, timer for 50 minutes. Press start to preheat the oven.
5. Line baking sheet with foil. Arrange marinated chicken legs on a baking sheet and bake for 45-50 minutes.
6. Serve and enjoy.

Nutritional Value (Amount per Serving):
- Calories 232
- Fat 14.2 g
- Carbohydrates 4.8 g
- Sugar 2.2 g
- Protein 21.9 g
- Cholesterol 95 mg

Creamy Cheese Chicken

Preparation Time: 10 minutes
Cooking Time: 45 minutes
Serve: 4

Ingredients:
- 4 chicken breasts, skinless, boneless & cut into chunks
- 1 cup mayonnaise
- 1 tsp garlic powder
- 1 cup parmesan cheese, shredded
- Pepper
- Salt

Directions:
1. Add chicken pieces into the bowl of buttermilk and soak for overnight.
2. Insert wire rack in rack position 6. Select bake, set temperature 375 F, timer for 45 minutes. Press start to preheat the oven.
3. Add marinated chicken pieces into the 9*13-inch baking dish. Mix together mayonnaise, garlic powder, 1/2 cup parmesan cheese, pepper, and salt and pour over chicken.
4. Sprinkle remaining cheese on top of the chicken and bake for 40-45 minutes.

5.   Serve and enjoy.
Nutritional Value (Amount per Serving):
- Calories 581
- Fat 35.3 g
- Carbohydrates 15.4 g
- Sugar 3.9 g
- Protein 50.1 g
- Cholesterol 161 mg

Protein Packed Baked Chicken Breasts

Preparation Time: 10 minutes
Cooking Time: 25 minutes
Serve: 6
Ingredients:
- 6 chicken breasts, skinless & boneless
- 1/4 tsp paprika
- 1/2 tsp garlic salt
- 1 tsp Italian seasoning
- 2 tbsp olive oil
- 1/4 tsp pepper

Directions:
1.   Insert wire rack in rack position 6. Select bake, set temperature 390 F, timer for 25 minutes. Press start to preheat the oven.
2.   Brush chicken with oil. Mix together Italian seasoning, garlic salt, paprika, and pepper and rub all over the chicken.
3.   Arrange chicken breasts on roasting pan and bake for 25 minutes or until internal temperature reaches 165 F.
4.   Slice and serve.
Nutritional Value (Amount per Serving):
- Calories 321
- Fat 15.7 g
- Carbohydrates 0.4 g
- Sugar 0.1 g
- Protein 42.3 g
- Cholesterol 130 mg

Flavors Balsamic Chicken

Preparation Time: 10 minutes
Cooking Time: 25 minutes
Serve: 4
Ingredients:
- 4 chicken breasts, skinless and boneless
- 2 tsp dried oregano
- 2 garlic cloves, minced
- 1/2 cup balsamic vinegar
- 2 tbsp soy sauce
- 1/4 cup olive oil
- Pepper
- Salt

Directions:
1.   Insert wire rack in rack position 6. Select bake, set temperature 390 F, timer for 25 minutes. Press start to preheat the oven.
2.   In a bowl, mix together soy sauce, oil, black pepper, oregano, garlic, and vinegar.

3.   Place chicken in a baking dish and pour soy sauce mixture over chicken. Let it sit for 10 minutes.
4.   Bake chicken for 25 minutes.
5.   Serve and enjoy.
Nutritional Value (Amount per Serving):
- Calories 401
- Fat 23.5 g
- Carbohydrates 1.9 g
- Sugar 0.3 g
- Protein 42.9 g
- Cholesterol 130 mg

Simple & Delicious Chicken Thighs

Preparation Time: 10 minutes
Cooking Time: 35 minutes
Serve: 6
Ingredients:
- 6 chicken thighs
- 2 tsp poultry seasoning
- 2 tbsp olive oil
- Pepper
- Salt

Directions:
1.   Insert wire rack in rack position 6. Select bake, set temperature 390 F, timer for 40 minutes. Press start to preheat the oven.
2.   Brush chicken with oil and rub with poultry seasoning, pepper, and salt.
3.   Arrange chicken on roasting pan and bake for 35-40 minutes or until internal temperature reaches 165 F.
4.   Serve and enjoy.
Nutritional Value (Amount per Serving):
- Calories 319
- Fat 15.5 g
- Carbohydrates 0.3 g
- Sugar 0 g
- Protein 42.3 g
- Cholesterol 130 mg

Perfect Baked Chicken Breasts

Preparation Time: 10 minutes
Cooking Time: 30 minutes
Serve: 4
Ingredients:
- 4 chicken breasts, bone-in & skin-on
- 1 tsp olive oil
- 1/4 tsp black pepper
- 1/2 tsp kosher salt

Directions:
1.   Insert wire rack in rack position 6. Select bake, set temperature 375 F, timer for 30 minutes. Press start to preheat the oven.
2.   Brush chicken with olive oil and season with pepper and salt.
3.   Place chicken on roasting pan and bake for 30 minutes.
4.   Serve and enjoy.
Nutritional Value (Amount per Serving):

- Calories 288
- Fat 12 g
- Carbohydrates 0.1 g
- Sugar 0 g
- Protein 42.3 g
- Cholesterol 130 mg

BBQ Chicken Wings

Preparation Time: 10 minutes
Cooking Time: 55 minutes
Serve: 8
Ingredients:
- 32 chicken wings
- 1 1/2 cups BBQ sauce
- 1/4 cup olive oil
- Pepper
- Salt

Directions:
1. Line baking sheet with parchment paper and set aside.
2. Insert wire rack in rack position 6. Select bake, set temperature 375 F, timer for 55 minutes. Press start to preheat the oven.
3. In a mixing bowl, toss chicken wings with olive oil, pepper, and salt.
4. Arrange chicken wings on a baking sheet and bake for 50 minutes.
5. Toss chicken wings with BBQ sauce and bake for 5 minutes more.
6. Serve and enjoy.

Nutritional Value (Amount per Serving):
- Calories 173
- Fat 8.3 g
- Carbohydrates 17 g
- Sugar 12.2 g
- Protein 7.4 g
- Cholesterol 23 mg

Delicious Honey Mustard Sauce Chicken

Preparation Time: 10 minutes
Cooking Time: 40 minutes
Serve: 6
Ingredients:
- 6 chicken thighs, bone-in & skin-on
- 1/4 cup yellow mustard
- 1/2 cup honey
- Pepper
- Salt

Directions:
1. Insert wire rack in rack position 6. Select bake, set temperature 350 F, timer for 30 minutes. Press start to preheat the oven.
2. Season chicken with pepper and salt and place into the baking dish.
3. Mix together yellow mustard and honey and pour over chicken and bake the chicken for 30 minutes.
4. Spoon honey mustard mixture over chicken and bake chicken 10 minutes more.

5. Serve and enjoy.
Nutritional Value (Amount per Serving):
- Calories 119
- Fat 1.4 g
- Carbohydrates 23.9 g
- Sugar 23.3 g
- Protein 4.5 g
- Cholesterol 12 mg

Baked Chicken & Potatoes

Preparation Time: 10 minutes
Cooking Time: 60 minutes
Serve: 5
Ingredients:
- 5 chicken thighs
- 1 lemon juice
- 1/2 cup olive oil
- 1 tbsp fresh rosemary, chopped
- 1 tsp dried oregano
- 2 lbs potatoes, cut into chunks
- 4 garlic cloves, minced
- Pepper
- Salt

Directions:
1. Insert wire rack in rack position 6. Select bake, set temperature 375 F, timer for 60 minutes. Press start to preheat the oven.
2. In a large mixing bowl, add chicken and remaining ingredients and mix well.
3. Place chicken in the baking dish and spread potatoes around the chicken.
4. Bake chicken for 60 minutes.
5. Serve and enjoy.

Nutritional Value (Amount per Serving):
- Calories 333
- Fat 21.6 g
- Carbohydrates 30.1 g
- Sugar 2.3 g
- Protein 7.3 g
- Cholesterol 12 mg

Crispy & Cheesy Parmesan Chicken

Preparation Time: 10 minutes
Cooking Time: 35 minutes
Serve: 4
Ingredients:
- 4 chicken breasts
- 1 cup breadcrumbs
- 1 cup parmesan cheese, shredded
- 1/4 cup olive oil
- Pepper
- Salt

Directions:
1. Insert wire rack in rack position 6. Select bake, set temperature 350 F, timer for 35 minutes. Press start to preheat the oven.
2. Season chicken with pepper and salt and brush with olive oil.

3. In a shallow dish, mix together parmesan cheese and breadcrumbs. Coat chicken with parmesan and breadcrumb mixture and place in the baking dish.

4. Bake chicken for 35 minutes.

5. Serve and enjoy.

Nutritional Value (Amount per Serving):
- Calories 564
- Fat 29.7 g
- Carbohydrates 20.3 g
- Sugar 1.7 g
- Protein 53.1 g
- Cholesterol 146 mg

Juicy Baked Chicken Wings

Preparation Time: 10 minutes
Cooking Time: 50 minutes
Serve: 5

Ingredients:
- 3 lbs chicken wings
- 4 garlic cloves, minced
- 1 cup honey
- 2 tbsp BBQ sauce
- 1/2 cup soy sauce
- 2 tbsp olive oil
- Pepper
- Salt

Directions:
1. Line baking sheet with foil and set aside.

2. Insert wire rack in rack position 6. Select bake, set temperature 350 F, timer for 50 minutes. Press start to preheat the oven.

3. Season chicken wings with pepper and salt and arrange on a baking sheet in a single layer.

4. In a bowl, stir together BBQ sauce, garlic, honey, soy sauce, and oil and pour over chicken wings.

5. Bake chicken wings for 50 minutes.

6. Serve and enjoy.

Nutritional Value (Amount per Serving):
- Calories 798
- Fat 25.8 g
- Carbohydrates 60.9 g
- Sugar 57.8 g
- Protein 80.7 g
- Cholesterol 242 mg

Delicious Curried Chicken

Preparation Time: 10 minutes
Cooking Time: 40 minutes
Serve: 4

Ingredients:
- 4 chicken breasts, skinless and boneless
- 4 tsp curry powder
- 1/4 cup mustard
- 1/3 cup butter
- 1/3 cup honey

Directions:

1. Insert wire rack in rack position 6. Select bake, set temperature 375 F, timer for 40 minutes. Press start to preheat the oven.

2. Add butter and honey in a small saucepan and heat over low heat until butter is melted.

3. Remove saucepan from heat and stir in curry powder and mustard.

4. Arrange chicken in a casserole dish and pour butter mixture over chicken and bake for 40 minutes.

5. Serve and enjoy.

Nutritional Value (Amount per Serving):
- Calories 552
- Fat 29.3 g
- Carbohydrates 27.9 g
- Sugar 23.9 g
- Protein 45.2 g
- Cholesterol 171 mg

BBQ Spice Chicken Wings

Preparation Time: 10 minutes
Cooking Time: 45 minutes
Serve: 6

Ingredients:
- 3 lbs chicken wings
- 2 tbsp olive oil
- 1/2 cup BBQ spice rub

Directions:
1. Insert wire rack in rack position 6. Select bake, set temperature 390 F, timer for 45 minutes. Press start to preheat the oven.

2. Brush chicken wings with olive oil and place in a large mixing bowl.

3. Add BBQ spice over chicken wings and toss until well coated.

4. Arrange chicken wings on rack in a single layer and bake for 45 minutes.

5. Serve and enjoy.

Nutritional Value (Amount per Serving):
- Calories 483
- Fat 22.2 g
- Carbohydrates 1.5 g
- Sugar 0.2 g
- Protein 65.8 g
- Cholesterol 202 mg

Italian Turkey Tenderloin

Preparation Time: 10 minutes
Cooking Time: 45 minutes
Serve: 4

Ingredients:
- 1 1/2 lbs turkey breast tenderloin
- 1/2 tbsp olive oil
- 1 tsp Italian seasoning
- 1/4 tsp pepper
- 1/2 tsp salt

Directions:

1. Insert wire rack in rack position 6. Select bake, set temperature 390 F, timer for 45 minutes. Press start to preheat the oven.
2. Brush turkey tenderloin with olive oil and rub with Italian seasoning, pepper, and salt.
3. Place tenderloin in a baking dish and bake for 40-45 minutes or until internal temperature reaches 165 F.
4. Serve and enjoy.

Nutritional Value (Amount per Serving):
- Calories 200
- Fat 4.3 g
- Carbohydrates 0.2 g
- Sugar 0.1 g
- Protein 42.2 g
- Cholesterol 69 mg

Scrumptious Chicken Meatballs

Preparation Time: 10 minutes
Cooking Time: 25 minutes
Serve: 4
Ingredients:
- 1 lb ground chicken
- 1/4 tsp red pepper flakes
- 1/2 tsp dried oregano
- 1 tsp dried onion flakes
- 1 garlic clove, minced
- 1 egg, lightly beaten
- 2 tbsp olive oil
- 1 tbsp parsley, chopped
- 1/2 cup breadcrumbs
- 1/2 cup parmesan cheese, grated
- 1/4 tsp pepper
- 1/2 tsp sea salt

Directions:
1. Line baking sheet with parchment paper and set aside.
2. Insert wire rack in rack position 6. Select bake, set temperature 390 F, timer for 25 minutes. Press start to preheat the oven.
3. Add all ingredients into the mixing bowl and mix until well combined.
4. Make small balls from the meat mixture and arrange on a baking sheet.
5. Bake meatballs for 25 minutes.
6. Serve and enjoy.

Nutritional Value (Amount per Serving):
- Calories 385
- Fat 19.7 g
- Carbohydrates 11.1 g
- Sugar 1.1 g
- Protein 39.8 g
- Cholesterol 150 mg

Herb Garlic Meatballs

Preparation Time: 10 minutes
Cooking Time: 25 minutes
Serve: 6
Ingredients:

- 2 lbs ground chicken
- 1 tsp dry parsley
- 4 garlic cloves, minced
- 1 onion, diced
- 2 cups breadcrumbs
- 1/2 cup milk
- 2 eggs, lightly beaten
- Pepper
- Salt

Directions:
1. Line baking sheet with parchment paper and set aside.
2. Insert wire rack in rack position 6. Select bake, set temperature 390 F, timer for 25 minutes. Press start to preheat the oven.
3. Add all ingredients into the mixing bowl and mix until well combined.
4. Make 1-inch balls from meat mixture and arrange on a baking sheet.
5. Bake meatballs for 25 minutes.
6. Serve and enjoy.

Nutritional Value (Amount per Serving):
- Calories 471
- Fat 15 g
- Carbohydrates 29.4 g
- Sugar 4.1 g
- Protein 51.4 g
- Cholesterol 191 mg

Parmesan Pesto Chicken

Preparation Time: 10 minutes
Cooking Time: 25 minutes
Serve: 4
Ingredients:
- 4 chicken breasts, skinless & boneless
- 1/2 cup parmesan cheese, shredded
- 1/2 cup pesto
- Pepper
- Salt

Directions:
1. Insert wire rack in rack position 6. Select bake, set temperature 390 F, timer for 25 minutes. Press start to preheat the oven.
2. Season chicken with pepper and salt and place into the baking dish.
3. Spread pesto on top of the chicken and sprinkle with shredded cheese.
4. Bake chicken for 25 minutes.
5. Serve and enjoy.

Nutritional Value (Amount per Serving):
- Calories 449
- Fat 26.2 g
- Carbohydrates 2.4 g
- Sugar 2 g
- Protein 48.9 g
- Cholesterol 145 mg

Simply Delicious Baked Chicken

Preparation Time: 10 minutes

Cooking Time: 45 minutes
Serve: 4
Ingredients:
- 4 chicken breasts, skinless and boneless
- 5 oz yogurt
- 1 tsp garlic powder
- 1/2 cup parmesan cheese, grated
- Pepper
- Salt

Directions:
1. Insert wire rack in rack position 6. Select bake, set temperature 375 F, timer for 45 minutes. Press start to preheat the oven.
2. Spray baking dish with cooking spray. Season chicken with pepper and salt and place in the baking dish.
3. Mix together yogurt, garlic powder, and parmesan cheese and pour over chicken.
4. Bake chicken for 45 minutes.
5. Serve and enjoy.

Nutritional Value (Amount per Serving):
- Calories 341
- Fat 13.7 g
- Carbohydrates 3.4 g
- Sugar 2.4 g
- Protein 48 g
- Cholesterol 140 mg

Chicken Meatballs

Preparation Time: 10 minutes
Cooking Time: 15 minutes
Serve: 4
Ingredients:
- 1 lb ground chicken
- 1 tsp cumin
- 3 garlic cloves, minced
- 2 tbsp soy sauce
- 1/4 cup breadcrumbs
- 1/2 cup parmesan cheese, grated
- 1 egg, lightly beaten
- Pepper
- Salt

Directions:
1. Line baking sheet with parchment paper and set aside.
2. Insert wire rack in rack position 6. Select bake, set temperature 390 F, timer for 15 minutes. Press start to preheat the oven.
3. Add all ingredients into the mixing bowl and mix until well combined.
4. Make small balls from the meat mixture and arrange on a baking sheet.
5. Bake meatballs for 15 minutes.
6. Serve and enjoy.

Nutritional Value (Amount per Serving):
- Calories 304
- Fat 12.4 g
- Carbohydrates 6.9 g
- Sugar 0.7 g

- Protein 39.4 g
- Cholesterol 150 mg

Lemon Pepper Baked Chicken Breasts

Preparation Time: 10 minutes
Cooking Time: 30 minutes
Serve: 4
Ingredients:
- 4 chicken breasts, skinless and boneless
- 4 tsp butter, sliced
- 1/2 tsp paprika
- 1 tsp garlic powder
- 1 tsp lemon pepper seasoning
- 4 tsp lemon juice
- Pepper
- Salt

Directions:
1. Insert wire rack in rack position 6. Select bake, set temperature 350 F, timer for 30 minutes. Press start to preheat the oven.
2. Season chicken with pepper and salt and place in the baking dish.
3. Pour lemon juice over chicken. Mix together paprika, garlic powder, and lemon pepper seasoning and sprinkle over chicken.
4. Add butter slices on top of the chicken and bake the chicken for 30 minutes.
5. Serve and enjoy.

Nutritional Value (Amount per Serving):
- Calories 323
- Fat 14.8 g
- Carbohydrates 2.5 g
- Sugar 1 g
- Protein 42.8 g
- Cholesterol 140 mg

Lemon Pepper Baked Chicken Legs

Preparation Time: 10 minutes
Cooking Time: 30 minutes
Serve: 6
Ingredients:
- 2 1/2 lbs chicken legs
- 2 tsp olive oil
- 2 tbsp lemon juice
- 1/2 tsp garlic powder
- 1 1/2 tbsp lemon pepper spice

Directions:
1. Add chicken legs into the zip-lock bag.
2. Add remaining ingredients over chicken. Seal bag and shake well and place in the refrigerator for 1 hour.
3. Insert wire rack in rack position 6. Select bake, set temperature 390 F, timer for 30 minutes. Press start to preheat the oven.
4. Arrange marinated chicken legs on a rack over a baking sheet and bake for 30 minutes.
5. Serve and enjoy.

Nutritional Value (Amount per Serving):
- Calories 374

- Fat 15.6 g
- Carbohydrates 0.3 g
- Sugar 0.2 g
- Protein 54.8 g
- Cholesterol 168 mg

Chicken Cheese Casserole

Preparation Time: 10 minutes
Cooking Time: 40 minutes
Serve: 8
Ingredients:
- 2 lbs cooked chicken, shredded
- 6 oz cream cheese, softened
- 4 oz butter, melted
- 5 oz Swiss cheese
- 1 oz fresh lemon juice
- 1 tbsp Dijon mustard
- 6 oz ham, cut into small pieces
- 1/2 tsp salt

Directions:
1. Insert wire rack in rack position 6. Select bake, set temperature 350 F, timer for 40 minutes. Press start to preheat the oven.
2. Arrange chicken in the baking dish and top with ham pieces.
3. Add butter, lemon juice, mustard, cream cheese, and salt into the blender and blend until a thick sauce.
4. Spread sauce on top of chicken in the baking dish.
5. Arrange Swiss cheese slices on top of the sauce and bake for 40 minutes.
6. Serve and enjoy.

Nutritional Value (Amount per Serving):
- Calories 451
- Fat 29.2 g
- Carbohydrates 2.5 g
- Sugar 0.4 g
- Protein 43 g
- Cholesterol 170 mg

Chicken Mushrooms Bake

Preparation Time: 10 minutes
Cooking Time: 30 minutes
Serve: 4
Ingredients:
- 2 lbs chicken breasts, halved
- 8 oz mushrooms, sliced
- 1/2 cup mayonnaise
- 1/3 cup sun-dried tomatoes
- 1 tsp salt

Directions:
1. Grease baking dish with butter and set aside.
2. Insert wire rack in rack position 6. Select bake, set temperature 390 F, timer for 30 minutes. Press start to preheat the oven.

3. Place chicken into the baking dish and top with sun-dried tomatoes, mushrooms, mayonnaise, and salt. Mix well.
4. Bake for 30 minutes.
5. Serve and enjoy.

Nutritional Value (Amount per Serving):
- Calories 560
- Fat 26.8 g
- Carbohydrates 9.5 g
- Sugar 3.2 g
- Protein 67.8 g
- Cholesterol 209 mg

Meatloaf

Preparation Time: 10 minutes
Cooking Time: 40 minutes
Serve: 8
Ingredients:
- 2 eggs
- 1/2 cup parmesan cheese, grated
- 1/2 cup marinara sauce, without sugar
- 1 cup cottage cheese
- 1 lb mozzarella cheese, cut into cubes
- 2 lbs ground turkey
- 2 tsp Italian seasoning
- 1/4 cup basil pesto
- 1 tsp salt

Directions:
1. A grease casserole dish with butter and set aside.
2. Insert wire rack in rack position 6. Select bake, set temperature 390 F, timer for 40 minutes. Press start to preheat the oven.
3. Add all ingredients into the large bowl and mix until well combined.
4. Transfer mixture into the casserole dish and bake for 40 minutes.
5. Serve and enjoy.

Nutritional Value (Amount per Serving):
- Calories 308
- Fat 16.7 g
- Carbohydrates 3.7 g
- Sugar 1.7 g
- Protein 39.4 g
- Cholesterol 166 mg

Italian Chicken

Preparation Time: 10 minutes
Cooking Time: 30 minutes
Serve: 4
Ingredients:
- 2 lbs chicken tenders
- 1 cup cherry tomatoes
- 2 tbsp olive oil
- 3 dill sprigs
- 1 large zucchini
- For topping:
- 2 tbsp feta cheese, crumbled
- 1 tbsp fresh dill, chopped

- 1 tbsp olive oil
- 1 tbsp fresh lemon juice

Directions:

1. Insert wire rack in rack position 6. Select bake, set temperature 390 F, timer for 30 minutes. Press start to preheat the oven.
2. Drizzle the olive oil on a roasting pan then place chicken, zucchini, dill, and tomatoes on the tray. Season with salt.
3. Bake chicken for 30 minutes.
4. Meanwhile, in a small bowl, stir together all topping ingredients.
5. Place chicken on the serving plate then tops with veggies. Discard dill sprigs.
6. Sprinkle topping mixture on top of chicken and vegetables.
7. Serve and enjoy.

Nutritional Value (Amount per Serving):
- Calories 531
- Fat 25.2 g
- Carbohydrates 6.1 g
- Sugar 2.9 g
- Protein 68.2 g
- Cholesterol 206 mg

Cheesy Meatloaf

Preparation Time: 10 minutes
Cooking Time: 35 minutes
Serve: 8
Ingredients:
- 1 egg
- 2 lbs ground turkey
- 1 tsp garlic powder
- 1 tsp garlic, minced
- 1 tbsp onion, minced
- 1 cup cheddar cheese, shredded
- 2 oz BBQ sauce, sugar-free
- 1 tsp ground mustard
- 1 tsp chili powder
- 1 tsp salt

Directions:

1. Spray 9*13-inch casserole dish with cooking spray and set aside.
2. Insert wire rack in rack position 6. Select bake, set temperature 390 F, timer for 35 minutes. Press start to preheat the oven.
3. In a large bowl, mix together all ingredients then transfer into the casserole dish.
4. Bake for 30-35 minutes.
5. Serve and enjoy.

Nutritional Value (Amount per Serving):
- Calories 302
- Fat 17.9 g
- Carbohydrates 3.6 g
- Sugar 2.2 g
- Protein 35.5 g
- Cholesterol 151 mg

Chicken Zucchini Casserole

Preparation Time: 10 minutes
Cooking Time: 40 minutes
Serve: 8
Ingredients:
- 2 1/2 lbs chicken breasts, boneless and cubed
- 1 tsp xanthan gum
- 1 tbsp tomato paste
- 5.5 oz coconut cream
- 5 zucchini, cut into cubes
- 12 oz roasted red peppers, drained and chopped
- 10 garlic cloves
- 2/3 cup mayonnaise
- 1 tsp salt

Directions:

1. Insert wire rack in rack position 6. Select bake, set temperature 390 F, timer for 35 minutes. Press start to preheat the oven.
2. Add zucchini and chicken into the casserole dish. Cover dish with foil. Bake for 35 minutes.
3. Meanwhile, in a bowl, stir together the remaining ingredients.
4. Pour bowl mixture over chicken and zucchini and broil for 5 minutes.
5. Serve and enjoy.

Nutritional Value (Amount per Serving):
- Calories 429
- Fat 22 g
- Carbohydrates 14.6 g
- Sugar 6.2 g
- Protein 43.9 g
- Cholesterol 131 mg

Yummy Chicken Fajita Casserole

Preparation Time: 10 minutes
Cooking Time: 15 minutes
Serve: 4
Ingredients:
- 1 lb cooked chicken, shredded
- 1 bell pepper, sliced
- 1/3 cup mayonnaise
- 7 oz cream cheese
- 7 oz cheddar cheese, shredded
- 2 tbsp tex-mix seasoning
- 1 onion, sliced
- Pepper
- Salt

Directions:

1. Grease baking dish with butter and set aside.
2. Insert wire rack in rack position 6. Select bake, set temperature 390 F, timer for 15 minutes. Press start to preheat the oven.
3. Mix all ingredients except 2 oz shredded cheese in a baking dish.
4. Spread remaining cheese on top and bake for 15 minutes.
5. Serve and enjoy.

Nutritional Value (Amount per Serving):
- Calories 641
- Fat 44.1 g
- Carbohydrates 13.3 g
- Sugar 4.3 g
- Protein 50.2 g
- Cholesterol 199 mg

Basil Pesto Chicken

Preparation Time: 10 minutes
Cooking Time: 40 minutes
Serve: 4

Ingredients:
- 4 chicken breasts, skinless, boneless, and cut in half
- 1 cup mozzarella cheese, shredded
- 1/2 cup basil pesto
- 3 tomatoes, sliced

Directions:
1. Line a roasting pan with aluminum foil and spray with cooking spray. Set aside.
2. Insert wire rack in rack position 6. Select bake, set temperature 390 F, timer for 35 minutes. Press start to preheat the oven.
3. In a bowl, mix together pesto and chicken until well coated.
4. Place chicken on roasting pan and bake for 35 minutes.
5. Remove from oven and top with cheese and tomatoes.
6. Bake for 5 minutes more.
7. Serve and enjoy.

Nutritional Value (Amount per Serving):
- Calories 315
- Fat 12.3 g
- Carbohydrates 3.9 g
- Sugar 2.4 g
- Protein 45.1 g
- Cholesterol 134 mg

Chicken with Vegetables

Preparation Time: 10 minutes
Cooking Time: 50 minutes
Serve: 4

Ingredients:
- 8 chicken thighs, skinless and boneless
- 10 oz roasted red peppers, sliced
- 2 cups cherry tomatoes
- 1 1/2 lbs potatoes, cut into chunks
- 4 tbsp olive oil
- 1 tsp dried oregano
- 5 garlic cloves, crushed
- 1/4 cup capers, drained
- Pepper
- Salt

Directions:
1. Insert wire rack in rack position 6. Select bake, set temperature 390 F, timer for 50 minutes. Press start to preheat the oven.

2. Season chicken with pepper and salt.
3. Heat 2 tablespoons of oil in a pan over medium-high heat. Add chicken and sear until brown from both the sides.
4. Place chicken in a roasting pan. Stir in potatoes, oregano, garlic, capers, red peppers, and tomatoes. Drizzle with olive oil.
5. Bake for 50 minutes.
6. Serve and enjoy.

Nutritional Value (Amount per Serving):
- Calories 837
- Fat 36.3 g
- Carbohydrates 36.7 g
- Sugar 7.6 g
- Protein 89.3 g
- Cholesterol 260 mg

Chicken Lasagna

Preparation Time: 10 minutes
Cooking Time: 1 hour 5 minutes
Serve: 8

Ingredients:
- 4 cups chicken, cooked and chopped
- 1 jar ragu cheese sauce
- 1 tsp garlic salt
- 10 oz frozen spinach, thawed, drained, and chopped
- 16 oz chive and onion cream cheese
- 12 lasagna noodles, cooked
- 3 cups mozzarella cheese, shredded

Directions:
1. Spray a 9*13-inch baking dish with cooking spray and set aside.
2. Insert wire rack in rack position 6. Select bake, set temperature 350 F, timer for 50 minutes. Press start to preheat the oven.
3. In a bowl, stir together chicken, garlic salt, spinach, and cream cheese.
4. Spread 1/3 tomato sauce in a baking dish then place 4 noodles, 1/3 chicken, and 1 cup cheese. Repeat layer twice.
5. Cover dish with foil and bake for 50 minutes. Remove foil and bake for 15 minutes more.
6. Serve and enjoy.

Nutritional Value (Amount per Serving):
- Calories 708
- Fat 33.3 g
- Carbohydrates 57.7 g
- Sugar 3.4 g
- Protein 38 g
- Cholesterol 174 mg

Bacon Chicken Lasagna

Preparation Time: 10 minutes
Cooking Time: 25 minutes
Serve: 8

Ingredients:
- 3 cups chicken, cooked and shredded
- 2 1/2 cups mozzarella cheese, grated

- 3/4 lb bacon, cooked and crumbled
- 1/2 cup sun-dried tomatoes, chopped
- 14 oz artichoke hearts, drained and chopped
- 1/2 cup parmesan cheese, grated
- 12 lasagna noodles, cooked
- 3 tbsp ranch dressing
- 1 1/4 cups milk
- 16 oz cream cheese

Directions:
1. Spray a 9*13-inch baking dish with cooking spray and set aside.
2. Insert wire rack in rack position 6. Select bake, set temperature 350 F, timer for 25 minutes. Press start to preheat the oven.
3. In a bowl, mix together chicken, tomatoes, artichokes, parmesan cheese, 1 cup mozzarella cheese, and bacon.
4. In a separate bowl, mix together milk, ranch dressing, and cream cheese.
5. Pour half milk mixture over the chicken and stir well. Pour half milk mixture in the baking dish.
6. Place 3 lasagna noodles in the baking dish then place 1/3 chicken mixture and half cup mozzarella cheese. Repeat layers twice.
7. Bake for 25 minutes.
8. Serve and enjoy.

Nutritional Value (Amount per Serving):
- Calories 851
- Fat 44.3 g
- Carbohydrates 60 g
- Sugar 2.8 g
- Protein 53.1 g
- Cholesterol 191 mg

Delicious Mexican Chicken Lasagna

Preparation Time: 10 minutes
Cooking Time: 15 minutes
Serve: 15
Ingredients:
- 1 1/2 lbs chicken breast, cooked and shredded
- 2 tsp ground cumin
- 2 tbsp chili powder
- 1 cup of salsa
- 3/4 cup sour cream
- 2 cup cheese, shredded
- 4 tortillas
- 1 tsp dry onion, minced

Directions:
1. Insert wire rack in rack position 6. Select bake, set temperature 390 F, timer for 15 minutes. Press start to preheat the oven.
2. Mix together chicken, dried onion, cumin, chili powder, salsa, and sour cream.
3. Spray baking dish with cooking spray.
4. Spread half chicken mixture in a baking dish then place 2 tortillas on top.

5. Sprinkle 1/2 cheese over the tortillas then repeat the layers.
6. Bake for 15 minutes.
7. Serve and enjoy.

Nutritional Value (Amount per Serving):
- Calories 160
- Fat 9 g
- Carbohydrates 5.3 g
- Sugar 0.8 g
- Protein 14.5 g
- Cholesterol 50 mg

Pumpkin Chicken Lasagna

Preparation Time: 10 minutes
Cooking Time: 35 minutes
Serve: 5
Ingredients:
- 1 lb chicken, boneless and chopped
- 1 tsp olive oil
- 1 cup milk
- 14 oz can cream of pumpkin soup
- 1 1/2 cups mozzarella cheese, shredded
- 9 lasagna noodles
- 16 oz pasta sauce

Directions:
1. Insert wire rack in rack position 6. Select bake, set temperature 390 F, timer for 35 minutes. Press start to preheat the oven.
2. In a bowl, combine together soup and milk. Set aside.
3. Heat oil in a saucepan over medium heat.
4. Add chicken in a saucepan and sauté until cooked.
5. Stir in pasta sauce and simmer for 15 minutes.
6. Spread 1/3 sauce mixture into the baking dish then place 3 noodles and top with 1/3 soup mixture. Repeat layers twice. Sprinkle cheese over noodles.
7. Bake for 35 minutes.
8. Serve and enjoy.

Nutritional Value (Amount per Serving):
- Calories 597
- Fat 10.9 g
- Carbohydrates 77.6 g
- Sugar 11.9 g
- Protein 45.1 g
- Cholesterol 116 mg

Cheesy Chicken Lasagna

Preparation Time: 10 minutes
Cooking Time: 45 minutes
Serve: 9
Ingredients:
- 3 cups chicken, cooked and diced
- 1/2 cup onion, chopped
- 8 lasagna noodles, cooked and drained
- 1/2 cup green bell pepper, chopped
- 1/2 cup parmesan cheese, grated

- 1/2 Tsp dried basil
- 2 cups processed cheese, shredded
- 16 oz cottage cheese
- 6 oz can mushroom, drained and sliced
- 10 oz can cream of chicken soup
- 1/4 cup pimento peppers, chopped
- 3/4 cup milk
- 3 tbsp butter

Directions:

1. Insert wire rack in rack position 6. Select bake, set temperature 350 F, timer for 45 minutes. Press start to preheat the oven.
2. Melt butter in a saucepan over medium heat. Add bell pepper, onion and sauté.
3. Stir in soup, pimento, basil, processed cheese, milk, and mushrooms.
4. Place 1/2 noodles in a baking dish then layer with 1/2 cream sauce, half cottage cheese, half chicken, and half parmesan cheese. Repeat layers.
5. Bake for 45 minutes.
6. Serve and enjoy.

Nutritional Value (Amount per Serving):

- Calories 449
- Fat 16.8 g
- Carbohydrates 38.8 g
- Sugar 3.8 g
- Protein 35 g
- Cholesterol 96 mg

Parmesan Chicken & Veggies

Preparation Time: 10 minutes
Cooking Time: 30 minutes
Serve: 4

Ingredients:

- 4 chicken breasts, skinless and boneless
- 2 tbsp olive oil
- 1/2 tsp garlic powder
- 1/2 cup Parmesan cheese, grated
- 1/2 cup Italian seasoned breadcrumbs
- 4 tbsp butter, melted
- 1/2 lb baby potatoes cut into fourths
- 1 yellow squash, sliced
- 1 zucchini, sliced
- Pepper
- Salt

Directions:

1. Spray a baking dish with cooking spray and set aside.
2. Insert wire rack in rack position 6. Select bake, set temperature 350 F, timer for 30 minutes. Press start to preheat the oven.
3. Place melted butter in a shallow dish.
4. In another dish mix together, parmesan cheese, breadcrumbs, and garlic powder.
5. Season chicken with pepper and salt then dip into the melted butter and coat with cheese mixture.
6. Place coated chicken in a baking dish.

7. In mixing bowl, add potatoes, yellow squash, zucchini, and olive oil toss well.
8. Add vegetables into the baking dish around the chicken and bake for 30 minutes.
9. Serve and enjoy.

Nutritional Value (Amount per Serving):

- Calories 579
- Fat 32.7 g
- Carbohydrates 20.4 g
- Sugar 2.3 g
- Protein 50.2 g
- Cholesterol 169 mg

Chicken Cheese Rice

Preparation Time: 10 minutes
Cooking Time: 25 minutes
Serve: 4

Ingredients:

- 1 cup chicken breast, cooked and shredded
- 2 tbsp all-purpose flour
- 2 cup cooked brown rice
- 1 tbsp garlic, minced
- 2 tbsp butter
- 1 cup cheddar cheese, shredded
- 1 cup chicken stock
- 1/2 tbsp fresh thyme, chopped
- 1/2 tsp pepper
- 1/1 tsp salt

Directions:

1. Spray a baking dish with cooking spray and set aside.
2. Insert wire rack in rack position 6. Select bake, set temperature 350 F, timer for 25 minutes. Press start to preheat the oven.
3. Melt butter in a pan over medium-high heat. Add garlic and cook for 1 minute. Add thyme, pepper, salt, and flour stir well.
4. Pour chicken stock into the pan and whisk constantly. Whisk until thick then add cheese and stir until melted.
5. Add chicken and cooked rice stir well to combine. Transfer pan mixture into the baking dish and bake for 25 minutes.
6. Serve and enjoy.

Nutritional Value (Amount per Serving):

- Calories 559
- Fat 18.5 g
- Carbohydrates 77 g
- Sugar 0.4 g
- Protein 20.3 g
- Cholesterol 61 mg

Lemon Rosemary Chicken

Preparation Time: 10 minutes
Cooking Time: 25 minutes
Serve: 2

Ingredients:

- 2 chicken breasts, boneless and skinless
- 1 garlic clove, minced

- 1 spring rosemary, chopped
- 1 tbsp rosemary leaves
- 12 oz small potatoes, halved
- 1/2 tbsp olive oil
- 1 lemon juice
- 1 tsp red chili flakes
- Salt

Directions:

1. Insert wire rack in rack position 6. Select bake, set temperature 390 F, timer for 25 minutes. Press start to preheat the oven.
2. Add potatoes into the boiling water and cook for 10 minutes. Drain well and set aside.
3. In a bowl, place chicken and add spring rosemary, garlic, chili flakes, lemon juice, rosemary leaves, and olive oil mix well.
4. In a pan, place chicken over medium-high heat for 5 minutes.
5. Transfer chicken in a baking tray and add potatoes in-tray.
6. Place the tray in oven and roast chicken for 25 minutes.
7. Serve and enjoy.

Nutritional Value (Amount per Serving):
- Calories 446
- Fat 15.5 g
- Carbohydrates 29.2 g
- Sugar 2.7 g
- Protein 46 g
- Cholesterol 132 mg

Spicy Chicken Wings

Preparation Time: 10 minutes
Cooking Time: 30 minutes
Serve: 4
Ingredients:
- 2 lbs fresh chicken wings
- 4 tbsp cayenne pepper sauce
- 2 tbsp spring onion, chopped
- 1 tbsp brown sugar
- 1 tbsp Worcestershire sauce
- 4 tbsp butter
- 1 tsp sea salt

Directions:

1. Line roasting pan with foil and set aside.
2. Insert wire rack in rack position 6. Select bake, set temperature 350 F, timer for 30 minutes. Press start to preheat the oven.
3. Arrange chicken wings on roasting pan and bake for 30 minutes.
4. In a large bowl, mix together brown sugar, Worcestershire sauce, butter, cayenne pepper sauce, and salt.
5. Remove wings from oven and place in sauce bowl toss well until all wings are coated well with the sauce.
6. Garnish with chopped spring onion.
7. Serve and enjoy.

Nutritional Value (Amount per Serving):

- Calories 563
- Fat 29.3 g
- Carbohydrates 6.2 g
- Sugar 3.6 g
- Protein 66.4 g
- Cholesterol 132 mg

Olive Tomato Chicken

Preparation Time: 10 minutes
Cooking Time: 22 minutes
Serve: 4
Ingredients:
- 4 chicken breast, boneless and halves
- 15 olives, pitted and halved
- 2 cups cherry tomatoes
- 3 tbsp olive oil
- 3 tbsp capers, rinsed and drained
- Pepper
- Salt

Directions:

1. Insert wire rack in rack position 6. Select bake, set temperature 390 F, timer for 20 minutes. Press start to preheat the oven.
2. In a bowl, toss tomatoes, capers, olives with 2 tablespoons of oil. Set aside.
3. Season chicken with pepper and salt.
4. Heat remaining oil in a pan over high heat.
5. Place chicken in the pan and cook for 4 minutes.
6. Transfer chicken onto the roasting pan and top with tomato mixture and bake for 20 minutes.
7. Serve and enjoy.

Nutritional Value (Amount per Serving):
- Calories 241
- Fat 15 g
- Carbohydrates 4.9 g
- Sugar 2.4 g
- Protein 22.3 g
- Cholesterol 64 mg

Chicken Paillard

Preparation Time: 10 minutes
Cooking Time: 25 minutes
Serve: 8
Ingredients:
- 4 chicken breasts, skinless and boneless
- 1/2 cup olives, diced
- 1 small onion, sliced
- 1 fennel bulb, sliced
- 28 oz can tomatoes, diced
- 1/4 cup fresh basil, chopped
- 1/4 cup fresh parsley, chopped
- 1/4 cup pine nuts
- 2 tbsp olive oil
- Pepper
- Salt

Directions:

1. Insert wire rack in rack position 6. Select bake, set temperature 390 F, timer for 25 minutes. Press start to preheat the oven.
2. Arrange chicken in baking dish and season with pepper and salt and drizzle with oil.
3. In a bowl, mix together olives, tomatoes, pine nuts, onion, fennel, pepper, and salt.
4. Pour olive mixture over chicken and bake for 25 minutes.
5. Garnish with basil and parsley.
6. Serve and enjoy.

Nutritional Value (Amount per Serving):
- Calories 242
- Fat 12.8 g
- Carbohydrates 9.3 g
- Sugar 3.9 g
- Protein 23.2 g
- Cholesterol 65 mg

Juicy Garlic Chicken

Preparation Time: 10 minutes
Cooking Time: 40 minutes
Serve: 6
Ingredients:
- 2 lbs chicken thighs, skinless and boneless
- 8 garlic cloves, sliced
- 2 tbsp olive oil
- 2 tbsp fresh parsley, chopped
- 1 fresh lemon juice
- Pepper
- Salt

Directions:
1. Insert wire rack in rack position 6. Select bake, set temperature 390 F, timer for 40 minutes. Press start to preheat the oven.
2. Place chicken on roasting pan and season with pepper and salt.
3. Sprinkle parsley and garlic over the chicken and drizzle with oil and lemon juice.
4. Bake for 40 minutes.
5. Serve and enjoy.

Nutritional Value (Amount per Serving):
- Calories 336
- Fat 16 g
- Carbohydrates 1.6 g
- Sugar 0.2 g
- Protein 44.1 g
- Cholesterol 135 mg

Lemon Pepper Chicken

Preparation Time: 10 minutes
Cooking Time: 35 minutes
Serve: 4
Ingredients:
- 4 chicken thighs
- 1 tsp garlic powder
- 1 tbsp lemon pepper seasoning
- 2 tbsp fresh lemon juice
- 1/2 tsp paprika

- 1/2 tsp Italian seasoning
- 1/2 tsp onion powder
- 2 tbsp olive oil
- 1 tsp salt

Directions:
1. Insert wire rack in rack position 6. Select bake, set temperature 390 F, timer for 35 minutes. Press start to preheat the oven.
2. Add chicken in the large bowl.
3. Mix together lemon juice and olive oil and pour over chicken.
4. Mix together paprika, Italian seasoning, onion powder, garlic powder, lemon pepper seasoning, and salt and rub all over the chicken.
5. Arrange chicken on a roasting pan and bake for 35 minutes.
6. Serve and enjoy.

Nutritional Value (Amount per Serving):
- Calories 338
- Fat 17.7 g
- Carbohydrates 2.2 g
- Sugar 0.5 g
- Protein 40.9 g
- Cholesterol 125 mg

Spicy Chicken Meatballs

Preparation Time: 10 minutes
Cooking Time: 25 minutes
Serve: 4
Ingredients:
- 1 lb ground chicken
- 1/2 cup cilantro, chopped
- 1 jalapeno pepper, minced
- 1 habanero pepper, minced
- 1 poblano chili pepper, minced
- Salt

Directions:
1. Insert wire rack in rack position 4. Select air fry, set temperature 400 F, timer for 25 minutes. Press start to preheat the oven.
2. Add all ingredients into the large bowl and mix until well combined.
3. Make small balls from meat mixture and place on an air fryer basket and air fry for 25 minutes.
4. Serve and enjoy.

Nutritional Value (Amount per Serving):
- Calories 226
- Fat 8.5 g
- Carbohydrates 2.3 g
- Sugar 0.7 g
- Protein 33.4 g
- Cholesterol 101 mg

Turkey Meatballs

Preparation Time: 10 minutes
Cooking Time: 20 minutes
Serve: 6
Ingredients:
- 1 lb ground turkey

- 1 tbsp basil, chopped
- 1/3 cup coconut flour
- 2 cups zucchini, grated
- 1 tsp dried oregano
- 1 tbsp garlic, minced
- 1 tsp cumin
- 1 tbsp dried onion flakes
- 2 eggs, lightly beaten
- 1 tbsp nutritional yeast
- Pepper
- Salt

Directions:
1. Insert wire rack in rack position 6. Select bake, set temperature 390 F, timer for 20 minutes. Press start to preheat the oven.
2. Add all ingredients into the mixing bowl and mix until well combined.
3. Make small balls from meat mixture and place on a roasting pan and bake for 20 minutes.
4. Serve and enjoy.

Nutritional Value (Amount per Serving):
- Calories 214
- Fat 10.7 g
- Carbohydrates 8.1 g
- Sugar 1.1 g
- Protein 24.9 g
- Cholesterol 132 mg

Tandoori Chicken

Preparation Time: 10 minutes
Cooking Time: 15 minutes
Serve: 4
Ingredients:
- 1 lb chicken tenders, cut in half
- 1/4 cup parsley, chopped
- 1 tbsp garlic, minced
- 1 tbsp ginger, minced
- 1/4 cup yogurt
- 1 tsp paprika
- 1 tsp garam masala
- 1 tsp turmeric
- 1 tsp cayenne pepper
- 1 tsp salt

Directions:
1. Insert wire rack in rack position 4. Select air fry, set temperature 350 F, timer for 15 minutes. Press start to preheat the oven.
2. Add all ingredients into the large bowl and mix well. Place in refrigerator for 30 minutes.
3. Add marinated chicken into the air fryer basket and cook for 15 minutes.
4. Serve and enjoy.

Nutritional Value (Amount per Serving):
- Calories 240
- Fat 8.9 g
- Carbohydrates 3.9 g
- Sugar 1.3 g
- Protein 34.2 g

- Cholesterol 102 mg

Hot Chicken Wings

Preparation Time: 10 minutes
Cooking Time: 25 minutes
Serve: 4
Ingredients:
- 2 lbs chicken wings
- 1/2 tsp Worcestershire sauce
- 1/2 tsp Tabasco
- 6 tbsp butter, melted
- 12 oz hot sauce

Directions:
1. Insert wire rack in rack position 4. Select air fry, set temperature 380 F, timer for 25 minutes. Press start to preheat the oven.
2. Add chicken wings into the air fryer basket and cook for 25 minutes.
3. Meanwhile, in a bowl, mix together hot sauce, Worcestershire sauce, and butter. Set aside.
4. Add cooked chicken wings into the sauce bowl and toss well.
5. Serve and enjoy.

Nutritional Value (Amount per Serving):
- Calories 594
- Fat 34.4 g
- Carbohydrates 1.6 g
- Sugar 1.2 g
- Protein 66.2 g
- Cholesterol 248 mg

Garlicky Chicken Wings

Preparation Time: 10 minutes
Cooking Time: 20 minutes
Serve: 4
Ingredients:
- 12 chicken wings
- 1 tbsp chili powder
- 1/2 tbsp baking powder
- 1 tsp granulated garlic
- 1/2 tsp sea salt

Directions:
1. Insert wire rack in rack position 4. Select air fry, set temperature 410 F, timer for 20 minutes. Press start to preheat the oven.
2. Add chicken wings into the large bowl and toss with remaining ingredients.
3. Transfer chicken wings into the air fryer basket and air fry for 20 minutes.
4. Serve and enjoy.

Nutritional Value (Amount per Serving):
- Calories 580
- Fat 22.6 g
- Carbohydrates 2.4 g
- Sugar 0.3 g
- Protein 87.1 g
- Cholesterol 267 mg

Fajita Chicken

Preparation Time: 10 minutes
Cooking Time: 15 minutes
Serve: 4

Ingredients:
- 4 chicken breasts, make horizontal cuts on each piece
- 2 tbsp fajita seasoning
- 2 tbsp olive oil
- 1 onion, sliced
- 1 bell pepper, sliced

Directions:
1. Insert wire rack in rack position 4. Select air fry, set temperature 380 F, timer for 15 minutes. Press start to preheat the oven.
2. Rub oil and seasoning all over the chicken breast.
3. Place chicken into the air fryer basket and top with bell peppers and onion.
4. Cook for 15 minutes.
5. Serve and enjoy.

Nutritional Value (Amount per Serving):
- Calories 374
- Fat 17.9 g
- Carbohydrates 8 g
- Sugar 2.7 g
- Protein 42.8 g
- Cholesterol 130 mg

Yummy Chicken Tenders

Preparation Time: 10 minutes
Cooking Time: 12 minutes
Serve: 4

Ingredients:
- 1 lb chicken tenderloin
- 1/3 cup breadcrumb
- 3 eggs, lightly beaten
- 2 tbsp olive oil
- 1/2 cup all-purpose flour
- Pepper
- Salt

Directions:
1. Insert wire rack in rack position 4. Select air fry, set temperature 330 F, timer for 12 minutes. Press start to preheat the oven.
2. In a shallow dish, mix together flour, pepper, and salt. Add breadcrumbs in a separate shallow dish. Add egg in a small bowl.
3. Roll chicken in flour then dips in egg and coat with breadcrumbs.
4. Place coated chicken on roasting pan and air fry for 12 minutes.
5. Serve and enjoy.

Nutritional Value (Amount per Serving):
- Calories 296
- Fat 11.5 g
- Carbohydrates 18.7 g
- Sugar 0.9 g
- Protein 29.9 g
- Cholesterol 171 mg

Old Bay Chicken Wings

Preparation Time: 10 minutes
Cooking Time: 45 minutes
Serve: 4

Ingredients:
- 3 lbs chicken wings
- 1 tbsp old bay seasoning
- 2 tsp xanthan gum
- 1 tsp fresh lemon juice
- 1/2 cup butter, melted

Directions:
1. Insert wire rack in rack position 4. Select air fry, set temperature 360 F, timer for 45 minutes. Press start to preheat the oven.
2. Add chicken wings, xanthan gum, and old bay seasoning to the large bowl and toss well.
3. Transfer chicken wings to the air fryer basket and air fry for 45 minutes.
4. In a large bowl mix together melted butter and lemon juice.
5. Add cooked chicken wings to the butter lemon mixture and toss well.
6. Serve and enjoy.

Nutritional Value (Amount per Serving):
- Calories 853
- Fat 48.2 g
- Carbohydrates 4.1 g
- Sugar 0.1 g
- Protein 99 g
- Cholesterol 364 mg

Chinese Chicken Wings

Preparation Time: 10 minutes
Cooking Time: 30 minutes
Serve: 2

Ingredients:
- 4 chicken wings
- 1 tsp mixed spice
- 1 tbsp soy sauce
- 1 tbsp Chinese spice
- Pepper
- Salt

Directions:
1. Insert wire rack in rack position 4. Select air fry, set temperature 350 F, timer for 30 minutes. Press start to preheat the oven.
2. Add chicken wings into the bowl. Add remaining ingredients and toss well.
3. Transfer chicken wings into the air fryer basket and air fry for 15 minutes.
4. Serve and enjoy.

Nutritional Value (Amount per Serving):
- Calories 429
- Fat 17.3 g
- Carbohydrates 2.1 g
- Sugar 0.6 g
- Protein 62.4 g
- Cholesterol 178 mg

Chicken Kabab

Preparation Time: 10 minutes
Cooking Time: 6 minutes
Serve: 3
Ingredients:
- 1 lb ground chicken
- 1/4 cup almond flour
- 2 green onion, chopped
- 1 egg, lightly beaten
- 1/3 cup fresh parsley, chopped
- 2 garlic cloves
- 4 oz onion, chopped
- 1/4 tsp turmeric powder
- 1/2 tsp black pepper
- 1 tbsp fresh lemon juice

Directions:
1. Insert wire rack in rack position 4. Select air fry, set temperature 400 F, timer for 6 minutes. Press start to preheat the oven.
2. Add all ingredients into the food processor and process until well combined.
3. Transfer chicken mixture to the bowl and place it in the refrigerator for 30 minutes.
4. Divide mixture into the 6 equal portions and roll around the soaked wooden skewers.
5. Place kabab into the air fryer basket air fry for 6 minutes.
6. Serve and enjoy.

Nutritional Value (Amount per Serving):
- Calories 391
- Fat 17.3 g
- Carbohydrates 7.9 g
- Sugar 2.1 g
- Protein 48.6 g
- Cholesterol 189 mg

Caribbean Chicken

Preparation Time: 10 minutes
Cooking Time: 10 minutes
Serve: 8
Ingredients:
- 3 lbs chicken thigh, skinless and boneless
- 1 tbsp cayenne
- 1 tbsp cinnamon
- 1 tbsp coriander powder
- 3 tbsp coconut oil, melted
- 1/2 tsp ground nutmeg
- 1/2 tsp ground ginger
- Pepper
- Salt

Directions:
1. Insert wire rack in rack position 4. Select air fry, set temperature 390 F, timer for 10 minutes. Press start to preheat the oven.
2. In a small bowl, mix together all ingredients except chicken.
3. Rub bowl mixture all over the chicken.
4. Place chicken into the air fryer basket and air fry for 10 minutes.
5. Serve and enjoy.

Nutritional Value (Amount per Serving):
- Calories 373
- Fat 17.9 g
- Carbohydrates 1.2 g
- Sugar 0.1 g
- Protein 49.3 g
- Cholesterol 151 mg

Chicken Coconut Meatballs

Preparation Time: 10 minutes
Cooking Time: 10 minutes
Serve: 4
Ingredients:
- 1 lb ground chicken
- 1 tbsp soy sauce
- 1 tbsp hoisin sauce
- 1/2 cup fresh cilantro, chopped
- 2 green onions, chopped
- 1/4 cup shredded coconut
- 1 tsp sesame oil
- 1 tsp sriracha
- Pepper
- Salt

Directions:
1. Insert wire rack in rack position 4. Select air fry, set temperature 350 F, timer for 10 minutes. Press start to preheat the oven.
2. Add all ingredients into the large bowl and mix until well combined.
3. Make small balls and place them into the air fryer basket and air fry for 10 minutes.
4. Serve and enjoy.

Nutritional Value (Amount per Serving):
- Calories 258
- Fat 11.4 g
- Carbohydrates 3.7 g
- Sugar 1.7 g
- Protein 33.5 g
- Cholesterol 101 mg

CHAPTER 4: MEAT RECIPES

Basil Pepper Beef

Preparation Time: 10 minutes
Cooking Time: 6 hours
Serve: 6
Ingredients:
- 2 lbs stew beef, cut into 1-inch cubes
- 1 tsp dried basil
- 1 tsp dried oregano
- 1 onion, diced
- 1 1/2 cups marinara sauce
- 12 oz roasted red peppers, drained and sliced
- 12 oz artichoke hearts, drained

Directions:
1. Insert wire rack in rack position 8. Select slow cook, Set LOW for 6 hours. Press start to preheat the oven.
2. Add all ingredients into the dutch oven and stir well.
3. Cover the dutch oven with lid and cook on low for 6 hours.
4. Serve and enjoy.

Nutritional Value (Amount per Serving):
- Calories 345
- Fat 12 g
- Carbohydrates 23 g
- Sugar 11.2 g
- Protein 37 g
- Cholesterol 2 mg

Italian Beef Roast

Preparation Time: 10 minutes
Cooking Time: 6 hours
Serve: 6
Ingredients:
- 2 lbs chuck roast, boneless
- 1/4 cup fresh parsley, chopped
- 1/4 cup olives, chopped
- 1/2 cup chicken stock
- 2 tbsp vinegar
- 2 tsp herb de Provence
- 1/3 cup sun-dried tomatoes, chopped
- 1 tbsp garlic, chopped

Directions:
1. Insert wire rack in rack position 8. Select slow cook, Set HIGH for 6 hours. Press start to preheat the oven.
2. Add all ingredients into the dutch oven and stir well.
3. Cover the dutch oven with lid and cook on high for 6 hours.
4. Shred meat using a fork.
5. Stir and serve.

Nutritional Value (Amount per Serving):
- Calories 345
- Fat 13 g
- Carbohydrates 2.3 g
- Sugar 0.5 g
- Protein 50 g
- Cholesterol 153 mg

Meatballs

Preparation Time: 10 minutes
Cooking Time: 20 minutes
Serve: 6
Ingredients:
- 2 lbs ground beef
- 1 egg, lightly beaten
- 1 tsp oregano
- 1 tsp cinnamon
- 2 tsp cumin
- 2 tsp coriander
- 1 tsp garlic, minced
- 1 small onion, grated
- 1 tbsp fresh mint, chopped
- 1/4 cup fresh parsley, minced
- 1/2 tsp allspice
- 1 tsp paprika
- Pepper
- Salt

Directions:
1. Insert wire rack in rack position 6. Select bake, set temperature 390 F, timer for 20 minutes. Press start to preheat the oven.
2. Add all ingredients into the large mixing bowl and mix until well combined.
3. Make small balls from the meat mixture and place them on a baking sheet and bake for 20 minutes.
4. Serve and enjoy.

Nutritional Value (Amount per Serving):
- Calories 304
- Fat 10.4 g
- Carbohydrates 2.7 g
- Sugar 10.7 g
- Protein 47.3 g
- Cholesterol 162 mg

Mediterranean Beef

Preparation Time: 10 minutes
Cooking Time: 8 hours
Serve: 8
Ingredients:
- 3 lbs beef pot roast, cut into small pieces
- 1/2 tsp ground cinnamon
- 1/2 tsp turmeric powder
- 1 tsp garlic, minced
- 15 oz frozen mixed vegetables
- 1/2 tsp ground ginger
- 1 tbsp beef bouillon granules
- 1 1/2 tbsp garam masala
- 2 cups of water

- 1 tsp salt

Directions:

1. Insert wire rack in rack position 8. Select slow cook, Set LOW for 8 hours. Press start to preheat the oven.
2. Add all ingredients into the dutch oven and stir everything well.
3. Cover the dutch oven with lid and cook on low for 8 hours.
4. Stir well and serve.

Nutritional Value (Amount per Serving):

- Calories 157
- Fat 3.2 g
- Carbohydrates 19.5 g
- Sugar 5.8 g
- Protein 13 g
- Cholesterol 17 mg

Balsamic Braised Beef

Preparation Time: 10 minutes
Cooking Time: 2 hours 30 minutes
Serve: 6

Ingredients:

- 2 1/2 lbs beef chuck shoulder pot roast, boneless
- 1/4 cup dates, pitted and chopped
- 2 tbsp olive oil
- 1/4 cup flour
- 4 medium shallots, sliced
- 1 medium onion, sliced
- 1/4 cup balsamic vinegar
- 1/4 tsp pepper
- 1/2 tsp salt

Directions:

1. Insert wire rack in rack position 6. Select bake, set temperature 325 F, timer for 2 hours 30 minutes. Press start to preheat the oven.
2. Coat beef with flour.
3. Heat oil in a Dutch oven over medium heat.
4. Add meat and cook until brown. Remove meat from the Dutch oven.
5. Add vinegar and 1 1/2 cups water to the Dutch oven and stir well.
6. Return meat to the Dutch oven along with shallots, onions, dates, pepper, and salt.
7. Cover and cook in the oven for 2 hours 30 minutes or until meat is tender.
8. Serve and enjoy.

Nutritional Value (Amount per Serving):

- Calories 169
- Fat 9 g
- Carbohydrates 12.5 g
- Sugar 5.5 g
- Protein 9.9 g
- Cholesterol 29 mg

Baked Lamb Patties

Preparation Time: 10 minutes
Cooking Time: 8 minutes

Serve: 4

Ingredients:

- 1 lb ground lamb
- 5 basil leaves, minced
- 10 mint leaves, minced
- 1/4 cup fresh parsley, chopped
- 1 tsp dried oregano
- 1 cup feta cheese, crumbled
- 1 tbsp garlic, minced
- 1 jalapeno pepper, minced
- 1/4 tsp pepper
- 1/2 tsp kosher salt

Directions:

1. Insert wire rack in rack position 6. Select bake, set temperature 390 F, timer for 8 minutes. Press start to preheat the oven.
2. Add all ingredients into the mixing bowl and mix until well combined.
3. Make four equal shape patties from meat mixture and place on a baking sheet and bake for 8 minutes.
4. Serve and enjoy.

Nutritional Value (Amount per Serving):

- Calories 330
- Fat 16.6 g
- Carbohydrates 5.4 g
- Sugar 1.7 g
- Protein 38.5 g
- Cholesterol 135 mg

Meatballs

Preparation Time: 10 minutes
Cooking Time: 20 minutes
Serve: 8

Ingredients:

- 2 lbs ground beef
- 1 1/2 cups whole wheat bread crumbs
- 12 oz jar roasted red peppers
- 1/4 cup fresh parsley, chopped
- 1/2 cup fresh basil, chopped
- 1/3 cup tomato sauce
- 2 eggs, lightly beaten
- 1/4 tsp pepper
- 1/2 tsp salt

Directions:

1. Spray a baking sheet with cooking spray and set aside.
2. Insert wire rack in rack position 6. Select bake, set temperature 350 F, timer for 20 minutes. Press start to preheat the oven.
3. Add all ingredients into the large mixing bowl and mix until well combined.
4. Make small meatballs from mixture and place on a prepared baking sheet and bake for 20 minutes.
5. Serve and enjoy.

Nutritional Value (Amount per Serving):

- Calories 304
- Fat 9.1 g

- Carbohydrates 12.6 g
- Sugar 0.5g
- Protein 38.1 g
- Cholesterol 142 mg

Olive Feta Beef

Preparation Time: 10 minutes
Cooking Time: 6 hours
Serve: 6
Ingredients:
- 2 lbs beef stew meat, cut into half-inch pieces
- 1 cup olives, pitted and cut in half
- 30 oz can tomatoes, diced
- 1/2 cup feta cheese, crumbled
- 1/4 tsp pepper
- 1/2 tsp salt

Directions:
1. Insert wire rack in rack position 8. Select slow cook, Set HIGH for 6 hours. Press start to preheat the oven.
2. Add all ingredients into the dutch oven and stir well.
3. Cover the dutch oven with lid and cook on high for 6 hours.
4. Season with pepper and salt.
5. Stir well and serve.

Nutritional Value (Amount per Serving):
- Calories 370
- Fat 14.5 g
- Carbohydrates 9.2 g
- Sugar 5.3 g
- Protein 49.1 g
- Cholesterol 8 mg

Olives Artichokes Beef

Preparation Time: 10 minutes
Cooking Time: 7 hours
Serve: 6
Ingredients:
- 2 lbs stew beef, cut into 1-inch cubes
- 14 oz can artichoke hearts, drained and halved
- 1/2 cup olives, pitted and chopped
- 14 oz can tomatoes, diced
- 15 oz can tomato sauce
- 32 oz chicken stock
- 2 garlic cloves, chopped
- 1 onion, diced
- 1 tsp dried basil
- 1 tsp dried parsley
- 1 bay leaf
- 1/2 tsp ground cumin
- 1 tsp dried oregano
- 1 tbsp olive oil

Directions:

1. Insert wire rack in rack position 8. Select slow cook, Set LOW for 7 hours. Press start to preheat the oven.
2. Heat olive oil in a large pan over medium-high heat.
3. Add meat and cook until brown, about 2 minutes on each side.
4. Transfer meat into the dutch oven.
5. Pour remaining ingredients over the meat and stir well.
6. Cover and dutch oven with lid and cook on low for 7 hours.
7. Serve and enjoy.

Nutritional Value (Amount per Serving):
- Calories 322
- Fat 13.2 g
- Carbohydrates 14.2 g
- Sugar 7.1 g
- Protein 36.8 g
- Cholesterol 10 mg

Baked Beef Casserole

Preparation Time: 10 minutes
Cooking Time: 1 hour 30 minutes
Serve: 6
Ingredients:
- 1 lb lean stew beef, cut into chunks
- 1/4 tsp garlic powder
- 1 tbsp tomato puree
- 2 cups beef stock
- 2 tbsp olive oil
- 2 tsp herb de Provence
- 3 tsp paprika
- 4 oz black olives, sliced
- 7 oz can tomatoes, chopped

Directions:
1. Insert wire rack in rack position 6. Select bake, set temperature 350 F, timer for 1 hour 30 minutes. Press start to preheat the oven.
2. Heat oil in a pan over medium heat. Add meat to the pan and cook until brown.
3. Add stock, olives, tomatoes, tomato puree, garlic powder, herb de Provence, and paprika. Stir well and bring to boil.
4. Transfer meat mixture into the casserole dish.
5. Cover dish with foil and cook in the oven for 1 hour 30 minutes.
6. Serve and enjoy.

Nutritional Value (Amount per Serving):
- Calories 228
- Fat 11.6 g
- Carbohydrates 5.8g
- Sugar 1.4 g
- Protein 26 g
- Cholesterol 11 mg

Roasted Sirloin Steak

Preparation Time: 10 minutes

Cooking Time: 30 minutes
Serve: 6
Ingredients:
- 2 lbs sirloin steak, cut into 1-inch cubes
- 2 garlic cloves, minced
- 3 tbsp fresh lemon juice
- 1/4 cup water
- 1/4 cup olive oil
- 2 cups fresh parsley, chopped
- 1 tsp dried oregano
- 1/2 tsp pepper
- 1 tsp salt

Directions:
1. Insert wire rack in rack position 6. Select bake, set temperature 390 F, timer for 30 minutes. Press start to preheat the oven.
2. Add all ingredients except beef into the large bowl and mix well.
3. Pour bowl mixture into the large zip-lock bag.
4. Add beef to the bag and shake well and place it in the refrigerator for 1 hour.
5. Place marinated beef on a roasting pan and bake for 30 minutes.
6. Serve and enjoy.

Nutritional Value (Amount per Serving):
- Calories 365
- Fat 18.1 g
- Carbohydrates 2 g
- Sugar 0.4 g
- Protein 46.6 g
- Cholesterol 135 mg

Garlic Rosemary Pork Chops

Preparation Time: 10 minutes
Cooking Time: 25 minutes
Serve: 4
Ingredients:
- 4 pork chops, boneless and cut 1/2-inch thick
- 1 tsp dried rosemary, crushed
- 2 garlic cloves, minced
- 1/4 tsp pepper
- 1/4 tsp salt

Directions:
1. Insert wire rack in rack position 6. Select bake, set temperature 350 F, timer for 35 minutes. Press start to preheat the oven.
2. Season pork chops with pepper and salt.
3. In a small bowl, mix together garlic and rosemary and rub all over pork chops.
4. Place pork chops on roasting pan and roast for 35 minutes.
5. Serve and enjoy.

Nutritional Value (Amount per Serving):
- Calories 208
- Fat 16 g
- Carbohydrates 0.6 g
- Sugar 0 g

- Protein 14.5 g
- Cholesterol 55 mg

Slow Cook Pork with Couscous

Preparation Time: 10 minutes
Cooking Time: 8 hours
Serve: 6
Ingredients:
- 2 1/2 lbs pork loin, boneless
- 1/4 tsp marjoram
- 1/4 tsp dried rosemary
- 2 tsp dried sage
- 1/2 tbsp garlic powder
- 1/2 tbsp paprika
- 3/4 cup chicken stock
- 2 tbsp olive oil
- 1 tsp basil
- 2 cups cooked couscous
- 1 tsp oregano
- 1/4 tsp dried thyme

Directions:
1. Insert wire rack in rack position 8. Select slow cook, Set LOW for 8 hours. Press start to preheat the oven.
2. Add all ingredients except couscous and meat into the dutch oven and stir well.
3. Place meat into the dutch oven. Cover the dutch oven with lid and cook on low for 8 hours.
4. Remove meat from pot and shred using a fork.
5. Return shredded meat to the pot and stir well.
6. Serve with couscous and enjoy.

Nutritional Value (Amount per Serving):
- Calories 721
- Fat 31.6 g
- Carbohydrates 45.9 g
- Sugar 0.3 g
- Protein 59.3 g
- Cholesterol 151mg

Artichoke Olive Pork Chops

Preparation Time: 10 minutes
Cooking Time: 20 minutes
Serve: 6
Ingredients:
- 1 1/2 lbs pork chops
- 2 lemons, sliced
- 15 oz can green olives, drained
- 1 onion, cut into wedges
- 1/2 tsp garlic powder
- 1 tsp oregano
- 6 tbsp olive oil
- 1 cup cherry tomatoes
- 12 oz marinated artichokes, drained
- 15 oz can black olives, drained
- 2 cups potatoes, diced
- 1/2 tsp pepper

- 1 tsp salt

Directions:

1.   Insert wire rack in rack position 6. Select bake, set temperature 375 F, timer for 20 minutes. Press start to preheat the oven.

2.   Place potatoes on a roasting pan. Drizzle potatoes with 2 tbsp oil and season with pepper and salt.

3.   Bake potatoes for 15 minutes.

4.   Season pork chops with garlic powder, oregano, pepper, and salt.

5.   Heat 2 tbsp oil in a pan over medium heat.

6.   Place pork chops in the pan and cook until brown from both the sides.

7.   Remove potatoes from the oven.

8.   Place pork chops, lemon slices, cherry tomatoes, artichokes, olives, and onion on a roasting pan and drizzle with 2 tbsp oil.

9.   Return to the oven and bake for 20 minutes more.

10.   Serve and enjoy.

Nutritional Value (Amount per Serving):

- Calories 666
- Fat 48.6 g
- Carbohydrates 28.4 g
- Sugar 2.8 g
- Protein 26.4 g
- Cholesterol 84 mg

Spicy Shredded Pork

Preparation Time: 10 minutes
Cooking Time: 8 hours
Serve: 8

Ingredients:

- 4 lbs pork shoulder, trimmed
- 2 lime juice
- 2 tsp dried oregano
- 2 tsp ground cumin
- 2 orange juices
- 2 onions, quartered
- 1 tbsp chili powder
- 4 garlic cloves, minced
- 1 tsp black pepper
- 2 tsp salt

Directions:

1.   Insert wire rack in rack position 8. Select slow cook, Set LOW for 8 hours. Press start to preheat the oven.

2.   In a small bowl, mix together chili powder, pepper, oregano, cumin, and salt.

3.   Rub spice mixture all over the pork.

4.   Place pork into the dutch oven.

5.   Add garlic, lime juice, orange juice and onions over the pork.

6.   Cover the dutch oven with lid and cook on low for 8 hours.

7.   Remove pork from Dutch oven and shred using a fork.

8.   Return shredded pork to the dutch oven and stir well.

9.   Serve and enjoy.

Nutritional Value (Amount per Serving):

- Calories 695
- Fat 48.9 g
- Carbohydrates 7.4 g
- Sugar 3.3 g
- Protein 53.7 g
- Cholesterol 56 mg

Pork Stew

Preparation Time: 10 minutes
Cooking Time: 8 hours
Serve: 4

Ingredients:

- 4 pork chops, boneless
- 2 1/4 cups vegetable stock
- 14 oz can tomatoes, chopped
- 1/2 cup olives
- 2 tsp garlic, minced
- 1 tbsp olive oil
- 2 tsp chili, diced
- 1 bay leaf
- 2 yellow bell pepper, sliced
- 2 red bell peppers, sliced
- 1 onion, sliced

Directions:

1.   Insert wire rack in rack position 8. Select slow cook, Set LOW for 8 hours. Press start to preheat the oven.

2.   Heat olive oil in a pan over medium heat. Add garlic, chili, and onion to the pan and sauté for 5 minutes.

3.   Add pork chops to the pan and cook for 5 minutes.

4.   Transfer pan mixture to the dutch oven along with remaining ingredients and stir well.

5.   Cover and cook on low for 8 hours.

6.   Stir and serve.

Nutritional Value (Amount per Serving):

- Calories 373
- Fat 26.6 g
- Carbohydrates 16.6 g
- Sugar 9.7 g
- Protein 20.4 g
- Cholesterol 46 mg

Italian Pork Chops

Preparation Time: 10 minutes
Cooking Time: 3 hours
Serve: 6

Ingredients:

- 6 pork chops, boneless
- 1/4 cup water
- 1 1/2 tsp garlic powder
- 1 1/2 tsp Italian seasoning
- 1/3 cup olive oil
- 15 oz can tomatoes, diced

- 1 onion, chopped

Directions:
1. Insert wire rack in rack position 8. Select slow cook, Set LOW for 3 hours. Press start to preheat the oven.
2. Add pork chops into the dutch oven.
3. Pour remaining ingredients on top of pork chops.
4. Cover and cook on low for 3 hours.
5. Serve and enjoy.

Nutritional Value (Amount per Serving):
- Calories 380
- Fat 31.5 g
- Carbohydrates 6 g
- Sugar 3.5 g
- Protein 18.9 g
- Cholesterol 70 mg

Cheese Stuff Pork Chops

Preparation Time: 10 minutes
Cooking Time: 35 minutes
Serve: 4

Ingredients:
- 4 pork chops, boneless and thick-cut
- 2 tbsp parsley, chopped
- 2 tbsp olives, chopped
- 2 tbsp sun-dried tomatoes, chopped
- 1/2 cup feta cheese, crumbled
- 2 garlic cloves, minced

Directions:
1. Insert wire rack in rack position 6. Select bake, set temperature 375 F, timer for 35 minutes. Press start to preheat the oven.
2. In a bowl, combine together garlic, parsley, olives, tomatoes, and feta cheese.
3. Cut a deep slit through each pork chop.
4. Stuff generous amount of stuffing mixture into each pork chop.
5. Season pork chop with pepper and salt and place into the baking dish and bake for 35 minutes.
6. Serve and enjoy.

Nutritional Value (Amount per Serving):
- Calories 314
- Fat 24.4 g
- Carbohydrates 1.9 g
- Sugar 1 g
- Protein 20.9 g
- Cholesterol 85 mg

Herb Pork Roast

Preparation Time: 10 minutes
Cooking Time: 1 hour 30 minutes
Serve: 6

Ingredients:
- 3 lbs pork roast, boneless
- 2 fresh oregano sprigs
- 1/4 tbsp black pepper
- 2 fresh thyme sprigs
- 1 cup of water

- 1 onion, chopped
- 3 garlic cloves, chopped
- 1 rosemary sprig
- 1 tbsp olive oil
- 1 tbsp kosher salt

Directions:
1. Insert wire rack in rack position 6. Select roast, set temperature 350 F, timer for 1 hour 30 minutes. Press start to preheat the oven.
2. Season pork roast with pepper and salt.
3. Heat olive oil in a stockpot and sear pork roast on each side, about 4 minutes.
4. Add onion and garlic. Pour in the water, oregano, and thyme and bring to boil for a minute.
5. Cover pot and roast in the preheated oven for 1 hour 30 minutes.
6. Serve and enjoy.

Nutritional Value (Amount per Serving):
- Calories 502
- Fat 23.8 g
- Carbohydrates 2.9 g
- Sugar 0.8 g
- Protein 65.1 g
- Cholesterol 195 mg

Perfect Steak

Preparation Time: 10 minutes
Cooking Time: 12 minutes
Serve: 2

Ingredients:
- 2 rib-eye steak
- 1 tsp Worcestershire sauce
- 2 tsp garlic, minced
- 2 tbsp fresh parsley, chopped
- 1 stick butter, softened
- Pepper
- Salt

Directions:
1. Insert wire rack in rack position 4. Select air fry, set temperature 400 F, timer for 12 minutes. Press start to preheat the oven.
2. In a bowl, mix together butter, Worcestershire sauce, garlic, parsley, and salt and place in the refrigerator.
3. Season steak with pepper and salt.
4. Place seasoned steak in the air fryer basket and cook for 12 minutes.
5. Remove steak from the air fryer and top with butter mixture.
6. Serve and enjoy.

Nutritional Value (Amount per Serving):
- Calories 593
- Fat 58.3 g
- Carbohydrates 2.9 g
- Sugar 0.6 g
- Protein 16.4 g
- Cholesterol 121 mg

Meatballs

Preparation Time: 10 minutes
Cooking Time: 20 minutes
Serve: 12
Ingredients:
- 1 lb ground beef
- 1/4 cup onion, chopped
- 3 tbsp mushrooms, chopped
- 2 tbsp fresh parsley, chopped
- 1/2 cup almond flour
- 1/4 tsp pepper
- 1 tsp salt

Directions:
1. Insert wire rack in rack position 4. Select air fry, set temperature 350 F, timer for 20 minutes. Press start to preheat the oven.
2. In a bowl, mix together ground beef, parsley, onions, and mushrooms.
3. Add remaining ingredients and mix until well combined.
4. Make small balls from the mixture.
5. Place prepared meatballs in the air fryer basket and cook for 20 minutes.
6. Serve and enjoy.

Nutritional Value (Amount per Serving):
- Calories 100
- Fat 4.6 g
- Carbohydrates 1.3 g
- Sugar 0.1 g
- Protein 12.6 g
- Cholesterol 34 mg

Simple Beef Roast

Preparation Time: 10 minutes
Cooking Time: 45 minutes
Serve: 6
Ingredients:
- 2 lbs beef roast
- 1 tbsp olive oil
- 1 tsp rosemary
- 1/4 tsp black pepper
- 1 tsp salt

Directions:
1. Insert wire rack in rack position 4. Select air fry, set temperature 360 F, timer for 45 minutes. Press start to preheat the oven.
2. Mix together oil, rosemary, pepper, and salt and rub all over the meat.
3. Place meat in the air fryer basket and cook for 45 minutes.
4. Serve and enjoy.

Nutritional Value (Amount per Serving):
- Calories 302
- Fat 11.8 g
- Carbohydrates 0.2 g
- Sugar 0 g
- Protein 45.9 g
- Cholesterol 135 mg

Broccoli & Beef

Preparation Time: 10 minutes
Cooking Time: 10 minutes
Serve: 4
Ingredients:
- 1 lb ground beef cubes
- 1 tbsp Worcestershire sauce
- 1/2 lb broccoli florets, steamed
- 1 tsp olive oil
- 1/2 onion, diced
- 1 tsp onion powder
- 1 tsp garlic powder

Directions:
1. Insert wire rack in rack position 4. Select air fry, set temperature 360 F, timer for 10 minutes. Press start to preheat the oven.
2. Add all ingredients except broccoli into the large bowl and toss until well combined.
3. Add bowl mixture into the air fryer basket and cook for 10 minutes.
4. Serve with broccoli and enjoy it.

Nutritional Value (Amount per Serving):
- Calories 227
- Fat 6 g
- Carbohydrates 6.8 g
- Sugar 2.7 g
- Protein 35.2 g
- Cholesterol 62 mg

Simple Sirloin Steak

Preparation Time: 10 minutes
Cooking Time: 10 minutes
Serve: 2
Ingredients:
- 2 sirloin steaks
- 2 tsp olive oil
- 2 tbsp steak seasoning

Directions:
1. Insert wire rack in rack position 4. Select air fry, set temperature 350 F, timer for 10 minutes. Press start to preheat the oven.
2. Brush steak with olive oil and season with steak seasoning.
3. Place steak in the air fryer basket and cook for 10 minutes.
4. Slice and serve.

Nutritional Value (Amount per Serving):
- Calories 198
- Fat 10 g
- Carbohydrates 0 g
- Sugar 0 g
- Protein 25.8 g
- Cholesterol 76 mg

Flavors Kebab

Preparation Time: 10 minutes
Cooking Time: 10 minutes
Serve: 4
Ingredients:
- 1 lb ground beef

- 1/4 cup fresh parsley, chopped
- 1 tbsp vegetable oil
- 2 tbsp kabab spice mix
- 1 tbsp garlic, minced
- 1 tsp salt

Directions:
1. Insert wire rack in rack position 4. Select air fry, set temperature 370 F, timer for 10 minutes. Press start to preheat the oven.
2. Add all ingredients into the mixing bowl and mix until well combined. Place in refrigerator for 30 minutes.
3. Divide the mixture equally and make sausage shape kabab.
4. Place kabab into the air fryer basket and cook for 10 minutes.
5. Serve and enjoy.

Nutritional Value (Amount per Serving):
- Calories 313
- Fat 14.6 g
- Carbohydrates 3.2 g
- Sugar 0.1 g
- Protein 40.2 g
- Cholesterol 101 mg

Meatballs

Preparation Time: 10 minutes
Cooking Time: 20 minutes
Serve: 4
Ingredients:
- 1/2 lb ground beef
- 1/2 lb Italian sausage
- 1/2 cup cheddar cheese, shredded
- 1/2 tsp black pepper
- 1/2 tsp garlic powder
- 1/2 tsp onion powder

Directions:
1. Insert wire rack in rack position 4. Select air fry, set temperature 370 F, timer for 20 minutes. Press start to preheat the oven.
2. Add all ingredients into the large mixing bowl and mix until well combined.
3. Make small balls from mixture and place in the air fryer basket and cook for 20 minutes.
4. Serve and enjoy.

Nutritional Value (Amount per Serving):
- Calories 357
- Fat 24.3 g
- Carbohydrates 0.8 g
- Sugar 0.3 g
- Protein 31.9 g
- Cholesterol 113 mg

Meatloaf

Preparation Time: 10 minutes
Cooking Time: 15 minutes
Serve: 4
Ingredients:
- 2 eggs

- 1 lb ground beef
- 1/2 tbsp ginger, minced
- 1/4 cup fresh cilantro, chopped
- 1 cup onion, diced
- 1/4 tsp cinnamon
- 1 tsp cayenne
- 1/2 tsp turmeric
- 1 tsp garam masala
- 1/2 tbsp garlic, minced
- 1 tsp salt

Directions:
1. Insert wire rack in rack position 4. Select air fry, set temperature 360 F, timer for 15 minutes. Press start to preheat the oven.
2. Add all ingredients into the mixing bowl and mix until well combined.
3. Transfer meat mixture into the 8-inch round pan and cook for 15 minutes.
4. Slices and serve.

Nutritional Value (Amount per Serving):
- Calories 261
- Fat 9.5 g
- Carbohydrates 4.3 g
- Sugar 1.5 g
- Protein 37.7 g
- Cholesterol 183 mg

Meatballs

Preparation Time: 10 minutes
Cooking Time: 8 minutes
Serve: 2
Ingredients:
- 5 oz minced beef
- 2 oz feta cheese, crumbled
- 2 tbsp almond flour
- 1/2 tbsp lemon zest, grated
- 1 tbsp fresh oregano, chopped
- Pepper
- Salt

Directions:
1. Insert wire rack in rack position 4. Select air fry, set temperature 390 F, timer for 8 minutes. Press start to preheat the oven.
2. Add all ingredients into the mixing bowl and mix until well combined.
3. Make small round balls from the meat mixture. Place meatballs into the air fryer basket and cook for 8 minutes.
4. Serve and enjoy.

Nutritional Value (Amount per Serving):
- Calories 256
- Fat 14 g
- Carbohydrates 4.5 g
- Sugar 1.3 g
- Protein 27.3 g
- Cholesterol 89 mg

Spiced Steak

Preparation Time: 10 minutes

Cooking Time: 9 minutes
Serve: 3
Ingredients:
- 1 lb ribeye steak
- 1/4 tsp paprika
- 1/4 tsp onion powder
- 1/4 tsp garlic powder
- 1/4 tsp chili powder
- 1/8 tsp cocoa powder
- 1/8 tsp coriander powder
- 1/4 tsp chipotle powder
- 1/2 tsp black pepper
- 1/2 tsp coffee powder
- 1 1/2 tsp sea salt

Directions:
1. Insert wire rack in rack position 4. Select air fry, set temperature 390 F, timer for 9 minutes. Press start to preheat the oven.
2. In a small bowl, mix together all ingredients except steak.
3. Rub spice mixture all over the steak and place steak in the air fryer basket and cook for 9 minutes.
4. Serve and enjoy.

Nutritional Value (Amount per Serving):
- Calories 967
- Fat 66.7 g
- Carbohydrates 7 g
- Sugar 0.2 g
- Protein 83.6 g
- Cholesterol 1 mg

Burger Patties

Preparation Time: 10 minutes
Cooking Time: 45 minutes
Serve: 4
Ingredients:
- 10 oz ground beef
- 1 tsp basil
- 1 tsp mustard
- 1 tsp tomato puree
- 1 tsp garlic puree
- 1 oz cheddar cheese
- 1 tsp mixed herbs
- Pepper
- Salt

Directions:
1. Insert wire rack in rack position 4. Select air fry, set temperature 350 F, timer for 20 minutes. Press start to preheat the oven.
2. Add all ingredients into the large bowl and mix until well combined.
3. Make four patties from mixture and place into the air fryer basket and cook for 45 minutes.
4. Serve and enjoy.

Nutritional Value (Amount per Serving):
- Calories 167
- Fat 7.3 g
- Carbohydrates 0.6 g

- Sugar 0.2 g
- Protein 23.5 g
- Cholesterol 71 mg

Meatloaf

Preparation Time: 10 minutes
Cooking Time: 25 minutes
Serve: 4
Ingredients:
- 1 lb ground beef
- 2 oz chorizo sausage, chopped
- 3 tbsp almond flour
- 1 egg, lightly beaten
- 2 mushrooms, sliced
- 1 tbsp thyme, chopped
- 1 onion, chopped
- Pepper
- Salt

Directions:
1. Insert wire rack in rack position 4. Select air fry, set temperature 390 F, timer for 25 minutes. Press start to preheat the oven.
2. Add all ingredients into the large bowl and mix until well combined.
3. Transfer bowl mixture into the baking dish and cook for 25 minutes.
4. Serve and enjoy.

Nutritional Value (Amount per Serving):
- Calories 321
- Fat 14.8 g
- Carbohydrates 4.5 g
- Sugar 1.4 g
- Protein 40.3 g
- Cholesterol 154 mg

Rosemary Dill Beef Roast

Preparation Time: 10 minutes
Cooking Time: 45 minutes
Serve: 8
Ingredients:
- 2 1/2 lbs beef roast
- 1/2 tsp onion powder
- 1 tsp rosemary
- 1 tsp dill
- 2 tbsp olive oil
- 1/2 tsp black pepper
- 1/2 tsp garlic powder

Directions:
1. Insert wire rack in rack position 4. Select air fry, set temperature 360 F, timer for 45 minutes. Press start to preheat the oven.
2. Mix together black pepper, garlic powder, onion powder, rosemary, dill, and olive oil. Rub all over the beef roast.
3. Place meat in the air fryer basket and cook for 45 minutes.
4. Serve and enjoy.

Nutritional Value (Amount per Serving):
- Calories 296

- Fat 12.4 g
- Carbohydrates 0.5 g
- Sugar 0.1 g
- Protein 43.1 g
- Cholesterol 127 mg

Meatballs

Preparation Time: 10 minutes
Cooking Time: 15 minutes
Serve: 6
Ingredients:
- 30 oz ground beef
- 1 tbsp Italian seasoning
- 1/4 cup parmesan cheese, grated
- 2 eggs, lightly beaten
- Pepper
- Salt

Directions:
1.   Insert wire rack in rack position 4. Select air fry, set temperature 375 F, timer for 15 minutes. Press start to preheat the oven.
2.   In a bowl, mix together meat, seasoning, parmesan cheese, and egg.
3.   Make small balls from the meat mixture and place it into the air fryer basket and cook for 15 minutes.
4.   Serve and enjoy.

Nutritional Value (Amount per Serving):
- Calories 304
- Fat 11.8 g
- Carbohydrates 0.5 g
- Sugar 0.3 g
- Protein 46.1 g
- Cholesterol 186 mg

Seasoned Steak

Preparation Time: 10 minutes
Cooking Time: 7 minutes
Serve: 2
Ingredients:
- 12 oz steaks
- 1 tbsp Montreal steak seasoning
- 1 tbsp soy sauce
- 1/2 tbsp cocoa powder
- Pepper
- Salt

Directions:
1.   Insert wire rack in rack position 4. Select air fry, set temperature 375 F, timer for 7 minutes. Press start to preheat the oven.
2.   Add steak, liquid smoke, soy sauce, and steak seasonings into the large zip-lock bag. Shake well and place it in the refrigerator overnight.
3.   Place marinated steaks into the air fryer basket and cook for 7 minutes.
4.   Serve and enjoy.

Nutritional Value (Amount per Serving):
- Calories 356
- Fat 8.7 g

- Carbohydrates 1.4 g
- Sugar 0.2 g
- Protein 62.2 g
- Cholesterol 153 mg

Meatballs

Preparation Time: 10 minutes
Cooking Time: 12 minutes
Serve: 4
Ingredients:
- 1 lb ground beef
- 1 egg, lightly beaten
- 1 tbsp onion, minced
- 1/4 cup marinara sauce, sugar-free
- 1/3 cup parmesan cheese, shredded
- 1 tsp garlic, minced
- 1 tsp Italian seasoning
- Pepper
- Salt

Directions:
1.   Insert wire rack in rack position 4. Select air fry, set temperature 350 F, timer for 12 minutes. Press start to preheat the oven.
2.   Add all ingredients into the mixing bowl and mix until well combined.
3.   Make small balls from mixture and place into the air fryer basket and cook for 12 minutes.
4.   Serve and enjoy.

Nutritional Value (Amount per Serving):
- Calories 270
- Fat 10.5 g
- Carbohydrates 3.1 g
- Sugar 1.7 g
- Protein 38.5 g
- Cholesterol 149 mg

Sausage Balls

Preparation Time: 10 minutes
Cooking Time: 15 minutes
Serve: 4
Ingredients:
- 4 oz sausage meat
- 1/2 tsp garlic paste
- 1/2 onion, diced
- 3 tbsp almond flour
- 1 tsp sage
- Pepper
- Salt

Directions:
1.   Insert wire rack in rack position 4. Select air fry, set temperature 360 F, timer for 15 minutes. Press start to preheat the oven.
2.   Add all ingredients into the mixing bowl and mix until well combined.
3.   Make small balls from mixture and place into the air fryer basket and cook for 15 minutes.
4.   Serve and enjoy.

Nutritional Value (Amount per Serving):
- Calories 134

- Fat 10.6 g
- Carbohydrates 2.7 g
- Sugar 0.6 g
- Protein 6.8 g
- Cholesterol 24 mg

BBQ Pork Chops

Preparation Time: 10 minutes
Cooking Time: 14 minutes
Serve: 2
Ingredients:
- 2 pork chops
- 1/2 tbsp garlic, minced
- 1/2 tsp sesame oil
- 1/4 cup BBQ sauce
- Pepper
- Salt

Directions:
1.   Insert wire rack in rack position 4. Select air fry, set temperature 350 F, timer for 14 minutes. Press start to preheat the oven.
2.   Add all ingredients into the mixing bowl and mix well and place in the refrigerator for 1 hour.
3.   Place marinated pork chops into the air fryer basket and cook for 14 minutes.
4.   Serve and enjoy.

Nutritional Value (Amount per Serving):
- Calories 316
- Fat 21.1 g
- Carbohydrates 12.1 g
- Sugar 8.2 g
- Protein 18.1 g
- Cholesterol 69 mg

Lamb Chops

Preparation Time: 10 minutes
Cooking Time: 12 minutes
Serve: 4
Ingredients:
- 4 lamb chops
- 3 tbsp olive oil
- 1 tbsp dried thyme
- 2 garlic clove, minced
- Pepper
- Salt

Directions:
1.   Insert wire rack in rack position 4. Select air fry, set temperature 390 F, timer for 12 minutes. Press start to preheat the oven.
2.   In a small bowl, mix together thyme, oil, and garlic. Season lamb chops with pepper and salt and rubs with thyme mixture.
3.   Place lamb chops into the air fryer basket and cook for 12 minutes.
4.   Serve and enjoy.

Nutritional Value (Amount per Serving):
- Calories 702
- Fat 34.5 g
- Carbohydrates 1 g

- Sugar 0 g
- Protein 92 g
- Cholesterol 294 mg

Pesto Pork Chops

Preparation Time: 10 minutes
Cooking Time: 18 minutes
Serve: 4
Ingredients:
- 4 pork chops
- 1 tbsp basil pesto
- 2 tbsp almond flour

Directions:
1.   Insert wire rack in rack position 4. Select air fry, set temperature 350 F, timer for 18 minutes. Press start to preheat the oven.
2.   Spread basil pesto on top of each pork chops and sprinkle with almond flour.
3.   Place pork chops into the air fryer basket and cook for 18 minutes.
4.   Serve and enjoy.

Nutritional Value (Amount per Serving):
- Calories 277
- Fat 21.5 g
- Carbohydrates 0.8 g
- Sugar 0 g
- Protein 18.8 g
- Cholesterol 69 mg

Moist Lamb Roast

Preparation Time: 10 minutes
Cooking Time: 1 hour 30 minutes
Serve: 4
Ingredients:
- 2.5 lbs lamb leg roast
- 3 garlic cloves, sliced
- 1 tbsp olive oil
- 1 tbsp dried rosemary
- Pepper
- Salt

Directions:
1.   Insert wire rack in rack position 4. Select air fry, set temperature 400 F, timer for 15 minutes. Press start to preheat the oven.
2.   Make small slits on meat using a sharp knife. Stuff garlic slices into the slits. Season meat with pepper and salt.
3.   Mix together oil and rosemary and rub all over the meat.
4.   Place meat into the air fryer basket and cook for 15 minutes.
5.   Serve and enjoy.

Nutritional Value (Amount per Serving):
- Calories 546
- Fat 22.6 g
- Carbohydrates 1.3 g
- Sugar 0 g
- Protein 80 g
- Cholesterol 247 mg

Flavors Herb Lamb Chops

Preparation Time: 10 minutes
Cooking Time: 7 minutes
Serve: 4

Ingredients:
- 1 lb lamb chops
- 1 tsp oregano
- 1 tsp thyme
- 1 tsp rosemary
- 2 tbsp fresh lemon juice
- 2 tbsp olive oil
- 1 tsp coriander
- 1 tsp salt

Directions:
1. Insert wire rack in rack position 4. Select air fry, set temperature 400 F, timer for 7 minutes. Press start to preheat the oven.
2. Add all ingredients except lamb chops into the zip-lock bag.
3. Add lamb chops to the bag. Seal bag and shake well and place it in the refrigerator overnight.
4. Place marinated lamb chops into the air fryer basket and cook for 7 minutes.
5. Serve and enjoy.

Nutritional Value (Amount per Serving):
- Calories 276
- Fat 15.5 g
- Carbohydrates 0.8 g
- Sugar 0.2 g
- Protein 32 g
- Cholesterol 102 mg

Simple & Quick Lamb Chops

Preparation Time: 10 minutes
Cooking Time: 5 minutes
Serve: 2

Ingredients:
- 2 lamb chops
- 1/2 tbsp fresh oregano, chopped
- 1 tbsp olive oil
- 1 garlic clove, minced
- Pepper
- Salt

Directions:
1. Insert wire rack in rack position 4. Select air fry, set temperature 400 F, timer for 5 minutes. Press start to preheat the oven.
2. Mix together garlic, olive oil, oregano, pepper, and salt and rub over lamb chops.
3. Place lamb chops into the air fryer basket and cook for 5 minutes.
4. Serve and enjoy.

Nutritional Value (Amount per Serving):
- Calories 674
- Fat 31.1 g
- Carbohydrates 1.3 g
- Sugar 0.1 g
- Protein 92.1 g

- Cholesterol 294 mg

Breaded Pork Chops

Preparation Time: 10 minutes
Cooking Time: 20 minutes
Serve: 4

Ingredients:
- 4 pork chops, boneless
- 2 eggs, lightly beaten
- 1 cup almond meal
- 1/4 cup parmesan cheese, grated
- 1 tbsp onion powder
- 1 tbsp garlic powder
- 1/4 tbsp black pepper
- 1/2 tsp sea salt

Directions:
1. Insert wire rack in rack position 4. Select air fry, set temperature 350 F, timer for 20 minutes. Press start to preheat the oven.
2. In a bowl, mix together almond meal, parmesan cheese, onion powder, garlic powder, pepper, and salt.
3. Whisk eggs in a shallow dish.
4. Dip pork chops into the egg then coat with almond meal mixture and place into the air fryer basket.
5. Cook pork chops for 20 minutes.
6. Serve and enjoy.

Nutritional Value (Amount per Serving):
- Calories 457
- Fat 35.2 g
- Carbohydrates 8.7 g
- Sugar 2.3 g
- Protein 28.2 g
- Cholesterol 155 mg

Cheese Garlic Pork Chops

Preparation Time: 10 minutes
Cooking Time: 20 minutes
Serve: 8

Ingredients:
- 8 pork chops, boneless
- 3/4 cup parmesan cheese
- 2 tbsp butter, melted
- 2 tbsp coconut oil
- 1 tsp thyme
- 1 tbsp parsley
- 6 garlic cloves, minced
- 1/4 tsp pepper
- 1/2 tsp sea salt

Directions:
1. Insert wire rack in rack position 4. Select air fry, set temperature 400 F, timer for 20 minutes. Press start to preheat the oven.
2. In a bowl, mix together butter, spices, parmesan cheese, and coconut oil.
3. Brush butter mixture on top of pork chops and place it into the air fryer basket and cook for 20 minutes.

4. Serve and enjoy.
Nutritional Value (Amount per Serving):
- Calories 342
- Fat 28 g
- Carbohydrates 1.2 g
- Sugar 0 g
- Protein 20.9 g
- Cholesterol 82 mg

Creole Pork Chops

Preparation Time: 10 minutes
Cooking Time: 12 minutes
Serve: 6
Ingredients:
- 1 1/2 lbs pork chops, boneless
- 1 tsp garlic powder
- 1/4 cup parmesan cheese, grated
- 1/3 cup almond flour
- 1 tsp paprika
- 1 tsp Creole seasoning

Directions:
1. Insert wire rack in rack position 4. Select air fry, set temperature 360 F, timer for 12 minutes. Press start to preheat the oven.
2. Add all ingredients except pork chops into the zip-lock bag.
3. Add pork chops into the bag. Seal bag and shake well.
4. Remove pork chops from the zip-lock bag and place it into the air fryer basket and cook for 12 minutes.
5. Serve and enjoy.
Nutritional Value (Amount per Serving):
- Calories 415
- Fat 32 g
- Carbohydrates 2 g
- Sugar 0.2 g
- Protein 28.2 g
- Cholesterol 100 mg

Tender Pork Chops

Preparation Time: 10 minutes
Cooking Time: 13 minutes
Serve: 4
Ingredients:
- 4 pork chops, boneless
- 1/2 tsp celery seeds
- 1/2 tsp parsley
- 1/2 tsp granulated onion
- 1/2 tsp granulated garlic
- 2 tsp olive oil
- 1/2 tsp salt

Directions:
1. Insert wire rack in rack position 4. Select air fry, set temperature 350 F, timer for 13 minutes. Press start to preheat the oven.
2. In a small bowl, mix together with seasonings and sprinkle onto the pork chops.

3. Place pork chops into the air fryer basket and cook for 13 minutes.
4. Serve and enjoy.
Nutritional Value (Amount per Serving):
- Calories 278
- Fat 22.3 g
- Carbohydrates 0.4 g
- Sugar 0.1 g
- Protein 18.1 g
- Cholesterol 69 mg

Simple Dash Seasoned Pork Chops

Preparation Time: 10 minutes
Cooking Time: 20 minutes
Serve: 2
Ingredients:
- 2 pork chops, boneless
- 1 tbsp dash seasoning

Directions:
1. Insert wire rack in rack position 4. Select air fry, set temperature 360 F, timer for 20 minutes. Press start to preheat the oven.
2. Rub seasoning all over the pork chops.
3. Place seasoned pork chops into the air fryer basket and cook for 20 minutes.
4. Serve and enjoy.
Nutritional Value (Amount per Serving):
- Calories 256
- Fat 19.9 g
- Carbohydrates 0 g
- Sugar 0 g
- Protein 18 g
- Cholesterol 69 mg

Jerk Pork Butt

Preparation Time: 10 minutes
Cooking Time: 20 minutes
Serve: 4
Ingredients:
- 1 1/2 lbs pork butt, cut into pieces
- 1/4 cup jerk paste

Directions:
1. Insert wire rack in rack position 4. Select air fry, set temperature 390 F, timer for 20 minutes. Press start to preheat the oven.
2. Add meat and jerk paste into the bowl and coat well. Place in refrigerator overnight.
3. Place marinated meat into the air fryer basket and cook for 20 minutes.
4. Serve and enjoy.
Nutritional Value (Amount per Serving):
- Calories 339
- Fat 12.1 g
- Carbohydrates 0.8 g
- Sugar 0.6 g
- Protein 53 g
- Cholesterol 156 mg

Asian Lamb

Preparation Time: 10 minutes
Cooking Time: 10 minutes
Serve: 4

Ingredients:

- 1 lb lamb, cut into 2-inch pieces
- 1 tbsp soy sauce
- 2 tbsp vegetable oil
- 1/2 tsp cayenne
- 1 1/2 tbsp ground cumin
- 2 red chili peppers, chopped
- 1 tbsp garlic, minced
- 1 tsp salt

Directions:

1. Insert wire rack in rack position 4. Select air fry, set temperature 360 F, timer for 10 minutes. Press start to preheat the oven.
2. Mix together cumin and cayenne in a small bowl. Rub meat with cumin mixture and place in a large bowl.
3. Add oil, soy sauce, garlic, chili peppers, and salt over the meat. Coat well and place it in the refrigerator overnight.
4. Add marinated meat to the air fryer basket and cook for 10 minutes.
5. Serve and enjoy.

Nutritional Value (Amount per Serving):

- Calories 286
- Fat 15.7 g
- Carbohydrates 2.3 g
- Sugar 0.3 g
- Protein 32.7 g
- Cholesterol 102 mg

Beef Stew

Preparation Time: 10 minutes
Cooking Time: 5 hours
Serve: 8

Ingredients:

- 3 lbs beef stew meat, trimmed
- 1/2 cup Thai red curry paste
- 1/3 cup tomato paste
- 13 oz can coconut milk
- 2 tsp ginger, minced
- 2 garlic cloves, minced
- 1 medium onion, sliced
- 2 tbsp extra virgin olive oil
- 2 cups carrots, julienned
- 2 cups broccoli florets
- 2 tsp fresh lime juice
- 2 tbsp fish sauce
- 2 tsp sea salt

Directions:

1. Insert wire rack in rack position 8. Select slow cook, Set HIGH for 5 hours. Press start to preheat the oven.
2. Heat 1 tbsp oil in a pan over medium-high heat. Add meat and brown the meat on all sides.
3. Transfer brown meat into the dutch oven.

4. Add remaining oil in a pan and sauté ginger, garlic, and onion over medium-high heat for 5 minutes. Add coconut milk and stir well.
5. Transfer pan mixture into the dutch oven.
6. Add remaining ingredients except for carrots and broccoli into the dutch oven.
7. Cover the dutch oven and cook on high for 5 hours.
8. Add carrots and broccoli during the last 30 minutes of cooking.
9. Serve and enjoy.

Nutritional Value (Amount per Serving):

- Calories 537
- Fat 28.6 g
- Carbohydrates 13 g
- Protein 54.4 g
- Cholesterol 152 mg

Mushroom Beef Stew

Preparation Time: 10 minutes
Cooking Time: 8 hours
Serve: 6

Ingredients:

- 3 lbs stewing steak, cut into pieces
- 4 cups mushrooms, quartered
- 1 tbsp Worcestershire sauce
- 2 tbsp tomato paste
- 1 1/4 cup beef stock
- 2 tbsp parsley, chopped
- 1 tbsp thyme leaves
- 1 bay leaf
- 3 medium carrots, peeled and cut into chunks
- Pepper
- Salt

Directions:

1. Insert wire rack in rack position 8. Select slow cook, Set LOW for 8 hours. Press start to preheat the oven.
2. Add beef, thyme, bay leaf, carrots, and mushrooms to the dutch oven.
3. Whisk together beef stock, Worcestershire sauce, and tomato paste and pour into the dutch oven. Season beef mixture with pepper and salt. Stir well.
4. Cover and cook on low for 8 hours.
5. Garnish with parsley and serve.

Nutritional Value (Amount per Serving):

- Calories 399
- Fat 15.3 g
- Carbohydrates 6.4 g
- Protein 57.5 g
- Cholesterol 0 mg

Spicy Pepper Beef

Preparation Time: 10 minutes
Cooking Time: 4 hours
Serve: 6

Ingredients:

- 2 lbs beef chuck, sliced

- 1 cup beef broth
- 1/2 medium onion, sliced
- 2 cups bell pepper, chopped
- 1 tbsp sriracha sauce
- 1/3 cup parsley, chopped
- 2 tsp garlic powder
- 1 tsp black pepper
- 2 tsp salt

Directions:

1. Insert wire rack in rack position 8. Select slow cook, Set HIGH for 4 hours. Press start to preheat the oven.
2. Place meat into the dutch oven.
3. Top meat with sliced onion and bell pepper. Season with garlic powder, pepper, and salt.
4. Mix together sriracha and broth and pour over meat mixture.
5. Cover and cook on high for 4 hours.
6. Garnish with chopped parsley and serve.

Nutritional Value (Amount per Serving):

- Calories 325
- Fat 11.5 g
- Carbohydrates 5.3 g
- Protein 47.5 g
- Cholesterol 137 mg

Slow Cooked Beef Brisket

Preparation Time: 10 minutes
Cooking Time: 7 hours
Serve: 6

Ingredients:

- 3 lbs beef brisket
- 1 tbsp chili powder
- 4 garlic cloves, chopped
- 1/2 onion, chopped
- 1 tsp cumin
- 3 tbsp chili sauce
- 1/4 cup beef broth
- 1 1/2 tsp liquid smoke
- 1 tbsp Worcestershire sauce
- 1/2 tsp black pepper

Directions:

1. Insert wire rack in rack position 8. Select slow cook, Set LOW for 7 hours. Press start to preheat the oven.
2. Mix together chili powder, pepper, cumin, Worcestershire sauce, and garlic and rub over brisket.
3. Place the beef brisket into the dutch oven. Mix together broth, chili sauce, onion, and liquid smoke and pour over brisket.
4. Cover and cook on low for 7 hours.
5. Remove brisket from dutch oven and cut into slices.
6. Serve and enjoy.

Nutritional Value (Amount per Serving):

- Calories 439
- Fat 14.5 g
- Carbohydrates 3.1 g

- Protein 69.5 g
- Cholesterol 203 mg

Slow Cooked Pork Chops

Preparation Time: 10 minutes
Cooking Time: 6 hours
Serve: 4

Ingredients:

- 4 pork chops
- 1 1/2 cups chicken broth
- 2 tbsp butter, melted
- 3 garlic cloves, minced
- 1 medium onion, chopped
- 3/4 tsp poultry seasoning
- 1/2 tsp salt

Directions:

1. Insert wire rack in rack position 8. Select slow cook, Set LOW for 6 hours. Press start to preheat the oven.
2. In a large bowl, mix together butter, broth, and poultry seasoning and salt.
3. Pour bowl mixture into the dutch oven.
4. Add pork chops, onion, and garlic into the dutch oven.
5. Cover and cook on low for 6 hours.
6. Serve and enjoy.

Nutritional Value (Amount per Serving):

- Calories 337
- Fat 26.2 g
- Carbohydrates 3.8 g
- Protein 20.3 g
- Cholesterol 84 mg

Cuban Pork

Preparation Time: 10 minutes
Cooking Time: 8 hours
Serve: 6

Ingredients:

- 3 lbs pork shoulder roast
- 1/4 tsp red pepper flakes, crushed
- 1 tsp dried oregano
- 1 tsp cumin
- 1/2 cup fresh lime juice
- 1 bay leaf
- 1 small onion, sliced
- 6 garlic cloves, minced
- 1/8 tsp black pepper
- 1/2 cup orange juice
- 2 tbsp olive oil
- 1 1/2 tsp salt

Directions:

1. Insert wire rack in rack position 8. Select slow cook, Set LOW for 8 hours. Press start to preheat the oven.
2. In a bowl, whisk together garlic, pepper, red pepper flakes, oregano, cumin, salt, lime juice, orange juice, and oil.
3. Pierce pork with knife and rub with garlic mixture.

4. Place pork into the dutch oven with bay leaf and onion.
5. Cover and cook on low for 8 hours.
6. Remove pork from Dutch oven and shred using the pork.
7. Serve and enjoy.

Nutritional Value (Amount per Serving):
- Calories 645
- Fat 51 g
- Carbohydrates 4.8 g
- Protein 38.7 g
- Cholesterol 161 mg

Steak Bites

Preparation Time: 10 minutes
Cooking Time: 8 hours
Serve: 4

Ingredients:
- 3 lbs round steak, cut into cubes
- 1/2 cup beef broth, low sodium
- 4 tbsp butter, sliced
- 1 tsp garlic powder
- 1 tbsp onion, minced
- 1/2 tsp black pepper
- 1/2 tsp salt

Directions:
1. Insert wire rack in rack position 8. Select slow cook, Set LOW for 8 hours. Press start to preheat the oven.
2. Add steak cubes into the dutch oven. Pour beef broth over the meat.
3. Sprinkle garlic powder, onion, pepper and salt over the meat.
4. Top with butter slices. Cover and cook on low for 8 hours.
5. Serve and enjoy.

Nutritional Value (Amount per Serving):
- Calories 845
- Fat 44.4 g
- Carbohydrates 1 g
- Protein 103.6 g
- Cholesterol 320 mg

Pot Roast

Preparation Time: 10 minutes
Cooking Time: 8 hours 30 minutes
Serve: 12

Ingredients:
- 3 lbs chuck roast, boneless
- 1 onion, quartered
- 4 celery stalks, sliced
- 1/2 cup beef broth
- 1 tsp garlic powder
- 1 tsp pepper
- 2 1/2 tsp salt

Directions:
1. Insert wire rack in rack position 8. Select slow cook, Set LOW for 8 hours. Press start to preheat the oven.

2. Mix together garlic powder, pepper, and salt and rub over the chuck roast.
3. Heat a few tablespoons of oil in a pan. Sear the meat in the pan from all sides.
4. Add meat, broth, and vegetables into the dutch oven.
5. Cover and cook on low for 8 hours.
6. Shred the meat using a fork and cook for 30 minutes more.
7. Serve and enjoy.

Nutritional Value (Amount per Serving):
- Calories 252
- Fat 9.5 g
- Carbohydrates 1.4 g
- Protein 37.8 g
- Cholesterol 115 mg

Flank Steak

Preparation Time: 10 minutes
Cooking Time: 8 hours
Serve: 8

Ingredients:
- 3 lbs flank steak
- 1 large onion, chopped
- 1 large carrot, chopped
- 1/2 cup water
- 1 bay leaf
- 1/4 tsp dried thyme
- Pepper
- Salt

Directions:
1. Insert wire rack in rack position 8. Select slow cook, Set HIGH for 8 hours. Press start to preheat the oven.
2. Season steak with pepper and salt.
3. Place season steak into the dutch oven.
4. Add onion and carrot over the steak.
5. Add thyme, bay leaves, and water over the steak.
6. Cover and cook on high for 8 hours.
7. Serve and enjoy.

Nutritional Value (Amount per Serving):
- Calories 292
- Fat 14 g
- Carbohydrates 2 g
- Protein 36 g
- Cholesterol 70 mg

Delicious Pork Carnitas

Preparation Time: 10 minutes
Cooking Time: 8 hours
Serve: 6

Ingredients:
- 3 lbs pork chops. boneless
- 2 garlic cloves, minced
- 1 red pepper, sliced
- 1 yellow pepper, sliced
- 1 onion, diced
- 1/2 cup water

- 1/2 cup taco sauce
- 2 bay leaves
- 1 tbsp cumin
- 2 tbsp chili powder
- Pepper
- Salt

Directions:
1. Insert wire rack in rack position 8. Select slow cook, Set LOW for 8 hours. Press start to preheat the oven.
2. Pour water into the dutch oven.
3. Add pork chops into the dutch oven.
4. Add all remaining ingredients over the pork chops and stir well.
5. Cover and cook on low for 8 hours.
6. Using fork shred the meat.
7. Serve and enjoy.

Nutritional Value (Amount per Serving):
- Calories 482
- Fat 16 g
- Carbohydrates 9.1 g
- Protein 72.2 g
- Cholesterol 209 mg

Flavors Caesar Pork Chops

Preparation Time: 10 minutes
Cooking Time: 8 hours 30
Serve: 5
Ingredients:
- 2 lbs pork chops
- 10.5 oz Caesar dressing
- 1/4 tsp pepper
- Salt

Directions:
1. Insert wire rack in rack position 8. Select slow cook, Set LOW for 8 hours. Press start to preheat the oven.
2. Season chops with pepper and salt.
3. Place seasoned pork chops into the dutch oven.
4. Sprinkle caesar dressing over the pork chops.
5. Cover and cook over low for 8 hours.
6. Serve and enjoy.

Nutritional Value (Amount per Serving):
- Calories 580
- Fat 43.8 g
- Carbohydrates 10.5 g
- Protein 34.4 g
- Cholesterol 131 mg

Beef Pot Roast

Preparation Time: 10 minutes
Cooking Time: 8 hours
Serve: 2
Ingredients:
- 8 oz beef chuck roast
- 15 baby carrots, sliced
- 3 small potatoes, cut into cubed

- 1/2 packet onion soup mix
- 1/2 medium onion, sliced

Directions:
1. Insert wire rack in rack position 8. Select slow cook, Set LOW for 8 hours. Press start to preheat the oven.
2. Place carrots and potatoes into the bottom of the dutch oven.
3. Place meat on top of veggies than add remaining ingredients.
4. Cover and cook on low for 8 hours.
5. Serve and enjoy.

Nutritional Value (Amount per Serving):
- Calories 630
- Fat 32 g
- Carbohydrates 50 g
- Sugar 7.8 g
- Protein 34.9 g
- Cholesterol 117 mg

Korean Beef

Preparation Time: 10 minutes
Cooking Time: 4 hours
Serve: 2
Ingredients:
- 1 lb flank steak, cut into strips
- 1/4 cup soy sauce
- 1/4 tsp garlic, minced
- 1 tbsp sesame oil
- 2 tbsp cornstarch
- 1/8 tsp red pepper flakes
- 1/2 small onion, chopped
- 6 tbsp brown sugar
- 1/4 cup beef broth

Directions:
1. Insert wire rack in rack position 8. Select slow cook, Set LOW for 4 hours. Press start to preheat the oven.
2. Add cornstarch and flank steak pieces into the ziplock bag and shake well to coat.
3. Add remaining ingredients into the dutch oven and stir well.
4. Add coated steak pieces into the dutch oven. Stir well.
5. Cover and cook on low for 4 hours.
6. Serve and enjoy.

Nutritional Value (Amount per Serving):
- Calories 663
- Fat 25.9 g
- Carbohydrates 38.1 g
- Sugar 27.6 g
- Protein 66 g
- Cholesterol 125 mg

Spicy Jalapeno Beef

Preparation Time: 10 minutes
Cooking Time: 6 hours
Serve: 2
Ingredients:

- 1 lb beef chuck roast
- 1/2 onion, sliced
- 1/4 cup Worcestershire sauce
- 1/4 cup beef broth
- 6 oz jar roasted bell peppers, drained and chopped
- 2 jalapenos, sliced
- 1/4 tsp black pepper
- 1/2 tsp salt

Directions:
1. Insert wire rack in rack position 8. Select slow cook, Set LOW for 6 hours. Press start to preheat the oven.
2. Place chuck roast into the dutch oven.
3. Pour Worcestershire sauce and beef broth over the roast. Season with pepper and salt.
4. Top roast with bell peppers, jalapenos, and sliced onions.
5. Cover and cook on low for 6 hours.
6. Shred the meat using a fork.
7. Serve and enjoy.

Nutritional Value (Amount per Serving):
- Calories 1299
- Fat 83.8 g
- Carbohydrates 65.8 g
- Sugar 11.1 g
- Protein 65.6 g
- Cholesterol 234 mg

Shredded Beef

Preparation Time: 10 minutes
Cooking Time: 6 hours
Serve: 2

Ingredients:
- 1 lb beef chuck shoulder roast, boneless and fat trimmed
- 2 banana peppers, seed discarded and sliced
- 1 cup beef broth
- 1/2 medium onion, sliced

Directions:
1. Insert wire rack in rack position 8. Select slow cook, Set LOW for 6 hours. Press start to preheat the oven.
2. Add all ingredients into the dutch oven.
3. Cover and cook on low for 6 hours.
4. Shred the meat using a fork.
5. Serve and enjoy.

Nutritional Value (Amount per Serving):
- Calories 490
- Fat 27.1 g
- Carbohydrates 12 g
- Sugar 7.5 g
- Protein 46.1 g
- Cholesterol 151 mg

Meatloaf

Preparation Time: 10 minutes
Cooking Time: 20 minutes

Serve: 4

Ingredients:
- 1 lb ground pork
- 1 onion, chopped
- 1 tbsp thyme, chopped
- 1/4 tsp garlic powder
- 1 egg, lightly beaten
- 3 tbsp breadcrumbs
- Pepper
- Salt

Directions:
1. Spray a loaf pan with cooking spray and set aside.
2. Insert wire rack in rack position 6. Select bake, set temperature 390 F, timer for 20 minutes. Press start to preheat the oven.
3. Add all ingredients into the mixing bowl and mix until well combined.
4. Pour meat mixture into the loaf pan and bake for 20 minutes.
5. Serve and enjoy.

Nutritional Value (Amount per Serving):
- Calories 211
- Fat 5.4 g
- Carbohydrates 6.9 g
- Sugar 1.6 g
- Protein 32.1 g
- Cholesterol 124 mg

Meatballs

Preparation Time: 10 minutes
Cooking Time: 12 minutes
Serve: 4

Ingredients:
- 1 egg, lightly beaten
- 1 tbsp oregano, chopped
- 4 oz ground lamb meat
- 1/2 tbsp lemon zest
- Pepper
- Salt

Directions:
1. Line baking tray with parchment paper and set aside.
2. Insert wire rack in rack position 6. Select bake, set temperature 390 F, timer for 12 minutes. Press start to preheat the oven.
3. Add all ingredients into the bowl and mix until well combined.
4. Make small balls from meat mixture and place them on a baking tray and bake for 12 minutes.
5. Serve and enjoy.

Nutritional Value (Amount per Serving):
- Calories 77
- Fat 5 g
- Carbohydrates 1 g
- Sugar 0.2 g
- Protein 6.8 g
- Cholesterol 61 mg

Italian Meatballs

Preparation Time: 10 minutes
Cooking Time: 20 minutes
Serve: 4
Ingredients:
- 1 lb ground beef
- 1/2 small onion, chopped
- 1 egg, lightly beaten
- 2 garlic cloves, minced
- 1 tbsp basil, chopped
- 1/4 cup parmesan cheese, grated
- 1/2 cup breadcrumbs
- 1 tbsp Italian parsley, chopped
- 1 tbsp rosemary, chopped
- 2 tbsp milk
- Pepper
- Salt

Directions:
1. Insert wire rack in rack position 6. Select bake, set temperature 375 F, timer for 20 minutes. Press start to preheat the oven.
2. Add all ingredients into the bowl and mix until well combined.
3. Make small balls from meat mixture and place them on a baking tray and cook for 20 minutes.
4. Serve and enjoy.

Nutritional Value (Amount per Serving):
- Calories 311
- Fat 10.4 g
- Carbohydrates 12.3 g
- Sugar 1.7 g
- Protein 39.9 g
- Cholesterol 147 mg

Cheesy Baked Patties

Preparation Time: 10 minutes
Cooking Time: 15 minutes
Serve: 6
Ingredients:
- 2 lbs ground beef
- 1 cup mozzarella cheese, grated
- 1 tsp onion powder
- 1 tsp garlic powder
- Pepper
- Salt

Directions:
1. Insert wire rack in rack position 6. Select bake, set temperature 390 F, timer for 15 minutes. Press start to preheat the oven.
2. Add all ingredients into the large bowl and mix until well combined.
3. Make patties from meat mixture and place on a baking tray and bake for 15 minutes.
4. Serve and enjoy.

Nutritional Value (Amount per Serving):
- Calories 297
- Fat 10.3 g
- Carbohydrates 0.8 g

- Sugar 0.3 g
- Protein 47.3 g
- Cholesterol 138 mg

Lamb Meatballs

Preparation Time: 10 minutes
Cooking Time: 15 minutes
Serve: 4
Ingredients:
- 1 lb ground lamb
- 1 tsp onion powder
- 1 tbsp garlic, minced
- 1 tsp ground coriander
- 1 tsp ground cumin
- Pepper
- Salt

Directions:
1. Insert wire rack in rack position 6. Select bake, set temperature 390 F, timer for 15 minutes. Press start to preheat the oven.
2. Add all ingredients into the large bowl and mix until well combined.
3. Make small balls from the meat mixture and place them on a baking tray and bake for 15 minutes.
4. Serve and enjoy.

Nutritional Value (Amount per Serving):
- Calories 218
- Fat 8.5 g
- Carbohydrates 1.4 g
- Sugar 0.2 g
- Protein 32.1 g
- Cholesterol 102 mg

Crispy Crusted Pork Chops

Preparation Time: 10 minutes
Cooking Time: 30 minutes
Serve: 3
Ingredients:
- 3 pork chops, boneless
- 3 tbsp parmesan cheese, grated
- 1/2 cup crushed crackers
- 2 tbsp milk
- 1 egg, lightly beaten
- Pepper
- Salt

Directions:
1. Spray a baking dish with cooking spray and set aside.
2. Insert wire rack in rack position 6. Select bake, set temperature 350 F, timer for 30 minutes. Press start to preheat the oven.
3. In a shallow bowl, whisk egg and milk.
4. In a separate shallow dish, mix together cheese, crackers, pepper, and salt.
5. Dip pork chops in egg then coat with cheese mixture and place in a baking dish and bake for 30 minutes.
6. Serve and enjoy.

Nutritional Value (Amount per Serving):

- Calories 320
- Fat 23.7 g
- Carbohydrates 3.3 g
- Sugar 1.1 g
- Protein 22.3 g
- Cholesterol 128 mg

Meatballs

Preparation Time: 10 minutes
Cooking Time: 20 minutes
Serve: 6
Ingredients:
- 8 oz ground beef
- 1/2 onion, diced
- 1 egg, lightly beaten
- 1/4 cup parmesan cheese, grated
- 1/2 cup breadcrumbs
- 1/4 cup parsley, chopped
- 1 tsp garlic, minced
- 8 oz ground pork
- Pepper
- Salt

Directions:
1. Insert wire rack in rack position 6. Select bake, set temperature 390 F, timer for 20 minutes. Press start to preheat the oven.
2. Add all ingredients into the large bowl and mix until well combined.
3. Make small balls from meat mixture and place them on a baking tray and bake for 20 minutes.
4. Serve and enjoy.

Nutritional Value (Amount per Serving):
- Calories 188
- Fat 5.7 g
- Carbohydrates 7.9 g
- Sugar 1 g
- Protein 24.9 g
- Cholesterol 91 mg

Tasty Crispy Crust Pork Chops

Preparation Time: 10 minutes
Cooking Time: 15 minutes
Serve: 2
Ingredients:
- 2 pork chops, bone-in
- 1 tbsp olive oil
- 1 cup crushed pork rinds
- 1/2 tsp garlic powder
- 1/2 tsp onion powder
- 1/2 tsp paprika
- 1/2 tsp parsley

Directions:
1. Insert wire rack in rack position 6. Select air fry, set temperature 400 F, timer for 15 minutes. Press start to preheat the oven.
2. In a large bowl, mix together pork rinds, garlic powder, onion powder, parsley, and paprika.

3. Brush pork chops with oil and coat with pork rind mixture and place on an air fryer basket and cook for 15 minutes.
4. Serve and enjoy.

Nutritional Value (Amount per Serving):
- Calories 362
- Fat 29.5 g
- Carbohydrates 1.3 g
- Sugar 0.4 g
- Protein 22.8 g
- Cholesterol 79 mg

Meatballs

Preparation Time: 10 minutes
Cooking Time: 20 minutes
Serve: 6
Ingredients:
- 1 lb ground beef
- 1 tbsp fresh rosemary, chopped
- 1/2 small onion, minced
- 2 garlic cloves, minced
- 1/4 cup parmesan cheese, grated
- 1/2 cup breadcrumbs
- 1 egg, lightly beaten
- 1 tbsp fresh basil, chopped
- 1 tbsp fresh parsley, chopped
- Pepper
- Salt

Directions:
1. Insert wire rack in rack position 6. Select bake, set temperature 375 F, timer for 20 minutes. Press start to preheat the oven.
2. Add all ingredients into the mixing bowl and mix until well combined.
3. Make small balls from meat mixture and place them on a baking tray and bake for 20 minutes.
4. Serve and enjoy.

Nutritional Value (Amount per Serving):
- Calories 205
- Fat 6.8 g
- Carbohydrates 8 g
- Sugar 0.9 g
- Protein 26.4 g
- Cholesterol 98 mg

Lemon Pepper Pork Chops

Preparation Time: 10 minutes
Cooking Time: 15 minutes
Serve: 4
Ingredients:
- 4 pork chops, boneless
- 1 tsp lemon pepper seasoning
- Salt

Directions:
1. Insert wire rack in rack position 6. Select air fry, set temperature 400 F, timer for 15 minutes. Press start to preheat oven

2.	Season pork chops with lemon pepper seasoning, and salt and place on an air fryer basket and cook for 15 minutes.
3.	Serve and enjoy.

Nutritional Value (Amount per Serving):
- Calories 257
- Fat 19.9 g
- Carbohydrates 0.3 g
- Sugar 0 g
- Protein 18 g
- Cholesterol 69 mg

Delicious Pork Patties

Preparation Time: 10 minutes
Cooking Time: 35 minutes
Serve: 6

Ingredients:
- 2 lbs ground pork
- 1 egg, lightly beaten
- 1 onion, minced
- 1 carrot, minced
- 1/2 cup breadcrumbs
- 1 tsp garlic powder
- 1 tsp paprika
- Pepper
- Salt

Directions:
1.	Insert wire rack in rack position 6. Select bake, set temperature 375 F, timer for 30 minutes. Press start to preheat the oven.
2.	Add all ingredients into the large bowl and mix until well combined.
3.	Make small patties from meat mixture and place on a baking tray and cook for 20 minutes.
4.	Turn patties bake for 15 minutes more.
5.	Serve and enjoy.

Nutritional Value (Amount per Serving):
- Calories 276
- Fat 6.6 g
- Carbohydrates 9.8 g
- Sugar 2.1 g
- Protein 42.1 g
- Cholesterol 138 mg

Lamb Chops

Preparation Time: 10 minutes
Cooking Time: 30 minutes
Serve: 4

Ingredients:
- 4 lamb chops
- 1 1/2 tsp tarragon
- 1 1/2 tsp ginger
- 1/4 cup brown sugar
- 1 tsp garlic powder
- 1 tsp ground cinnamon
- Pepper
- Salt

Directions:

1.	Insert wire rack in rack position 6. Select bake, set temperature 375 F, timer for 30 minutes. Press start to preheat the oven.
2.	Add garlic powder, cinnamon, tarragon, ginger, brown sugar, pepper, and salt into the zip-lock bag and mix well.
3.	Add lamb chops in a zip-lock bag. The sealed bag shakes well and places it in the refrigerator for 2 hours.
4.	Place marinated lamb chops on a roasting pan and bake for 30 minutes.
5.	Serve and enjoy.

Nutritional Value (Amount per Serving):
- Calories 650
- Fat 24.1 g
- Carbohydrates 10.5 g
- Sugar 9 g
- Protein 92.1 g
- Cholesterol 294 mg

Meatballs

Preparation Time: 10 minutes
Cooking Time: 15 minutes
Serve: 4

Ingredients:
- 1 lb ground pork
- 1/2 tsp dried thyme
- 1 tsp paprika
- 1 tsp garlic powder
- 1/2 tsp ground cumin
- 1/2 tsp coriander
- 1 tsp onion powder
- Pepper
- Salt

Directions:
1.	Insert wire rack in rack position 6. Select bake, set temperature 390 F, timer for 15 minutes. Press start to preheat the oven.
2.	Add all ingredients into the large bowl and mix until well combined.
3.	Make small balls from the meat mixture and place them on a baking tray and bake for 15 minutes.
4.	Serve and enjoy.

Nutritional Value (Amount per Serving):
- Calories 170
- Fat 4.1 g
- Carbohydrates 1.5 g
- Sugar 0.4 g
- Protein 30 g
- Cholesterol 83 mg

Ranch Pork Chops

Preparation Time: 10 minutes
Cooking Time: 35 minutes
Serve: 6

Ingredients:
- 6 pork chops, boneless
- 1 oz ranch seasoning
- 2 tbsp olive oil

- 1 tsp dried parsley

Directions:
1. Line baking tray with parchment paper and set aside.
2. Insert wire rack in rack position 6. Select bake, set temperature 390 F, timer for 35 minutes. Press start to preheat the oven.
3. Mix together oil, dried parsley, and ranch seasoning and rub over pork chops.
4. Place pork chops on a baking tray and cook for 35 minutes.
5. Serve and enjoy.

Nutritional Value (Amount per Serving):
- Calories 311
- Fat 24.6 g
- Carbohydrates 0 g
- Sugar 0 g
- Protein 18 g
- Cholesterol 69 mg

Country Style Baked Pork Chops

Preparation Time: 10 minutes
Cooking Time: 35 minutes
Serve: 2
Ingredients:
- 2 pork chops
- 2 onion sliced
- 2 tbsp ketchup
- 2 tbsp brown sugar
- Pepper
- Salt

Directions:
1. Insert wire rack in rack position 6. Select bake, set temperature 375 F, timer for 35 minutes. Press start to preheat the oven.
2. Season pork chops with pepper and salt.
3. Place pork chops in a baking dish. Mix together ketchup and brown sugar and pour over pork chops.
4. Top with onion slices. Cover baking dish with foil and bake for 35 minutes.
5. Serve and enjoy.

Nutritional Value (Amount per Serving):
- Calories 308
- Fat 19.9 g
- Carbohydrates 13.5 g
- Sugar 12.5 g
- Protein 18.2 g
- Cholesterol 69 mg

Baked Patties

Preparation Time: 10 minutes
Cooking Time: 15 minutes
Serve: 4
Ingredients:
- 1 lb ground lamb
- 1 tsp ground coriander
- 1 tsp ground cumin
- 1/4 cup fresh parsley, chopped
- 1/4 cup onion, minced
- 1/4 tsp cayenne pepper
- 1/2 tsp ground allspice
- 1 tsp ground cinnamon
- 1 tbsp garlic, minced
- 1/4 tsp pepper
- 1 tsp kosher salt

Directions:
1. Insert wire rack in rack position 6. Select bake, set temperature 390 F, timer for 15 minutes. Press start to preheat the oven.
2. Add all ingredients into the large bowl and mix until well combined.
3. Make small balls from meat mixture and place on a baking tray and lightly flatten the meatballs with back on spoon.
4. Bake for 15 minutes.
5. Serve and enjoy.

Nutritional Value (Amount per Serving):
- Calories 223
- Fat 8.5 g
- Carbohydrates 2.6 g
- Sugar 0.4 g
- Protein 32.3 g
- Cholesterol 102 mg

Lamb Roast

Preparation Time: 10 minutes
Cooking Time: 8 hours
Serve: 8
Ingredients:
- 4 lbs lamb roast, boneless
- 4 garlic cloves, cut into slivers
- 1 tsp oregano
- 1/4 tsp pepper
- 1/2 tsp marjoram
- 1/2 tsp thyme
- 2 tsp salt

Directions:
1. Insert wire rack in rack position 8. Select slow cook, Set LOW for 8 hours. Press start to preheat the oven.
2. Using a sharp knife make small cuts all over lamb roast then insert garlic slivers into the cuts.
3. In a small bowl, mix together marjoram, thyme, oregano, pepper, and salt and rub all over lamb roast.
4. Place lamb roast into the dutch oven.
5. Cover and cook on low for 8 hours.
6. Serve and enjoy.

Nutritional Value (Amount per Serving):
- Calories 605
- Fat 48.2 g
- Carbohydrates 0.7 g
- Sugar 0 g
- Protein 38.3 g
- Cholesterol 161 mg

Italian Pork Roast

Preparation Time: 10 minutes
Cooking Time: 6 hours
Serve: 8
Ingredients:
- 2 lbs lean pork roast, boneless
- 1 tbsp parsley
- 1/2 cup parmesan cheese, grated
- 28 oz can tomatoes, diced
- 1 tsp dried oregano
- 1 tsp dried basil
- 1 tsp garlic powder
- Pepper
- Salt

Directions:
1. Insert wire rack in rack position 8. Select slow cook, Set LOW for 6 hours. Press start to preheat the oven.
2. Add the meat into the dutch oven.
3. Mix together tomatoes, oregano, basil, garlic powder, parsley, cheese, pepper, and salt and pour over meat.
4. Cover and cook on low for 6 hours.
5. Serve and enjoy.

Nutritional Value (Amount per Serving):
- Calories 237
- Fat 8.4 g
- Carbohydrates 5.7 g
- Sugar 3.5 g
- Protein 33.7 g
- Cholesterol 94 mg

Meatballs

Preparation Time: 10 minutes
Cooking Time: 20 minutes
Serve: 4
Ingredients:
- 1 lb ground lamb
- 3 tbsp olive oil
- 1/4 tsp red pepper flakes
- 1 tbsp garlic, minced
- 1 egg, lightly beaten
- 1 tsp ground cumin
- 2 tsp fresh oregano, chopped
- 2 tbsp fresh parsley, chopped
- 1/4 tsp pepper
- 1 tsp kosher salt

Directions:
1. Line baking tray with parchment paper.
2. Insert wire rack in rack position 6. Select bake, set temperature 390 F, timer for 20 minutes. Press start to preheat the oven.
3. Add all ingredients except oil into the mixing bowl and mix until well combined.
4. Make small meatballs from meat mixture and place on a prepared baking tray.
5. Drizzle oil over meatballs and bake in for 20 minutes.
6. Serve and enjoy.

Nutritional Value (Amount per Serving):

- Calories 325
- Fat 20.2 g
- Carbohydrates 1.7 g
- Sugar 0.2 g
- Protein 33.6 g
- Cholesterol 143 mg

Garlicky Beef Roast

Preparation Time: 10 minutes
Cooking Time: 8 hours
Serve: 6
Ingredients:
- 2 lbs lean top round beef roast
- 1 tbsp Italian seasoning
- 6 garlic cloves, minced
- 1 onion, sliced
- 2 cups beef broth
- 1/2 cup red wine
- 1 tsp red pepper flakes
- Pepper
- Salt

Directions:
1. Insert wire rack in rack position 8. Select slow cook, Set LOW for 8 hours. Press start to preheat the oven.
2. Season meat with pepper and salt and place into the dutch oven.
3. Pour remaining ingredients over meat.
4. Cover and cook on low for 8 hours.
5. Remove meat from dutch oven and shred using a fork.
6. Return shredded meat to the dutch oven and stir well.
7. Serve and enjoy.

Nutritional Value (Amount per Serving):
- Calories 231
- Fat 6.7 g
- Carbohydrates 4 g
- Sugar 1.4 g
- Protein 35.8 g
- Cholesterol 76 mg

Tender Pork Tenderloin

Preparation Time: 10 minutes
Cooking Time: 15 minutes
Serve: 4
Ingredients:
- 1 1/2 lbs pork tenderloin
- 1 tsp garlic powder
- 1 tsp Italian seasoning
- 2 tbsp olive oil
- 1 tsp ground coriander
- 1/4 tsp pepper
- 1 tsp sea salt

Directions:
1. Insert wire rack in rack position 6. Select bake, set temperature 390 F, timer for 15 minutes. Press start to preheat the oven.

2. Rub pork tenderloin with 1 tablespoon of olive oil.
3. Mix together coriander, garlic powder, Italian seasoning, pepper, and salt and rub over pork tenderloin.
4. Heat remaining oil in a pan over medium-high heat.
5. Add pork tenderloin in hot oil and cook until brown from all the sides.
6. Place pork tenderloin on a baking tray and cook for 15 minutes.
7. Slice and serve.

Nutritional Value (Amount per Serving):
- Calories 310
- Fat 13.3 g
- Carbohydrates 0.7 g
- Sugar 0.3 g
- Protein 44.7 g
- Cholesterol 125 mg

Creole Pork Chops

Preparation Time: 10 minutes
Cooking Time: 10 minutes
Serve: 6
Ingredients:
- 6 pork chops, boneless
- 2 tbsp Creole mustard
- 1/2 cup zesty Italian dressing
- 1 tbsp Italian seasoning

Directions:
1. Insert wire rack in rack position 6. Select bake, set temperature 375 F, timer for 30 minutes. Press start to preheat the oven.
2. Add pork chops in a mixing bowl.
3. Pour remaining ingredients over pork chops and coat well and place them in the refrigerator for 30 minutes.
4. Arrange marinated pork chops on a baking tray and cook 10 minutes or until internal temperature reaches 145 F.
5. Serve and enjoy.

Nutritional Value (Amount per Serving):
- Calories 280
- Fat 21.8 g
- Carbohydrates 0.5 g
- Sugar 0.4 g
- Protein 18 g
- Cholesterol 70 mg

Delicious Burger Patties

Preparation Time: 10 minutes
Cooking Time: 12 minutes
Serve: 4
Ingredients:
- 1 lb ground beef
- 1/4 tsp red pepper flakes
- 1/2 tsp garlic powder
- 1/2 tsp onion powder
- Pepper

- Salt

Directions:
1. Insert wire rack in rack position 6. Select bake, set temperature 350 F, timer for 12 minutes. Press start to preheat the oven.
2. Add all ingredients into the mixing bowl and mix until well combined.
3. Make four patties from meat mixture and place on a baking tray and bake for 12 minutes.
4. Serve and enjoy.

Nutritional Value (Amount per Serving):
- Calories 213
- Fat 7.1 g
- Carbohydrates 0.6 g
- Sugar 0.2 g
- Protein 34.5 g
- Cholesterol 101 mg

Meatballs

Preparation Time: 10 minutes
Cooking Time: 10 minutes
Serve: 4
Ingredients:
- 1 egg
- 1 lb ground beef
- 2 tbsp taco seasoning
- 1 tbsp garlic, minced
- 1/4 cup cilantro, chopped
- 1/4 cup onion, chopped
- 1/2 cup cheddar cheese, shredded
- Pepper
- Salt

Directions:
1. Insert wire rack in rack position 6. Select bake, set temperature 390 F, timer for 10 minutes. Press start to preheat the oven.
2. Add ground beef and remaining ingredients into the mixing bowl and mix until well combined.
3. Make small meatballs and place them on a baking tray and bake for 10 minutes.
4. Serve and enjoy.

Nutritional Value (Amount per Serving):
- Calories 293
- Fat 13 g
- Carbohydrates 1.9 g
- Sugar 0.5 g
- Protein 39.7 g
- Cholesterol 158 mg

Creamy Pork Chops

Preparation Time: 10 minutes
Cooking Time: 6 hours
Serve: 4
Ingredients:
- 4 pork chops, boneless
- 2 chicken bouillon cubes, crushed
- 1 cup milk
- 10 oz can cream chicken soup
- 10 oz can cream mushrooms soup

- 1/2 tsp dried basil
- 1 tsp onion powder
- 1 tsp garlic powder
- 1/2 tsp dried dill
- 2 tbsp dried parsley
- 1/2 tsp pepper

Directions:

1. Insert wire rack in rack position 8. Select slow cook, Set LOW for 6 hours. Press start to preheat the oven.
2. Spray dutch oven from inside with cooking spray.
3. Place pork chops into the dutch oven.
4. In a bowl, mix together the remaining ingredients and pour over pork chops.
5. Cover the dutch oven with lid and cook on low for 6 hours.
6. Serve and enjoy.

Nutritional Value (Amount per Serving):

- Calories 398
- Fat 26.6 g
- Carbohydrates 15.6 g
- Sugar 5.3 g
- Protein 23.1 g
- Cholesterol 82 mg

Slow Cooked Balsamic Pork Tenderloin

Preparation Time: 10 minutes
Cooking Time: 6 hours
Serve: 6

Ingredients:

- 2 lbs pork tenderloin
- 1 tbsp cornstarch
- 1/2 cup brown sugar
- 1 garlic clove, crushed
- 1/4 tsp pepper
- 1/2 cup water
- 2 tbsp soy sauce
- 1/2 cup water
- 1/4 cup balsamic vinegar
- 1 tsp ground sage
- 1/2 tsp salt

Directions:

1. Insert wire rack in rack position 8. Select slow cook, Set LOW for 6 hours. Press start to preheat the oven.
2. In a small bowl, mix together sage, garlic, pepper, and salt and rub over pork tenderloin.
3. Pour 1/2 cup water in the dutch oven and then place pork tenderloin in the dutch oven.
4. Cover with lid and cook on low for 6 hours.
5. For the glaze: in a saucepan, add brown sugar, soy sauce, water, vinegar, and cornstarch and heat over medium heat until thickens, about 4 minutes.
6. Brush glaze on pork during the last hour of cooking.
7. Serve and enjoy.

Nutritional Value (Amount per Serving):

- Calories 273
- Fat 5.3 g
- Carbohydrates 13.9 g
- Sugar 11.9 g
- Protein 40 g
- Cholesterol 110 mg

CHAPTER 5: SNACK & APPETIZER

Crispy Potato Wedges

Preparation Time: 10 minutes
Cooking Time: 15 minutes
Serve: 4
Ingredients:
- 2 medium potatoes, cut into wedges
- 1/8 tsp cayenne pepper
- 1/4 tsp garlic powder
- 1/2 tsp paprika
- 1 1/2 tbsp olive oil
- 1/4 tsp pepper
- 1 tsp sea salt

Directions:
1. Soak potato wedges into the cold water for 30 minutes. Drain well and pat dry with a paper towel.
2. In a mixing bowl, toss potato wedges with remaining ingredients.
3. Insert wire rack in rack position 4. Select air fry, set temperature 400 F, timer for 15 minutes. Press start to preheat the oven.
4. Arrange potato wedges in the air fryer basket and cook for 15 minutes.
5. Serve and enjoy.

Nutritional Value (Amount per Serving):
- Calories 120
- Fat 5.4 g
- Carbohydrates 17.1 g
- Sugar 1.3 g
- Protein 1.9 g
- Cholesterol 0 mg

Thyme Parmesan Potatoes

Preparation Time: 10 minutes
Cooking Time: 45 minutes
Serve: 4
Ingredients:
- 5 potatoes, cut into wedges
- 2 tbsp lemon juice
- 1/3 cup olive oil
- 2 garlic cloves, minced
- 2 thyme sprigs
- 1/2 cup parmesan cheese, grated
- Pepper
- Salt

Directions:
1. Spray a 9*13-inch baking dish with cooking spray and set aside.
2. Insert wire rack in rack position 4. Select bake, set temperature 325 F, timer for 45 minutes. Press start to preheat the oven.
3. Add potato wedges into the baking dish.
4. Mix together lemon juice, oil, garlic, thyme, cheese, pepper, and salt and pour over potatoes and toss well.
5. Bake for 45 minutes.

6. Serve and enjoy.
Nutritional Value (Amount per Serving):
- Calories 374
- Fat 19.7 g
- Carbohydrates 44.3 g
- Sugar 3.3 g
- Protein 8.5 g
- Cholesterol 8 mg

Easy Buffalo Chicken Dip

Preparation Time: 10 minutes
Cooking Time: 25 minutes
Serve: 8
Ingredients:
- 2 chicken breasts, skinless, boneless, cooked and shredded
- 1 cup Monterey jack cheese, shredded
- 1 cup cheddar cheese, shredded
- 1/4 cup blue cheese, crumbled
- 1/2 cup ranch dressing
- 1/2 cup buffalo wing sauce
- 8 oz cream cheese, softened

Directions:
1. Spray a 1.5-quart casserole dish with cooking spray and set aside.
2. Insert wire rack in rack position 4. Select bake, set temperature 350 F, timer for 25 minutes. Press start to preheat the oven.
3. Add cream cheese into the casserole dish and top with shredded chicken, ranch dressing, and buffalo sauce.
4. Sprinkle cheddar cheese, Monterey jack cheese and blue cheese on top of chicken mixture.
5. Bake for 25 minutes.
6. Serve and enjoy.

Nutritional Value (Amount per Serving):
- Calories 298
- Fat 22.8 g
- Carbohydrates 2 g
- Sugar 0.6 g
- Protein 20.8 g
- Cholesterol 94 mg

Perfect Goat Cheese Dip

Preparation Time: 10 minutes
Cooking Time: 20 minutes
Serve: 8
Ingredients:
- 12 oz goat cheese
- 2 tsp rosemary, chopped
- 1 tsp red pepper flakes
- 4 garlic cloves, minced
- 2 tbsp olive oil
- 1/2 cup parmesan cheese, shredded
- 4 oz cream cheese
- 1/2 tsp salt

Directions:

1. Spray a baking dish with cooking spray and set aside.
2. Insert wire rack in rack position 4. Select bake, set temperature 390 F, timer for 20 minutes. Press start to preheat the oven.
3. Add all ingredients into the mixing bowl and mix until well combined. Pour mixture into the baking dish and bake for 20 minutes.
4. Serve and enjoy.

Nutritional Value (Amount per Serving):
- Calories 294
- Fat 24.9 g
- Carbohydrates 2.3 g
- Sugar 1 g
- Protein 16 g
- Cholesterol 64 mg

Easy Taco Dip

Preparation Time: 10 minutes
Cooking Time: 25 minutes
Serve: 2

Ingredients:
- 1/4 cup salsa
- 2 tbsp red pepper, chopped
- 2 tbsp onion, chopped
- 1 cup cheddar cheese, shredded
- 1/2 cup sour cream
- 1/2 cup miracle whip
- 1 oz taco seasoning

Directions:
1. Spray a baking dish with cooking spray and set aside.
2. Insert wire rack in rack position 4. Select bake, set temperature 350 F, timer for 25 minutes. Press start to preheat the oven.
3. In a bowl, mix together all ingredients and pour into the baking dish and bake for 25 minutes.
4. Serve and enjoy.

Nutritional Value (Amount per Serving):
- Calories 661
- Fat 52.5 g
- Carbohydrates 31.4 g
- Sugar 11.6 g
- Protein 19.9 g
- Cholesterol 105 mg

Spicy Mexican Cheese Dip

Preparation Time: 10 minutes
Cooking Time: 30 minutes
Serve: 10

Ingredients:
- 16 oz cream cheese, softened
- 1/2 cup hot salsa
- 3 cups cheddar cheese, shredded
- 1 cup sour cream

Directions:
1. Spray an 8*8-inch baking dish with cooking spray and set aside.

2. Insert wire rack in rack position 4. Select bake, set temperature 350 F, timer for 25 minutes. Press start to preheat the oven.
3. In a mixing bowl, mix together all ingredients until well combined and pour into the baking dish and bake for 30 minutes.
4. Serve and enjoy.

Nutritional Value (Amount per Serving):
- Calories 348
- Fat 31.9 g
- Carbohydrates 3.4 g
- Sugar 0.7 g
- Protein 12.8 g
- Cholesterol 96 mg

Cheese Garlic Dip

Preparation Time: 10 minutes
Cooking Time: 8 minutes
Serve: 6

Ingredients:
- 13 oz brie cheese, remove the rind and cubed
- 1 tbsp dried thyme
- 2 tsp rosemary, chopped
- 3 garlic cloves, chopped
- Pepper
- Salt

Directions:
1. Spray a baking dish with cooking spray and set aside.
2. Insert wire rack in rack position 4. Select bake, set temperature 375 F, timer for 8 minutes. Press start to preheat the oven.
3. Add all ingredients into the mixing bowl and mix well. Pour mixture into the baking dish and bake for 8 minutes.
4. Serve and enjoy.

Nutritional Value (Amount per Serving):
- Calories 210
- Fat 17.1 g
- Carbohydrates 1.3 g
- Sugar 0.3 g
- Protein 12.9 g
- Cholesterol 61 mg

Cheesy Crab Dip

Preparation Time: 10 minutes
Cooking Time: 15 minutes
Serve: 4

Ingredients:
- 8 oz crab meat
- 1/4 tsp paprika
- 1/2 tsp garlic powder
- 1/4 cup onion, chopped
- 1 1/2 tsp garlic, minced
- 1 cup cheddar cheese, shredded
- 1/2 cup sour cream
- 1/4 cup mayonnaise
- 8 oz cream cheese, softened

- Pepper
- Salt

Directions:

1. Spray a baking dish with cooking spray and set aside.
2. Insert wire rack in rack position 4. Select bake, set temperature 390 F, timer for 15 minutes. Press start to preheat the oven.
3. Add all ingredients into the bowl and mix until well combined. Pour mixture into the baking dish and bake for 15 minutes.
4. Serve and enjoy.

Nutritional Value (Amount per Serving):
- Calories 487
- Fat 41.1 g
- Carbohydrates 9 g
- Sugar 1.7 g
- Protein 19.7 g
- Cholesterol 139 mg

Broccoli Nuggets

Preparation Time: 10 minutes
Cooking Time: 20 minutes
Serve: 4

Ingredients:
- 1/4 cup almond flour
- 2 cups broccoli florets, cooked until soften
- 1 cup cheddar cheese, shredded
- 2 egg whites
- 1/8 tsp salt

Directions:

1. Line baking sheet with parchment paper and set aside.
2. Insert wire rack in rack position 6. Select bake, set temperature 350 F, timer for 20 minutes. Press start to preheat the oven.
3. Add cooked broccoli to the bowl and using masher mash broccoli into the small pieces.
4. Add remaining ingredients to the bowl and mix until well combined.
5. Drop 20 scoops of broccoli mixture onto the prepared baking sheet and press into a nugget shape.
6. Bake for 20 minutes.
7. Serve and enjoy.

Nutritional Value (Amount per Serving):
- Calories 180
- Fat 12.9 g
- Carbohydrates 5 g
- Sugar 1 g
- Protein 11.6 g
- Cholesterol 30 mg

Stuffed Jalapenos

Preparation Time: 10 minutes
Cooking Time: 25 minutes
Serve: 12

Ingredients:
- 6 jalapenos, halved
- 1/4 cup green onion, sliced

- 1/4 cup Monterey jack cheese, shredded
- 1/4 tsp dried basil
- 1/2 cup chicken, cooked and shredded
- 1/4 tsp garlic powder
- 4 oz cream cheese
- 1/4 tsp dried oregano
- 1/4 tsp salt

Directions:

1. Line baking sheet with parchment paper and set aside.
2. Insert wire rack in rack position 6. Select bake, set temperature 390 F, timer for 25 minutes. Press start to preheat the oven.
3. Mix all ingredients in a bowl except jalapenos.
4. Spoon 1 tablespoon mixture into each jalapeno half and place on a baking sheet.
5. Bake for 25 minutes.
6. Serve and enjoy.

Nutritional Value (Amount per Serving):
- Calories 54
- Fat 4.2 g
- Carbohydrates 0.9 g
- Sugar 0.3 g
- Protein 3.1 g
- Cholesterol 17 mg

Broccoli Fritters

Preparation Time: 10 minutes
Cooking Time: 30 minutes
Serve: 4

Ingredients:
- 3 cups broccoli florets, steam & chopped
- 2 cups cheddar cheese, shredded
- 1/4 cup almond flour
- 2 eggs, lightly beaten
- 2 garlic cloves, minced
- Pepper
- Salt

Directions:

1. Line baking sheet with parchment paper and set aside.
2. Insert wire rack in rack position 6. Select bake, set temperature 375 F, timer for 15 minutes. Press start to preheat the oven.
3. Add all ingredients into the large bowl and mix until well combined.
4. Make patties from broccoli mixture and place on a baking sheet and bake for 15 minutes.
5. Turn patties and bake for 15 minutes more.
6. Serve and enjoy.

Nutritional Value (Amount per Serving):
- Calories 327
- Fat 24.5 g
- Carbohydrates 7.4 g
- Sugar 2.6 g
- Protein 20.4 g
- Cholesterol 141 mg

Ranch Potatoes

Preparation Time: 10 minutes
Cooking Time: 20 minutes
Serve: 2
Ingredients:
- 1/2 lb baby potatoes, wash and cut in half
- 1/2 tbsp olive oil
- 1/4 tsp dill
- 1/4 tsp chives
- 1/4 tsp paprika
- 1/4 tsp onion powder
- 1/4 tsp garlic powder
- 1/4 tsp parsley
- Salt

Directions:
1. Insert wire rack in rack position 4. Select air fry, set temperature 400 F, timer for 10 minutes. Press start to preheat the oven.
2. Add all ingredients into the mixing bowl and toss well.
3. Spread potatoes on an air fryer basket and air fry for 20 minutes.
4. Serve and enjoy.

Nutritional Value (Amount per Serving):
- Calories 99
- Fat 3.7 g
- Carbohydrates 14.8 g
- Sugar 0.2 g
- Protein 3.1 g
- Cholesterol 0 mg

Potato Nuggets

Preparation Time: 10 minutes
Cooking Time: 42 minutes
Serve: 4
Ingredients:
- 2 cups potatoes, chopped
- 1 garlic clove, minced
- 1 tsp olive oil
- 2 tbsp almond milk
- 4 cups kale, chopped
- Pepper
- Salt

Directions:
1. Insert wire rack in rack position 4. Select air fry, set temperature 390 F, timer for 12 minutes. Press start to preheat the oven.
2. Add potatoes in boiling water and cook for 30 minutes or until tender. Drain well.
3. Heat oil in a pan over medium-high heat.
4. Add garlic and sauté for 30 seconds. Add kale and sauté for 2 minutes.
5. Transfer sautéed garlic and kale in a large bowl. Add potatoes, almond milk, pepper, and salt and mash potato using a fork and stir to combine.
6. Make small nuggets from potato mixture and place on an air fryer basket and air fry for 12 minutes.
7. Serve and enjoy.

Nutritional Value (Amount per Serving):
- Calories 113
- Fat 3 g
- Carbohydrates 19.5 g
- Sugar 1.1 g
- Protein 3.5 g
- Cholesterol 0 mg

Tasty Zucchini Patties

Preparation Time: 10 minutes
Cooking Time: 25 minutes
Serve: 6
Ingredients:
- 1 cup zucchini, shredded and squeeze out all liquid
- 2 tbsp onion, minced
- 1 egg, lightly beaten
- 1/4 tsp red pepper flakes
- 1/4 cup parmesan cheese, grated
- 1/2 tbsp Dijon mustard
- 1/2 tbsp mayonnaise
- 1/2 cup breadcrumbs
- Pepper
- Salt

Directions:
1. Insert wire rack in rack position 4. Select air fry, set temperature 400 F, timer for 25 minutes. Press start to preheat the oven.
2. Add all ingredients into the bowl and mix until well combined.
3. Make small patties from the zucchini mixture and place it on an air fryer basket and air fry for 25 minutes.
4. Serve and enjoy.

Nutritional Value (Amount per Serving):
- Calories 68
- Fat 2.5 g
- Carbohydrates 8 g
- Sugar 1.2 g
- Protein 3.7 g
- Cholesterol 30 mg

Sweet Potato Fries

Preparation Time: 10 minutes
Cooking Time: 16 minutes
Serve: 2
Ingredients:
- 2 sweet potatoes, peeled and cut into fries shape
- 1/4 tsp chili powder
- 1 tbsp olive oil
- Salt

Directions:
1. Insert wire rack in rack position 4. Select air fry, set temperature 380 F, timer for 16 minutes. Press start to preheat the oven.
2. In a mixing bowl, add sweet potato fries, chili powder, garlic powder, olive oil, and salt and toss until well coated.

3.　　　　Arrange sweet potato fries on an air fryer basket and air fry for 16 minutes.
4.　　　　Serve and enjoy.
Nutritional Value (Amount per Serving):
- Calories 238
- Fat 7.3 g
- Carbohydrates 42 g
- Sugar 0.8 g
- Protein 2.3 g
- Cholesterol 0 mg

Crispy Tofu

Preparation Time: 10 minutes
Cooking Time: 15 minutes
Serve: 4
Ingredients:
- 15 oz extra firm tofu, cut into bite-sized chunks
- 1 tbsp olive oil
- 2 tbsp soy sauce

Directions:
1.　　　　Insert wire rack in rack position 4. Select air fry, set temperature 370 F, timer for 15 minutes. Press start to preheat the oven.
2.　　　　Add tofu, oil, and soy sauce in a mixing bowl and toss well. Let it sit for 15 minutes.
3.　　　　Arrange tofu pieces on an air fryer basket and air fry for 15 minutes.
4.　　　　Serve and enjoy.
Nutritional Value (Amount per Serving):
- Calories 109
- Fat 7.9 g
- Carbohydrates 2.4 g
- Sugar 0.8 g
- Protein 9.2 g
- Cholesterol 0 mg

Maple Chickpeas

Preparation Time: 10 minutes
Cooking Time: 12 minutes
Serve: 4
Ingredients:
- 15 oz can chickpeas, rinsed, drained and pat dry
- 1 tbsp olive oil
- 1/2 tsp ground cinnamon
- 1 tbsp maple syrup
- Pepper
- Salt

Directions:
1.　　　　Insert wire rack in rack position 4. Select air fry, set temperature 375 F, timer for 12 minutes. Press start to preheat the oven.
2.　　　　Spread chickpeas on air fryer basket and air fry for 12 minutes.
3.　　　　In a large bowl, mix together cinnamon, maple syrup, oil, pepper, and salt. Add chickpeas and toss well.
4.　　　　Serve and enjoy.

Nutritional Value (Amount per Serving):
- Calories 170
- Fat 4.7 g
- Carbohydrates 27.6 g
- Sugar 3 g
- Protein 5.3 g
- Cholesterol 0 mg

Air Fryer Pecans

Preparation Time: 5 minutes
Cooking Time: 6 minutes
Serve: 6
Ingredients:
- 2 cups pecan halves
- 1 tbsp butter, melted
- 1 tsp brown sugar
- Salt

Directions:
1.　　　　Insert wire rack in rack position 4. Select air fry, set temperature 400 F, timer for 6 minutes. Press start to preheat the oven.
2.　　　　Add pecans, butter, and salt in a mixing bowl and toss well.
3.　　　　Transfer pecans on air fryer basket and air fry for 6 minutes.
4.　　　　Serve and enjoy.
Nutritional Value (Amount per Serving):
- Calories 51
- Fat 5.3 g
- Carbohydrates 1.2 g
- Sugar 0.7 g
- Protein 0.5 g
- Cholesterol 5 mg

Carrot Fries

Preparation Time: 10 minutes
Cooking Time: 15 minutes
Serve: 4
Ingredients:
- 4 carrots, peeled and cut into fries
- 2 tbsp olive oil
- 2 tbsp parmesan cheese, grated
- 1 1/2 tbsp garlic, minced
- Pepper
- Salt

Directions:
1.　　　　Insert wire rack in rack position 4. Select air fry, set temperature 350 F, timer for 15 minutes. Press start to preheat the oven.
2.　　　　Add carrots and remaining ingredients into the mixing bowl and toss well.
3.　　　　Add carrots fries into the air fryer basket and air fry for 15 minutes.
4.　　　　Serve and enjoy.
Nutritional Value (Amount per Serving):
- Calories 99
- Fat 7.6 g
- Carbohydrates 7.2 g
- Sugar 3 g

- Protein 1.6 g
- Cholesterol 2 mg

Chili Chickpeas

Preparation Time: 10 minutes
Cooking Time: 12 minutes
Serve: 4
Ingredients:
- 14 oz can chickpeas, rinsed, drained and pat dry
- 1/2 tsp chili powder
- 1 tbsp olive oil
- Pepper
- Salt

Directions:
1. Insert wire rack in rack position 4. Select air fry, set temperature 375 F, timer for 12 minutes. Press start to preheat the oven.
2. Add chickpeas, chili powder, oil, pepper, and salt into the mixing bowl and toss well.
3. Spread chickpeas on air fryer basket and air fry for 12 minutes.
4. Serve and enjoy.

Nutritional Value (Amount per Serving):
- Calories 149
- Fat 4.7 g
- Carbohydrates 22.6 g
- Sugar 0 g
- Protein 5 g
- Cholesterol 0 mg

Parmesan Air Fried Brussels Sprouts

Preparation Time: 10 minutes
Cooking Time: 12 minutes
Serve: 4
Ingredients:
- 1 lb Brussels sprouts, cut stems and halved
- 1/4 cup parmesan cheese, grated
- 1 tbsp olive oil
- Pepper
- Salt

Directions:
1. Insert wire rack in rack position 4. Select air fry, set temperature 350 F, timer for 12 minutes. Press start to preheat the oven.
2. Toss Brussels sprouts, oil, pepper, and salt into the bowl.
3. Transfer Brussels sprouts into the air fryer basket and air fry for 12 minutes.
4. Sprinkle with parmesan cheese and serve.

Nutritional Value (Amount per Serving):
- Calories 97
- Fat 5.1 g
- Carbohydrates 10.5 g
- Sugar 2.5 g
- Protein 5.7 g
- Cholesterol 4 mg

Garlicky Cauliflower Florets

Preparation Time: 10 minutes
Cooking Time: 20 minutes
Serve: 4
Ingredients:
- 5 cups cauliflower florets
- 1/2 tsp cumin powder
- 6 garlic cloves, chopped
- 4 tablespoons olive oil
- 1/2 tsp salt

Directions:
1. Insert wire rack in rack position 4. Select air fry, set temperature 400 F, timer for 20 minutes. Press start to preheat the oven.
2. Add all ingredients into the large bowl and toss well.
3. Add cauliflower florets into the air fryer basket and air fry for 20 minutes.
4. Serve and enjoy.

Nutritional Value (Amount per Serving):
- Calories 159
- Fat 14.2 g
- Carbohydrates 8.2 g
- Sugar 3.1 g
- Protein 2.8 g
- Cholesterol 0 mg

Beetroot Chips

Preparation Time: 10 minutes
Cooking Time: 15 minutes
Serve: 4
Ingredients:
- 2 beetroot, wash, peeled, and sliced thinly
- 1 tsp olive oil
- Salt

Directions:
1. Insert wire rack in rack position 4. Select air fry, set temperature 300 F, timer for 15 minutes. Press start to preheat the oven.
2. Sprinkle salt on the beetroot slices.
3. Arrange beetroot slices in a single layer on an air fryer basket and drizzle with oil and air fry for 15 minutes.
4. Serve and enjoy.

Nutritional Value (Amount per Serving):
- Calories 29
- Fat 1.3 g
- Carbohydrates 4.2 g
- Sugar 3.4 g
- Protein 0.7 g
- Cholesterol 0 mg

Buffalo Cauliflower

Preparation Time: 10 minutes
Cooking Time: 15 minutes
Serve: 4
Ingredients:
- 8 oz cauliflower florets
- 1 tsp cayenne pepper
- 1 tsp chili powder

- 6 tbsp almond flour
- 1 tsp olive oil
- 1 tsp garlic, minced
- 1 tomato, diced
- 1 tsp black pepper
- 1/2 tsp salt

Directions:

1. Insert wire rack in rack position 4. Select air fry, set temperature 350 F, timer for 15 minutes. Press start to preheat the oven.
2. Add tomato, garlic, black pepper, olive oil, cayenne pepper, and chili powder into the blender and blend until smooth.
3. Add cauliflower florets into the mixing bowl. Season with pepper and salt.
4. Pour blended tomato mixture over cauliflower florets and mix well.
5. Coat cauliflower florets with almond flour and place into the air fryer basket and air fry for 15 minutes.
6. Serve and enjoy.

Nutritional Value (Amount per Serving):

- Calories 96
- Fat 6.5 g
- Carbohydrates 7 g
- Sugar 1.9 g
- Protein 3.7 g
- Cholesterol 0 mg

Air Fryer Green Beans

Preparation Time: 10 minutes
Cooking Time: 10 minutes
Serve: 2

Ingredients:

- 2 cups green beans
- 2 tbsp olive oil
- 1/8 tsp ground allspice
- 1/4 tsp ground cinnamon
- 1/2 tsp dried oregano
- 1/4 tsp ground coriander
- 1/4 tsp ground cumin
- 1/8 tsp cayenne pepper
- 1/2 tsp salt

Directions:

1. Insert wire rack in rack position 4. Select air fry, set temperature 370 F, timer for 10 minutes. Press start to preheat the oven.
2. Add all ingredients into the mixing bowl and toss well.
3. Spray air fryer basket with cooking spray.
4. Add bowl mixture into the air fryer basket and air fry for 10 minutes.
5. serve and enjoy.

Nutritional Value (Amount per Serving):

- Calories 158
- Fat 14.3 g
- Carbohydrates 8.6 g
- Sugar 1.6 g
- Protein 2.1 g

- Cholesterol 0 mg

Tasty Carrot Fries

Preparation Time: 10 minutes
Cooking Time: 15 minutes
Serve: 2

Ingredients:

- 1/2 lb carrots, peeled and cut into fries shape
- 1/4 tsp paprika
- 1/4 tsp cumin
- 1/2 tbsp olive oil
- 1/4 tsp onion powder
- 1/4 tsp kosher salt

Directions:

1. Insert wire rack in rack position 4. Select air fry, set temperature 400 F, timer for 15 minutes. Press start to preheat the oven.
2. In a large bowl, add all ingredients and toss until well coated.
3. Pour carrots fries in the air fryer basket and air fry for 15 minutes.
4. Serve and enjoy.

Nutritional Value (Amount per Serving):

- Calories 79
- Fat 3.6 g
- Carbohydrates 11.7 g
- Sugar 5.7 g
- Protein 1.1 g
- Cholesterol 0 mg

Delicious Crisp Okra

Preparation Time: 10 minutes
Cooking Time: 10 minutes
Serve: 2

Ingredients:

- 3 cups okra, wash and dry
- 1 tsp dry mango powder
- 1 tsp fresh lemon juice
- 1 tsp red chili powder
- 3 tbsp chickpea flour
- 1/2 tsp coriander powder
- 1 tsp cumin powder
- Salt

Directions

1. Insert wire rack in rack position 4. Select air fry, set temperature 400 F, timer for 10 minutes. Press start to preheat the oven.
2. Cut top of okra then makes a deep horizontal cut in each okra and set aside.
3. In a bowl, combine together the chickpea flour, lemon juice, chili powder, coriander powder, cumin powder, mango powder, and salt.
4. Add little water in chickpea flour mixture and make a thick batter.
5. Fill the batter in each okra and place it in the air fryer basket and air fry for 10 minutes.
6. Serve and enjoy.

Nutritional Value (Amount per Serving):

- Calories 102
- Fat 1.3 g
- Carbohydrates 17.4 g
- Sugar 3.3 g
- Protein 5.2 g
- Cholesterol 0 mg

Taro Fries

Preparation Time: 10 minutes
Cooking Time: 20 minutes
Serve: 2
Ingredients:
- 8 small taro, peel and cut into fries shape
- 1 tbsp olive oil
- 1/4 tsp pepper
- 1/2 tsp salt

Directions:
1. Insert wire rack in rack position 4. Select air fry, set temperature 400 F, timer for 15 minutes. Press start to preheat the oven.
2. Add taro fries in a bowl and drizzle with olive oil. Season with pepper and salt.
3. Transfer taro slices to the air fryer basket and air fry for 20 minutes.
4. Serve and enjoy.

Nutritional Value (Amount per Serving):
- Calories 118
- Fat 7.1 g
- Carbohydrates 13.8 g
- Sugar 0.2 g
- Protein 0.8 g
- Cholesterol 0 mg

Veggie Cheese Fritters

Preparation Time: 10 minutes
Cooking Time: 15 minutes
Serve: 2
Ingredients:
- 1 egg, lightly beaten
- 1/4 tsp garlic powder
- 1/4 cup parmesan cheese, shredded
- 1 1/2 cups frozen vegetable
- 1/2 tbsp coconut flour
- Pepper
- Salt

Directions:
1. Insert wire rack in rack position 4. Select air fry, set temperature 390 F, timer for 15 minutes. Press start to preheat the oven.
2. Steam frozen vegetables and mash vegetables in a bowl.
3. Add egg in mash vegetables and stir well.
4. Add parmesan cheese, coconut flour, garlic powder, pepper, and salt and stir well.
5. Make small patties from the mixture and place on an air fryer basket and air fry for 15 minutes.
6. Serve and enjoy.

Nutritional Value (Amount per Serving):
- Calories 183

- Fat 6.2 g
- Carbohydrates 20.7 g
- Sugar 4.8 g
- Protein 11 g
- Cholesterol 89 mg

BBQ Chickpeas

Preparation Time: 10 minutes
Cooking Time: 12 minutes
Serve: 4
Ingredients:
- 14 oz can chickpeas, rinsed, drained and pat dry
- 1 tbsp olive oil
- 1/2 tsp dry mustard
- 1/2 tsp garlic powder
- 1 tsp brown sugar
- 1 1/2 tsp paprika
- 1/4 tsp pepper
- 1/2 tsp celery salt

Directions:
1. Insert wire rack in rack position 4. Select air fry, set temperature 375 F, timer for 12 minutes. Press start to preheat the oven.
2. Add chickpeas into the mixing bowl and toss with remaining ingredients.
3. Spread chickpeas on air fryer basket and air fry for 12 minutes.
4. Serve and enjoy.

Nutritional Value (Amount per Serving):
- Calories 154
- Fat 4.7 g
- Carbohydrates 24.1 g
- Sugar 0.6 g
- Protein 5.1 g
- Cholesterol 0 mg

Asian Tofu

Preparation Time: 10 minutes
Cooking Time: 20 minutes
Serve: 4
Ingredients:
- 1 block firm tofu, cut into 1-inch cubes
- 1 tsp vinegar
- 2 tbsp soy sauce
- 1 tbsp cornstarch
- 2 tsp sesame oil

Directions:
1. Insert wire rack in rack position 4. Select air fry, set temperature 370 F, timer for 20 minutes. Press start to preheat the oven.
2. Add tofu, sesame oil, vinegar, and soy sauce in a large bowl and let marinate for 15 minutes.
3. Toss marinated tofu with cornstarch and place in the air fryer basket and air fry for 20 minutes.
4. Serve and enjoy.

Nutritional Value (Amount per Serving):
- Calories 48

- Fat 3.2 g
- Carbohydrates 2.8 g
- Sugar 0.3 g
- Protein 2.4 g
- Cholesterol 0 mg

Sweet Potato Fries

Preparation Time: 10 minutes
Cooking Time: 8 minutes
Serve: 4

Ingredients:
- 2 medium sweet potatoes, peeled and cut into fries shape
- 1/2 tsp garlic powder
- 1 tbsp olive oil
- 1/4 tsp chili powder
- 1/4 tsp cumin
- Pepper
- Salt

Directions:
1. Insert wire rack in rack position 4. Select air fry, set temperature 400 F, timer for 8 minutes. Press start to preheat the oven.
2. Add sweet potato fries in a large bowl and drizzle with olive oil.
3. Sprinkle with chili powder, cumin, garlic powder, pepper, and salt and toss until well coated.
4. Transfer sweet potato fries in the air fryer basket and air fry for 8 minutes.
5. Serve and enjoy.

Nutritional Value (Amount per Serving):
- Calories 78
- Fat 2.4 g
- Carbohydrates 13.5 g
- Sugar 2.8 g
- Protein 1.1 g
- Cholesterol 0 mg

Chicken Tenders

Preparation Time: 10 minutes
Cooking Time: 6 minutes
Serve: 8

Ingredients:
- 1 egg
- 3 tbsp butter, melted
- 1/2 cup parmesan cheese, grated
- 8 piece chicken tenders
- 1 tsp Italian herbs
- 1 tsp garlic powder
- 1 cup breadcrumbs

Directions
1. Insert wire rack in rack position 4. Select air fry, set temperature 400 F, timer for 15 minutes. Press start to preheat the oven.
2. In a bowl, combine together egg, Italian herbs, garlic powder, and butter.
3. Add chicken tenders in the egg mixture and coat well.

4. In a shallow dish, combine together parmesan cheese and breadcrumbs.
5. Coat chicken with cheese and breadcrumbs mixture and set aside for 5 minutes.
6. Place coated chicken tenders in the air fryer basket and air fry for 6 minutes.
7. Serve and enjoy.

Nutritional Value (Amount per Serving):
- Calories 398
- Fat 17.6 g
- Carbohydrates 13.2 g
- Sugar 1 g
- Protein 46.3 g
- Cholesterol 161 mg

Jicama Fries

Preparation Time: 10 minutes
Cooking Time: 20 minutes
Serve: 8

Ingredients:
- 2 eggs, lightly beaten
- 1 tsp sea salt
- 1/2 large jicama, cut into fries
- 1 tbsp thyme, dried
- 3/4 cup arrowroot flour

Directions
1. Insert wire rack in rack position 4. Select air fry, set temperature 400 F, timer for 15 minutes. Press start to preheat the oven.
2. Add beaten eggs into the bowl.
3. Take one more bowl and combine together salt, thyme, and arrowroot flour.
4. Add jicama fries in eggs bowl and toss well.
5. Add jicama fries in flour mixture and toss until well coated.
6. Place coated jicama fries in the air fryer basket and air fry for 20 minutes.
7. Serve and enjoy.

Nutritional Value (Amount per Serving):
- Calories 52
- Fat 1.2 g
- Carbohydrates 8.4 g
- Sugar 1.4 g
- Protein 2.4 g
- Cholesterol 41 mg

Onion Rings

Preparation Time: 10 minutes
Cooking Time: 8 minutes
Serve: 2

Ingredients:
- 1 large egg, lightly beaten
- 1 medium onion, sliced into whole slices
- 1/2 cup breadcrumbs
- Pepper
- Salt

Directions

1.   Insert wire rack in rack position 4. Select air fry, set temperature 350 F, timer for 8 minutes. Press start to preheat the oven.
2.   Add breadcrumbs, pepper, and salt in a shallow dish.
3.   In another shallow dish add lightly beaten egg.
4.   Dip onion ring in egg then coats with breadcrumbs.
5.   Place coated onion rings in the air fryer basket and air fry for 8 minutes.
6.   Serve and enjoy.
Nutritional Value (Amount per Serving):
- Calories 165
- Fat 4 g
- Carbohydrates 24.8 g
- Sugar 4.2 g
- Protein 7.4 g
- Cholesterol 93 mg

Kale Chips

Preparation Time: 10 minutes
Cooking Time: 3 minutes
Serve: 2
Ingredients:
- 1 head kale, tear into 1 1/2 inch pieces
- 1 tsp soy sauce
- 1 tbsp olive oil

Directions
1.   Insert wire rack in rack position 4. Select air fry, set temperature 400 F, timer for 3 minutes. Press start to preheat the oven.
2.   Add kale in a bowl and toss with soy sauce and oil.
3.   Add kale on the air fryer basket and air fry for 3 minutes.
4.   Serve and enjoy.
Nutritional Value (Amount per Serving):
- Calories 78
- Fat 7 g
- Carbohydrates 3.7 g
- Sugar 0.1 g
- Protein 1.2 g
- Cholesterol 0 mg

Cod Sticks

Preparation Time: 10 minutes
Cooking Time: 12 minutes
Serve: 4
Ingredients:
- 1 lb cod
- 2 large eggs
- 1/2 tsp pepper
- 3 tbsp milk
- 1 cup almond flour
- 2 cups breadcrumbs
- 1/4 tsp sea salt

Directions

1.   Insert wire rack in rack position 4. Select air fry, set temperature 350 F, timer for 12 minutes. Press start to preheat the oven.
2.   In a small bowl, whisk together milk and eggs.
3.   In a shallow dish, mix together breadcrumbs, pepper, and salt.
4.   In another shallow dish, add the almond flour.
5.   Roll cod sticks into the almond flour then dip in the egg mixture and finally coat with breadcrumbs.
6.   Place coated cod sticks in the air fryer basket and air fry for 12 minutes.
7.   Serve and enjoy.
Nutritional Value (Amount per Serving):
- Calories 543
- Fat 19.9 g
- Carbohydrates 45.8 g
- Sugar 4.1 g
- Protein 42.7 g
- Cholesterol 156 mg

Chicken Tikka

Preparation Time: 10 minutes
Cooking Time: 15 minutes
Serve: 4
Ingredients:
- 1 lb boneless chicken, cut into pieces
- 1 cup cherry tomatoes
- 1 tsp turmeric powder
- 2 tbsp coriander powder
- 2 tbsp cumin powder
- 2 tsp olive oil
- 1 cup yogurt
- 1 tbsp ginger garlic paste
- 2 tbsp red chili powder
- 3 bell peppers, cut into chunks
- Salt

Directions
1.   Insert wire rack in rack position 4. Select air fry, set temperature 400 F, timer for 15 minutes. Press start to preheat the oven.
2.   Add all ingredients into the mixing bowl and place it in the refrigerator for 2 hours.
3.   Threading marinated chicken, pepper, and tomatoes alternately on soaked wooden skewers.
4.   Place chicken skewers on air fryer basket and air fry for 15 minutes.
5.   Serve and enjoy.
Nutritional Value (Amount per Serving):
- Calories 343
- Fat 13.2 g
- Carbohydrates 17.1 g
- Sugar 10.4 g
- Protein 38.7 g
- Cholesterol 105 mg

Baked Okra

Preparation Time: 10 minutes
Cooking Time: 15 minutes
Serve: 4
Ingredients:
- 1 lb fresh okra, cut into 3/4-inch pieces
- 1 tsp paprika
- 1/4 tsp chili powder
- 2 tbsp olive oil
- Salt

Directions:
1. Line roasting pan with parchment paper and set aside.
2. Insert wire rack in rack position 6. Select bake, set temperature 390 F, timer for 15 minutes. Press start to preheat the oven.
3. Add okra, chili powder, paprika, oil, and salt into the bowl and toss well.
4. Spread okra on a roasting pan and bake for 15 minutes.
5. Serve and enjoy.

Nutritional Value (Amount per Serving):
- Calories 107
- Fat 7.3 g
- Carbohydrates 8.8 g
- Sugar 1.7 g
- Protein 2.3 g
- Cholesterol 0 mg

Salmon Croquettes

Preparation Time: 10 minutes
Cooking Time: 7 minutes
Serve: 4
Ingredients:
- 1 lb can red salmon, drained and mashed
- 2 eggs, beaten
- 1/3 cup olive oil
- 1 cup breadcrumbs

Directions :
1. Insert wire rack in rack position 4. Select air fry, set temperature 400 F, timer for 7 minutes. Press start to preheat the oven.
2. In a bowl, add drained salmon, eggs, and parsley. Mix well.
3. In a shallow dish, combine together breadcrumbs and oil.
4. Make 16 croquettes from the salmon mixture and coat with breadcrumbs.
5. Place coated croquettes in the air fryer basket and air fry for 7 minutes.
6. Serve and enjoy.

Nutritional Value (Amount per Serving):
- Calories 330
- Fat 22.6 g
- Carbohydrates 19.6 g
- Sugar 1.8 g
- Protein 13.3 g
- Cholesterol 95 mg

Crispy Broccoli Florets

Preparation Time: 10 minutes
Cooking Time: 10 minutes
Serve: 3
Ingredients:
- 1 lb broccoli florets
- 2 tbsp plain yogurt
- 1 tbsp chickpea flour
- 1/2 tsp red chili powder
- 1/4 tsp turmeric powder
- 1/2 tsp salt

Directions
1. Insert wire rack in rack position 4. Select air fry, set temperature 400 F, timer for 10 minutes. Press start to preheat the oven.
2. Add all ingredients to the bowl and toss well.
3. Place marinated broccoli in a refrigerator for 15 minutes.
4. Place marinated broccoli into the air fryer basket and air fry for 10 minutes.
5. Serve and enjoy.

Nutritional Value (Amount per Serving):
- Calories 76
- Fat 1 g
- Carbohydrates 13.7 g
- Sugar 3.8 g
- Protein 5.7 g
- Cholesterol 1 mg

Eggplant Fries

Preparation Time: 10 minutes
Cooking Time: 20 minutes
Serve: 4
Ingredients:
- 1 eggplant, cut into 3-inch pieces
- 1 tbsp olive oil
- 4 tbsp cornstarch
- 2 tbsp water
- Salt

Directions
1. Insert wire rack in rack position 4. Select air fry, set temperature 390 F, timer for 20 minutes. Press start to preheat the oven.
2. In a bowl, mix together water, oil, eggplant, and cornstarch.
3. Place eggplant fries in the air fryer basket and air fry for 20 minutes.
4. Serve and enjoy.

Nutritional Value (Amount per Serving):
- Calories 89
- Fat 3.7 g
- Carbohydrates 14 g
- Sugar 3.4 g
- Protein 1.1 g
- Cholesterol 0 mg

Fish Nuggets

Preparation Time: 10 minutes
Cooking Time: 20 minutes

Serve: 4

Ingredients:
- 1 lb cod fillet, cut into nuggets
- 1 cup almond flour
- 1 cup breadcrumbs
- 4 tbsp olive oil
- 3 eggs, beaten
- 1 tsp salt

Directions
1. Insert wire rack in rack position 4. Select air fry, set temperature 490 F, timer for 20 minutes. Press start to preheat the oven.
2. Add beaten eggs in a bowl.
3. Add almond flour in a shallow dish.
4. In another bowl, combine together breadcrumbs, salt, and oil.
5. Coat fish pieces with flour then dip in eggs and finally coat with breadcrumbs.
6. Place coated fish nuggets in the air fryer basket and air fry for 20 minutes.
7. Serve and enjoy.

Nutritional Value (Amount per Serving):
- Calories 533
- Fat 33 g
- Carbohydrates 25.7 g
- Sugar 1.9 g
- Protein 34 g
- Cholesterol 178 mg

Herb Chicken Wings

Preparation Time: 10 minutes
Cooking Time: 15 minutes
Serve: 6

Ingredients:
- 4 lb chicken wings
- 1/4 tsp cinnamon
- 1 habanero, chopped
- 6 garlic cloves, minced
- 2 tbsp soy sauce
- 1 tbsp olive oil
- 4 tbsp vinegar
- 1 fresh lime juice
- 1/2 tbsp ginger, minced
- 1 tbsp brown sugar
- 1 tsp thyme, chopped
- 1/2 tsp white pepper
- 1/2 tsp salt

Directions
1. Insert wire rack in rack position 4. Select air fry, set temperature 390 F, timer for 15 minutes. Press start to preheat the oven.
2. Add all ingredients into the mixing bowl and mix well.
3. Place marinated chicken wings in a refrigerator for 2 hours.
4. Add chicken wings into the air fryer basket and air fry for 15 minutes.
5. Serve and enjoy.

Nutritional Value (Amount per Serving):

- Calories 617
- Fat 24.8 g
- Carbohydrates 4.9 g
- Sugar 2.2 g
- Protein 88.3 g
- Cholesterol 269 mg

Crab Croquettes

Preparation Time: 10 minutes
Cooking Time: 18 minutes
Serve: 6

Ingredients:
- 1 lb crab meat
- 2 egg whites
- 1/2 tsp parsley
- 1/4 tsp chives
- 1/4 tsp tarragon
- 2 tbsp celery, chopped
- 1/4 cup red pepper, chopped
- 1 cup breadcrumbs
- 1 tsp olive oil
- 1/2 tsp fresh lime juice
- 4 tbsp sour cream
- 4 tbsp mayonnaise
- 1/4 cup onion, chopped
- 1/4 tsp salt

Directions
1. Insert wire rack in rack position 4. Select air fry, set temperature 400 F, timer for 18 minutes. Press start to preheat the oven.
2. Place breadcrumbs and salt in a shallow dish.
3. In a small bowl, add egg whites.
4. Add all remaining ingredients into the mixing bowl and mix well.
5. Make small croquettes from the mixture and dip in egg white and coat with breadcrumbs.
6. Place croquettes in air fryer basket and air fry for 18 minutes.
7. Serve and enjoy.

Nutritional Value (Amount per Serving):
- Calories 211
- Fat 8.1 g
- Carbohydrates 18.3 g
- Sugar 2.4 g
- Protein 13.5 g
- Cholesterol 47 mg

Roasted Cashew

Preparation Time: 10 minutes
Cooking Time: 10 minutes
Serve: 4

Ingredients:
- 1 2/3 cups cashews
- 1 tsp olive oil
- 1 tsp red chili powder
- 1 tsp coriander powder
- 1/2 tsp black pepper

- 1/2 tsp salt

Directions

1. Insert wire rack in rack position 4. Select air fry, set temperature 250 F, timer for 10 minutes. Press start to preheat the oven.
2. Add all ingredients into the mixing bowl and toss well.
3. Add cashews in the air fryer basket and air fry for 10 minutes.
4. Serve or store.

Nutritional Value (Amount per Serving):

- Calories 340
- Fat 27.8 g
- Carbohydrates 19.2 g
- Sugar 2.9 g
- Protein 8.9 g
- Cholesterol 0 mg

Salmon Patties

Preparation Time: 10 minutes
Cooking Time: 15 minutes
Serve: 4

Ingredients:

- 1 egg
- 4 tbsp cup cornmeal
- 4 tbsp onion, minced
- 1/2 tsp garlic powder
- 2 tbsp mayonnaise
- 14 oz can salmon, drained
- 4 tbsp flour
- Pepper
- Salt

Directions

1. Insert wire rack in rack position 4. Select air fry, set temperature 350 F, timer for 15 minutes. Press start to preheat the oven.
2. Add drained salmon in a bowl and using a fork to make salmon flake.
3. Add garlic powder, mayonnaise, flour, cornmeal, egg, onion, pepper, and salt in a bowl. Mix well.
4. Make patties from mixture and place in air fryer basket and air fry for 15 minutes.
5. Serve and enjoy.

Nutritional Value (Amount per Serving):

- Calories 255
- Fat 10.9 g
- Carbohydrates 11.6 g
- Sugar 1.2 g
- Protein 26.2 g
- Cholesterol 86 mg

Roasted Mix Nuts

Preparation Time: 10 minutes
Cooking Time: 5 minutes
Serve: 4

Ingredients:

- 2 cup mix nuts
- 1 tsp ground cumin

- 1 tsp chipotle chili powder
- 1 tbsp butter, melted
- 1 tsp pepper
- 1 tsp salt

Directions

1. Insert wire rack in rack position 4. Select air fry, set temperature 350 F, timer for 5 minutes. Press start to preheat the oven.
2. In a mixing bowl, toss together all ingredients and until well mixed.
3. Add mix nuts in the air fryer basket and roast for 5 minutes.
4. Serve and enjoy.

Nutritional Value (Amount per Serving):

- Calories 473
- Fat 43.5 g
- Carbohydrates 16.8 g
- Sugar 3.3 g
- Protein 11.4 g
- Cholesterol 8 mg

Tasty Fishcakes

Preparation Time: 10 minutes
Cooking Time: 15 minutes
Serve: 2

Ingredients:

- 1 1/2 cups white fish, cooked
- 1 tbsp butter
- 1/2 cup mashed potatoes
- 1 1/2 tbsp milk
- 1/2 tsp sage
- 1 tsp parsley
- 2 tsp flour
- Pepper
- Salt

Directions

1. Insert wire rack in rack position 4. Select air fry, set temperature 400 F, timer for 15 minutes. Press start to preheat the oven.
2. Add all ingredients in a bowl and mix well.
3. Make patties from mixture and place in the refrigerator for 1 hour.
4. Place patties in the air fryer basket and air fry for 15 minutes.
5. Serve and enjoy.

Nutritional Value (Amount per Serving):

- Calories 206
- Fat 15 g
- Carbohydrates 12.5 g
- Sugar 0.5 g
- Protein 5.9 g
- Cholesterol 17 mg

Roasted Almond, Peanuts & Cashew

Preparation Time: 10 minutes
Cooking Time: 15 minutes
Serve: 6

Ingredients:

- 1/2 cup cashew nuts

- 1 cup peanuts
- 1 cup almonds
- 1 tbsp olive oil
- 1/2 tsp salt

Directions

1. Insert wire rack in rack position 4. Select air fry, set temperature 320 F, timer for 5 minutes. Press start to preheat the oven.
2. Add nuts in the air fryer basket and air fry for 10 minutes.
3. Transfer nuts into the bowl and toss with oil and salt.
4. Add nuts again in the air fryer basket and air fry for 5 minutes more.
5. Serve and enjoy.

Nutritional Value (Amount per Serving):
- Calories 315
- Fat 27.5 g
- Carbohydrates 11 g
- Sugar 2.2 g
- Protein 11.4 g
- Cholesterol 0 mg

Sweet Potato Fries

Preparation Time: 10 minutes
Cooking Time: 15 minutes
Serve: 4

Ingredients:
- 2 sweet potatoes, peel and cut into fries shape
- 1 tbsp olive oil
- 1/4 tsp garlic powder
- 1/4 tsp pepper
- 1/4 tsp salt

Directions:

1. Insert wire rack in rack position 4. Select air fry, set temperature 400 F, timer for 15 minutes. Press start to preheat the oven.
2. Toss sweet potato fries in a bowl with oil, garlic powder, pepper, and salt.
3. Place sweet potatoes fries in the air fryer basket and cook for 15 minutes.
4. Serve and enjoy.

Nutritional Value (Amount per Serving):
- Calories 87
- Fat 3.5 g
- Carbohydrates 13.3 g
- Sugar 2.8 g
- Protein 1.1 g
- Cholesterol 0 mg

Healthy Carrots Chips

Preparation Time: 10 minutes
Cooking Time: 15 minutes
Serve: 4

Ingredients:
- 12 oz carrot chips
- 1/2 tsp garlic powder
- 1 tbsp olive oil

- 1/4 tsp paprika
- 1/4 tsp pepper
- 1/2 tsp salt

Directions:

1. Insert wire rack in rack position 4. Select air fry, set temperature 375 F, timer for 12 minutes. Press start to preheat the oven.
2. Add all ingredients into the bowl and toss well.
3. Spray air fryer basket with cooking spray.
4. Transfer carrot chips to the air fryer basket and air fry for 15 minutes.
5. Serve and enjoy.

Nutritional Value (Amount per Serving):
- Calories 67
- Fat 3.5 g
- Carbohydrates 8.4 g
- Sugar 5.1 g
- Protein 1.1 g
- Cholesterol 0 mg

Sweet Pepper Poppers

Preparation Time: 10 minutes
Cooking Time: 15 minutes
Serve: 10

Ingredients:
- 1 lb mini sweet peppers, halved
- 1/2 cup feta cheese, crumbled
- 8 oz cream cheese
- 8 oz gouda cheese, grated
- 2 tbsp cilantro, chopped
- 2 garlic cloves, minced
- 1/4 cup onion, grated

Directions:

1. Insert wire rack in rack position 4. Select air fry, set temperature 425 F, timer for 15 minutes. Press start to preheat the oven.
2. Add all ingredients except peppers into the bowl and mix well to combine.
3. Stuff each pepper halves with cheese mixture and place on an air fryer basket and air fry for 15 minutes.
4. Serve and enjoy.

Nutritional Value (Amount per Serving):
- Calories 186
- Fat 15.8 g
- Carbohydrates 2.8 g
- Protein 8.6 g
- Sugar 1.6 g
- Cholesterol 57mg

Potato Chips

Preparation Time: 10 minutes
Cooking Time: 30 minutes
Serve: 2

Ingredients:
- 1 medium potato, thinly sliced
- 1/8 tsp pepper
- 1/2 tsp oregano

- 1/4 tsp chili powder
- 2 tsp olive oil
- 1/8 tsp thyme
- 1/8 tsp rosemary
- Salt

Directions:
1. Insert wire rack in rack position 4. Select air fry, set temperature 400 F, timer for 30 minutes. Press start to preheat the oven.
2. Add potato slices in a bowl.
3. Add remaining ingredients and toss well.
4. Arrange potato slices in the air fryer basket and air fry for 30 minutes.
5. Serve and enjoy.

Nutritional Value (Amount per Serving):
- Calories 124
- Fat 4.8 g
- Carbohydrates 19 g
- Sugar 0.9 g
- Protein 2.2 g
- Cholesterol 0 mg

Buffalo Baby Potatoes

Preparation Time: 10 minutes
Cooking Time: 20 minutes
Serve: 4

Ingredients:
- 1 lb baby potatoes
- 2 tbsp olive oil
- 1/4 cup buffalo sauce
- Pepper
- Salt

Directions:
1. Insert wire rack in rack position 4. Select air fry, set temperature 375 F, timer for 20 minutes. Press start to preheat the oven.
2. Add baby potatoes in a large bowl with remaining ingredients and toss well.
3. Transfer potatoes in the air fryer basket and air fry for 20 minutes.
4. Serve and enjoy.

Nutritional Value (Amount per Serving):
- Calories 131
- Fat 7.6 g
- Carbohydrates 14.4 g
- Sugar 0.1 g
- Protein 2.9 g
- Cholesterol 0 mg

Cajun Potato Wedges

Preparation Time: 10 minutes
Cooking Time: 25 minutes
Serve: 4

Ingredients:
- 4 potatoes, cut into wedges
- 1 tbsp Cajun spice
- 1 tbsp olive oil
- Pepper
- Salt

Directions:
1. Insert wire rack in rack position 4. Select air fry, set temperature 375 F, timer for 25 minutes. Press start to preheat the oven.
2. Add potato wedges in the air fryer basket and drizzle with olive oil and air fry for 25 minutes.
3. Transfer potato wedges in a mixing bowl and season with Cajun spice, pepper, and salt. Toss well.
4. Serve and enjoy.

Nutritional Value (Amount per Serving):
- Calories 177
- Fat 3 g
- Carbohydrates 33 g
- Sugar 2 g
- Protein 3 g
- Cholesterol 0 mg

Garlic Chili Okra

Preparation Time: 10 minutes
Cooking Time: 12 minutes
Serve: 2

Ingredients:
- 1/2 lb okra, trimmed and sliced
- 1 tsp olive oil
- 1/2 tsp chili powder
- 1/2 tsp garlic powder
- 1/8 tsp pepper
- 1/4 tsp salt

Directions:
1. Insert wire rack in rack position 4. Select air fry, set temperature 350 F, timer for 12 minutes. Press start to preheat the oven.
2. Add all ingredients into the bowl and toss well.
3. Transfer okra into the air fryer basket and air fry for 12 minutes.
4. Serve and enjoy.

Nutritional Value (Amount per Serving):
- Calories 68
- Fat 2.6 g
- Carbohydrates 9 g
- Sugar 1.8 g
- Protein 2.3 g
- Cholesterol 0 mg

Crispy Chicken Wings

Preparation Time: 10 minutes
Cooking Time: 15 minutes
Serve: 2

Ingredients:
- 1 lb chicken wings
- 1/2 tsp smoked paprika
- 1/2 tsp herb de Provence
- Pepper
- Salt

Directions:

1. Insert wire rack in rack position 4. Select air fry, set temperature 350 F, timer for 15 minutes. Press start to preheat the oven.
2. Season chicken wings with herb de Provence, paprika, pepper, and salt.
3. Place seasoned chicken wings in the air fryer basket and air fry for 15 minutes.
4. Serve and enjoy.

Nutritional Value (Amount per Serving):
- Calories 433
- Fat 16.9 g
- Carbohydrates 0.3 g
- Sugar 0.1 g
- Protein 65.7 g
- Cholesterol 202 mg

Tangy Chicken Tenders

Preparation Time: 10 minutes
Cooking Time: 18 minutes
Serve: 4

Ingredients:
- 1 lb chicken tenders
- 1/2 tsp ginger, minced
- 3 garlic cloves, minced
- 2 tbsp sesame oil
- 5 tbsp pineapple juice
- 1/2 tsp pepper

Directions:
1. Insert wire rack in rack position 4. Select air fry, set temperature 350 F, timer for 18 minutes. Press start to preheat the oven.
2. Add all ingredients except chicken in a mixing bowl and mix well.
3. Skewer chicken and place in a bowl and marinate for 2 hours.

4. Place marinated chicken in the air fryer basket and air fry for 18 minutes.
5. Serve and enjoy.

Nutritional Value (Amount per Serving):
- Calories 299
- Fat 15 g
- Carbohydrates 5 g
- Sugar 2 g
- Protein 33 g
- Cholesterol 101 mg

Air Fryer Apple Chips

Preparation Time: 10 minutes
Cooking Time: 8 minutes
Serve: 4

Ingredients :
- 1 large apple, sliced thinly
- 1/4 tsp ground cinnamon
- 1/4 tsp ground nutmeg

Directions:
1. Insert wire rack in rack position 4. Select air fry, set temperature 375 F, timer for 8 minutes. Press start to preheat the oven.
2. Season apple slices with nutmeg and cinnamon.
3. Place apple slice in the air fryer basket and air fry for 8 minutes.
4. Serve and enjoy.

Nutritional Value (Amount per Serving):
- Calories 30
- Fat 0.2 g
- Carbohydrates 7.9 g
- Sugar 5.8 g
- Protein 0.2 g
- Cholesterol 0 mg

CHAPTER 6: FISH & SEAFOOD

Tender & Flaky Chili Lime Salmon

Preparation Time: 10 minutes
Cooking Time: 15 minutes
Serve: 3

Ingredients:
- 1 lb salmon
- 1 tsp lime zest
- 1 tsp chili powder
- 1 tsp cumin powder
- 2 tbsp butter
- 1 garlic clove, minced
- 2 tsp honey
- 2 tbsp lime juice
- 1/2 tsp salt

Directions:
1. Insert wire rack in rack position 6. Select bake, set temperature 350 F, timer for 15 minutes. Press start to preheat the oven.
2. Place salmon skin side down onto the piece of aluminum foil. Make sure the foil piece is large enough to cover the salmon.
3. In a saucepan, heat honey, garlic, lime juice, and salt over medium heat.
4. Remove saucepan from heat and add butter and stir until butter is melted.
5. Pour honey mixture over salmon and sprinkle with lime zest, chili powder, and cumin.
6. Cover salmon with foil and bake for 15 minutes.
7. Serve and enjoy.

Nutritional Value (Amount per Serving):
- Calories 297
- Fat 17.4 g
- Carbohydrates 7.6 g
- Sugar 4.5 g
- Protein 29.8 g
- Cholesterol 87 mg

Sweet & Spicy Salmon

Preparation Time: 10 minutes
Cooking Time: 12 minutes
Serve: 4

Ingredients:
- 4 salmon fillets
- 2 tsp Cajun seasoning
- 4 tbsp brown sugar
- Salt

Directions:
1. Line baking sheet with foil and set aside.
2. Insert wire rack in rack position 6. Select bake, set temperature 390 F, timer for 12 minutes. Press start to preheat the oven.
3. Mix together Cajun seasoning, brown sugar, and salt and rub all over salmon.
4. Place salmon on a baking sheet and bake for 12 minutes.

5. Serve and enjoy.

Nutritional Value (Amount per Serving):
- Calories 270
- Fat 11 g
- Carbohydrates 8.8 g
- Sugar 8.7 g
- Protein 34.6 g
- Cholesterol 78 mg

Maple Dijon Salmon

Preparation Time: 10 minutes
Cooking Time: 12 minutes
Serve: 4

Ingredients:
- 4 salmon fillets
- 2 tbsp ground Dijon mustard
- 3 tbsp maple syrup

Directions:
1. Line baking sheet with foil and set aside.
2. Insert wire rack in rack position 6. Select bake, set temperature 390 F, timer for 12 minutes. Press start to preheat the oven.
3. Arrange salmon fillets on a baking sheet.
4. Mix together Dijon mustard and maple syrup and brush over salmon fillets.
5. Bake salmon fillets for 12 minutes.
6. Serve and enjoy.

Nutritional Value (Amount per Serving):
- Calories 282
- Fat 11 g
- Carbohydrates 10.1 g
- Sugar 8.9 g
- Protein 34.5 g
- Cholesterol 78 mg

Lemon Butter Cod

Preparation Time: 10 minutes
Cooking Time: 20 minutes
Serve: 4

Ingredients:
- 1 1/2 lb cod fillet
- 1 lemon, sliced
- 1/4 cup butter, diced
- 4 garlic cloves, minced
- 2 lemon juice
- 2 tbsp olive oil
- Pepper
- Salt

Directions:
1. Insert wire rack in rack position 6. Select bake, set temperature 390 F, timer for 20 minutes. Press start to preheat the oven.
2. Place codpieces in the baking dish and season with pepper and salt.
3. Whisk together garlic, lemon juice, and olive oil and pour over cod.

4. Arrange butter pieces and lemon slices on top of cod.
5. Bake for 15-20 minutes.
6. Serve and enjoy.

Nutritional Value (Amount per Serving):
- Calories 309
- Fat 20.3 g
- Carbohydrates 1.7 g
- Sugar 0.6 g
- Protein 30.9 g
- Cholesterol 114 mg

Spicy Tilapia Fish Fillets

Preparation Time: 10 minutes
Cooking Time: 15 minutes
Serve: 2

Ingredients:
- 4 tilapia fillets
- 2 tsp fresh parsley, chopped
- 1 lemon, sliced
- 1/2 tsp red chili powder
- 1 tsp garlic, minced
- 3 tbsp butter, melted
- 1 tbsp fresh lemon juice
- Pepper
- Salt

Directions:
1. Insert wire rack in rack position 6. Select bake, set temperature 350 F, timer for 15 minutes. Press start to preheat the oven.
2. Place fish fillets in the baking dish and season with pepper and salt.
3. Mix together butter, red chili powder, garlic, and lemon juice and pour over fish fillets.
4. Arrange lemon slices on top of fish fillets.
5. Bake fish for 15 minutes.
6. Garnish with parsley and serve.

Nutritional Value (Amount per Serving):
- Calories 914
- Fat 25.7 g
- Carbohydrates 3.7 g
- Sugar 1 g
- Protein 169.5 g
- Cholesterol 488 mg

Perfect Baked Shrimp

Preparation Time: 10 minutes
Cooking Time: 12 minutes
Serve: 4

Ingredients:
- 1 1/4 lbs shrimp, peeled and deveined
- 2 tbsp parsley, minced
- 2 tbsp fresh lemon juice
- 1 tbsp garlic, minced
- 1/4 cup butter
- Pepper
- Salt

Directions:

1. Insert wire rack in rack position 6. Select bake, set temperature 350 F, timer for 12 minutes. Press start to preheat the oven.
2. Melt butter in a saucepan over low heat. Add garlic and saute for 30 seconds.
3. Remove saucepan from heat. Add lemon juice in melted butter and stir well.
4. Season shrimp with pepper and salt and place in baking dish. Pour melted butter mixture over shrimp.
5. Bake shrimp for 12 minutes.
6. Garnish with parsley and serve.

Nutritional Value (Amount per Serving):
- Calories 276
- Fat 14 g
- Carbohydrates 3.2 g
- Sugar 0.2 g
- Protein 32.7 g
- Cholesterol 329 mg

Buttery Baked Scallops

Preparation Time: 10 minutes
Cooking Time: 15 minutes
Serve: 4

Ingredients:
- 1 1/2 lbs sea scallops
- 2 tbsp olive oil
- 4 tbsp butter, melted
- 2 tbsp parsley, chopped
- 4 tbsp parmesan cheese, grated
- 1/2 cup breadcrumbs
- 1/4 tsp paprika
- 1/8 tsp cayenne pepper
- Pepper
- Salt

Directions:
1. Insert wire rack in rack position 6. Select bake, set temperature 390 F, timer for 15 minutes. Press start to preheat the oven.
2. Add scallops in the 8*10-inch baking dish.
3. Mix together breadcrumbs, cayenne, paprika, parmesan cheese, parsley, butter, oil, pepper, and salt and spread over scallops.
4. Bake scallops for 15 minutes.
5. Serve and enjoy.

Nutritional Value (Amount per Serving):
- Calories 384
- Fat 21.8 g
- Carbohydrates 14.2 g
- Sugar 0.9 g
- Protein 32.4 g
- Cholesterol 91 mg

Cheesy Scallop Gratin

Preparation Time: 10 minutes
Cooking Time: 8 minutes
Serve: 4

Ingredients:
- 1 1/2 lbs sea scallops

- 1/4 cup parmesan cheese, shaved
- 1 tbsp tarragon, chopped
- 1 lemon juice
- 1/4 cup white wine
- 1/4 cup cream cheese, softened
- Pepper
- Salt

Directions:

1. Insert wire rack in rack position 6. Select bake, set temperature 390 F, timer for 8 minutes. Press start to preheat the oven.
2. Add scallops in the baking dish.
3. In a bowl, whisk together lemon juice, cream cheese, white wine, tarragon, parmesan cheese, pepper, and salt and pour over scallops.
4. Bake for 8-10 minutes.
5. Serve and enjoy.

Nutritional Value (Amount per Serving):

- Calories 235
- Fat 7.7 g
- Carbohydrates 5.5 g
- Sugar 0.4 g
- Protein 31.6 g
- Cholesterol 76 mg

Baked Basa Fish Fillets

Preparation Time: 10 minutes
Cooking Time: 12 minutes
Serve: 4

Ingredients:

- 4 basa fish fillets
- 2 tbsp parsley, chopped
- 1/4 cup green onion, sliced
- 1/2 tsp garlic powder
- 1/4 tsp lemon pepper seasoning
- 4 tbsp lemon juice
- 8 tsp butter, melted
- Pepper
- Salt

Directions:

1. Insert wire rack in rack position 6. Select bake, set temperature 390 F, timer for 12 minutes. Press start to preheat the oven.
2. Place fish fillets in the baking dish.
3. Pour melted butter and lemon juice over fish fillets.
4. Sprinkle lemon pepper seasoning, garlic powder, pepper, salt, parsley, and green onion over fish fillets.
5. Bake fish fillets for 12 minutes.
6. Serve and enjoy.

Nutritional Value (Amount per Serving):

- Calories 297
- Fat 19.7 g
- Carbohydrates 5.9 g
- Sugar 3.4 g
- Protein 24.2 g
- Cholesterol 20 mg

Dill Mustard Fish Fillets

Preparation Time: 10 minutes
Cooking Time: 15 minutes
Serve: 4

Ingredients:

- 16 oz white fish fillets
- 1/2 tsp dried dill
- 1 tbsp olive oil
- 2 tbsp fresh lemon juice
- 1 tbsp Dijon mustard
- 1/4 tsp pepper

Directions:

1. Insert wire rack in rack position 6. Select bake, set temperature 390 F, timer for 15 minutes. Press start to preheat the oven.
2. Place white fish fillets in the baking dish.
3. Mix together olive oil, lemon juice, dill, Dijon mustard, and pepper and brush over fish fillets.
4. Bake for 12-15 minutes.
5. Serve and enjoy.

Nutritional Value (Amount per Serving):

- Calories 230
- Fat 12.3 g
- Carbohydrates 0.5 g
- Sugar 0.2 g
- Protein 28 g
- Cholesterol 87 mg

Easy Lemon Pepper Tilapia

Preparation Time: 10 minutes
Cooking Time: 15 minutes
Serve: 4

Ingredients:

- 16 oz tilapia fish fillets
- 2 tbsp fresh parsley, chopped
- 1/4 cup green onions, sliced
- 1/8 tsp paprika
- 1/2 tsp garlic powder
- 1/4 tsp lemon pepper seasoning
- 4 tbsp lemon juice
- 8 tsp butter, melted
- Pepper
- Salt

Directions:

1. Insert wire rack in rack position 6. Select bake, set temperature 390 F, timer for 15 minutes. Press start to preheat the oven.
2. Place tilapia fish fillets in the baking dish.
3. Pour butter and lemon juice over fish fillets.
4. Sprinkle lemon pepper seasoning, garlic powder, paprika, pepper, salt, parsley, and green onion over fish fillets.
5. Bake fish fillets for 12-15 minutes.
6. Serve and enjoy.

Nutritional Value (Amount per Serving):

- Calories 328
- Fat 19.8 g
- Carbohydrates 24.8 g

- Sugar 1.6 g
- Protein 12.6 g
- Cholesterol 45 mg

Baked Crab Cakes

Preparation Time: 10 minutes
Cooking Time: 30 minutes
Serve: 6
Ingredients:
- 16 oz lump crab meat
- 1/4 cup celery, diced
- 1/4 cup onion, diced
- 1 cup crushed crackers
- 1 tsp old bay seasoning
- 1 tsp brown mustard
- 2/3 cup mashed avocado

Directions:
1. Line roasting pan with parchment paper and set aside.
2. Insert wire rack in rack position 6. Select bake, set temperature 350 F, timer for 30 minutes. Press start to preheat the oven.
3. Add all ingredients into the mixing bowl and mix until well combined.
4. Make small patties from mixture and place on a roasting pan.
5. Bake for 30 minutes or until crab patties is firm.
6. Serve and enjoy.

Nutritional Value (Amount per Serving):
- Calories 156
- Fat 12.1 g
- Carbohydrates 12.2 g
- Sugar 2.1 g
- Protein 12.6 g
- Cholesterol 43 mg

Garlicky Shrimp

Preparation Time: 10 minutes
Cooking Time: 10 minutes
Serve: 4
Ingredients:
- 1 lb shrimp, peel and deveined
- 1/4 cup fresh cilantro, chopped
- 3 garlic cloves, pressed
- 2 tbsp lime juice
- 2 tbsp butter, melted

Directions:
1. Insert wire rack in rack position 6. Select bake, set temperature 375 F, timer for 10 minutes. Press start to preheat the oven.
2. Add shrimp into the baking dish.
3. Mix together garlic, lime juice, and butter and pour over shrimp. Toss shrimp well and let it sit for 15 minutes.
4. Bake shrimp for 10 minutes.
5. Garnish with cilantro and serve.

Nutritional Value (Amount per Serving):
- Calories 195

- Fat 7.7 g
- Carbohydrates 4.4 g
- Sugar 0.4 g
- Protein 26.1 g
- Cholesterol 254 mg

Healthy Salmon Patties

Preparation Time: 10 minutes
Cooking Time: 20 minutes
Serve: 6
Ingredients:
- 1 lb salmon, cooked and flakes
- 2 tsp old bay seasoning
- 3 tbsp fresh dill, chopped
- 1/4 cup onion, diced
- 1 1/2 cups bell peppers, diced
- 3/4 cup breadcrumbs
- 1/4 cup mayonnaise
- 2 eggs, lightly beaten

Directions:
1. Line roasting pan with parchment paper and set aside.
2. Insert wire rack in rack position 6. Select bake, set temperature 390 F, timer for 20 minutes. Press start to preheat the oven.
3. Add all ingredients into the mixing bowl and mix until well combined.
4. Make small patties from mixture and place on a roasting pan.
5. Bake salmon patties for 15 minutes. Turn patties and bake for 5 minutes more.
6. Serve and enjoy.

Nutritional Value (Amount per Serving):
- Calories 228
- Fat 10.3 g
- Carbohydrates 15.7 g
- Sugar 3.3 g
- Protein 19.1 g
- Cholesterol 90 mg

Perfectly Tender Baked Salmon

Preparation Time: 10 minutes
Cooking Time: 15 minutes
Serve: 4
Ingredients:
- 1 1/4 lbs salmon fillets
- 1/2 tsp garlic, minced
- 1 1/2 tsp thyme
- 3/4 tsp lemon zest
- 1 tbsp soy sauce
- 2 tsp brown sugar
- 3 tbsp butter, melted
- 1/4 tsp pepper
- 1/4 tsp salt

Directions:
1. Insert wire rack in rack position 6. Select bake, set temperature 390 F, timer for 15 minutes. Press start to preheat the oven.
2. Place salmon fillets into the baking dish.

3.   Mix together garlic, thyme, lemon zest, soy sauce, brown sugar, butter, pepper, and salt and pour over fish fillets.
4.   Bake for 12-15 minutes or until fish fillets are opaque.
5.   Serve and enjoy.
Nutritional Value (Amount per Serving):
- Calories 274
- Fat 17.4 g
- Carbohydrates 2.3 g
- Sugar 1.6 g
- Protein 27.9 g
- Cholesterol 85 mg

Tasty Parmesan Baked Shrimp

Preparation Time: 10 minutes
Cooking Time: 10 minutes
Serve: 4
Ingredients:
- 1 1/2 lbs shrimp, peeled and deveined
- 1/4 cup parmesan cheese, grated
- 1/2 tsp red pepper, crushed
- 1 tsp garlic powder
- 1/4 cup butter, melted
- Pepper
- Salt

Directions:
1.   Insert wire rack in rack position 6. Select bake, set temperature 390 F, timer for 10 minutes. Press start to preheat the oven.
2.   Season shrimp with pepper and salt and add into the baking dish. Pour melted butter over shrimp.
3.   Sprinkle garlic powder, crushed red pepper, and grated cheese over shrimp.
4.   Bake shrimp for 10 minutes.
5.   Serve and enjoy.
Nutritional Value (Amount per Serving):
- Calories 329
- Fat 15.7 g
- Carbohydrates 4.5 g
- Sugar 0.9 g
- Protein 40.9 g
- Cholesterol 393 mg

Baked Catfish Fillets

Preparation Time: 10 minutes
Cooking Time: 15 minutes
Serve: 4
Ingredients:
- 4 catfish fillets
- 1 tbsp Cajun seasoning
- 1 cup cornmeal
- 1/4 cup olive oil
- Pepper
- Salt

Directions:
1.   Drizzle 2 tablespoons of olive oil on roasting pan and set aside.

2.   Insert wire rack in rack position 6. Select bake, set temperature 390 F, timer for 15 minutes. Press start to preheat the oven.
3.   In a shallow dish, mix together cornmeal, pepper, cajun seasoning, and salt.
4.   Coat fish fillets with cornmeal mixture and place them on a roasting pan. Drizzle with remaining olive oil.
5.   Bake fish fillets for 15 minutes or until fish flakes with a fork.
6.   Serve and enjoy.
Nutritional Value (Amount per Serving):
- Calories 434
- Fat 25.8 g
- Carbohydrates 23.5 g
- Sugar 0.2 g
- Protein 27.4 g
- Cholesterol 75 mg

Crispy Crusted Salmon Patties

Preparation Time: 10 minutes
Cooking Time: 20 minutes
Serve: 6
Ingredients:
- 2 cans wild Alaska salmon, drain and remove bones
- 1 egg, lightly beaten
- 1 tbsp curry paste
- 2 green onion, minced
- 3 tbsp cilantro, chopped
- 1/2 tsp lemon zest
- Salt

Directions:
1.   Spray a roasting pan with cooking spray and set aside.
2.   Insert wire rack in rack position 6. Select bake, set temperature 375 F, timer for 20 minutes. Press start to preheat the oven.
3.   Add all ingredients into the mixing bowl and mix until well combined.
4.   Make patties from mixture and place on a roasting pan.
5.   Bake salmon patties for 20 minutes.
6.   Serve and enjoy.
Nutritional Value (Amount per Serving):
- Calories 113
- Fat 6.9 g
- Carbohydrates 1.2 g
- Sugar 0.2 g
- Protein 12.3 g
- Cholesterol 65 mg

Baked Lemon Cod

Preparation Time: 10 minutes
Cooking Time: 30 minutes
Serve: 4
Ingredients:
- 1 lb cod fish fillets
- 1/4 cup all-purpose flour

- 2 tbsp lemon juice
- 1/4 cup butter, melted
- Pepper
- Salt

Directions:
1.   Insert wire rack in rack position 6. Select bake, set temperature 350 F, timer for 30 minutes. Press start to preheat the oven.
2.   In a shallow dish, mix together lemon juice and butter.
3.   In a separate shallow dish, mix together flour, pepper, and salt.
4.   Dip fish fillet in lemon butter mixture and coat with flour mixture.
5.   Place coated fish fillets in the baking dish and bake for 25-30 minutes.
6.   Serve and enjoy.

Nutritional Value (Amount per Serving):
- Calories 251
- Fat 12.6 g
- Carbohydrates 6.2 g
- Sugar 0.2 g
- Protein 26.9 g
- Cholesterol 93 mg

Moist & Juicy Cod

Preparation Time: 10 minutes
Cooking Time: 12 minutes
Serve: 4
Ingredients:
- 1 lb cod fillets
- 1 tbsp parsley, chopped
- 1 1/2 tbsp olive oil
- 1 tbsp lemon juice
- 1/8 tsp cayenne pepper
- 1/4 tsp salt

Directions:
1.   Insert wire rack in rack position 6. Select bake, set temperature 390 F, timer for 12 minutes. Press start to preheat the oven.
2.   Place fish fillets in the baking dish and drizzle with olive oil and lemon juice.
3.   Sprinkle cayenne pepper and salt over fish fillets.
4.   Bake fish fillets for 10-12 minutes.
5.   Garnish with parsley and serve.

Nutritional Value (Amount per Serving):
- Calories 28
- Fat 1.3 g
- Carbohydrates 0 g
- Sugar 0 g
- Protein 4.1 g
- Cholesterol 11 mg

Delicious Dijon Salmon

Preparation Time: 10 minutes
Cooking Time: 12 minutes
Serve: 4
Ingredients:

- 4 salmon fillets
- 2 garlic cloves, minced
- 2 tbsp olive oil
- 1/4 cup Dijon mustard
- 1/4 cup maple syrup
- Pepper
- Salt

Directions:
1.   Insert wire rack in rack position 6. Select bake, set temperature 390 F, timer for 12 minutes. Press start to preheat the oven.
2.   Place salmon fillets into the baking dish.
3.   Mix together garlic, olive oil, Dijon mustard, maple syrup, pepper, and salt and pour over salmon fillets. Coat well and let it sit for 10 minutes.
4.   Bake salmon fillets for 10-12 minutes.
5.   Serve and enjoy.

Nutritional Value (Amount per Serving):
- Calories 360
- Fat 18.7 g
- Carbohydrates 14.6 g
- Sugar 11.9 g
- Protein 35.3 g
- Cholesterol 78 mg

Delicious Seafood Bake

Preparation Time: 10 minutes
Cooking Time: 30 minutes
Serve: 6
Ingredients:
- 1 lb shrimp, cooked
- 1 lb crab meat
- 2 tbsp butter, melted
- 1/2 cup breadcrumbs
- 1 cup sour cream
- 1 tbsp Worcestershire sauce
- 1/2 cup bell pepper, chopped
- 1 cup mayonnaise
- 1 cup celery, chopped
- 1 cup onion, chopped
- 1/2 tsp salt

Directions:
1.   Spray a 3-quart baking dish with cooking spray and set aside.
2.   Insert wire rack in rack position 6. Select bake, set temperature 390 F, timer for 12 minutes. Press start to preheat the oven.
3.   In a bowl, mix together crabmeat, sour cream, Worcestershire sauce, bell pepper, mayonnaise, celery, onion, shrimp, pepper, and salt.
4.   Pour crabmeat mixture into the baking dish.
5.   In a small bowl, mix together butter and breadcrumbs and sprinkle over the crabmeat mixture.
6.   Bake for 30 minutes.
7.   Serve and enjoy.

Nutritional Value (Amount per Serving):
- Calories 478
- Fat 28.1 g

- Carbohydrates 23.5 g
- Sugar 5.2 g
- Protein 29.9 g
- Cholesterol 237 mg

Parmesan Herb Crust Salmon

Preparation Time: 10 minutes
Cooking Time: 15 minutes
Serve: 4
Ingredients:
- 2 lbs salmon fillet
- 1/2 cup parmesan cheese, grated
- 1/4 cup parsley, minced
- 3 garlic cloves, minced

Directions:
1. Line roasting pan with parchment paper and set aside.
2. Insert wire rack in rack position 6. Select bake, set temperature 390 F, timer for 15 minutes. Press start to preheat the oven.
3. Place a salmon fillet, skin side down on roasting pan and cover with another piece of parchment paper. Bake salmon for 10 minutes.
4. Mix together cheese, parsley, and garlic and spread over salmon and bake for 5 minutes more.
5. Serve and enjoy.

Nutritional Value (Amount per Serving):
- Calories 341
- Fat 16.5 g
- Carbohydrates 1.4 g
- Sugar 0.1 g
- Protein 47.9 g
- Cholesterol 108 mg

Shrimp Fajitas

Preparation Time: 10 minutes
Cooking Time: 15 minutes
Serve: 4
Ingredients:
- 1 lb shrimp, peeled and deveined
- 1/2 lime juice
- 1 1/2 tbsp taco seasoning
- 1 1/2 tbsp olive oil
- 3 bell peppers, sliced
- 1 medium onion, sliced

Directions:
1. Line roasting pan with parchment paper and set aside.
2. Insert wire rack in rack position 6. Select bake, set temperature 390 F, timer for 15 minutes. Press start to preheat the oven.
3. In a mixing bowl, toss shrimp with remaining ingredients.
4. Spread shrimp mixture on roasting pan and bake for 12-15 minutes or until shrimp are cooked through.
5. Serve and enjoy.

Nutritional Value (Amount per Serving):
- Calories 229

- Fat 7.9 g
- Carbohydrates 12.1 g
- Sugar 5.8 g
- Protein 27.5 g
- Cholesterol 240 mg

Asian Seafood Bake

Preparation Time: 10 minutes
Cooking Time: 30 minutes
Serve: 4
Ingredients:
- 6 oz shrimp
- 1/2 cup mozzarella cheese
- 2 tbsp green onions, sliced
- 1 cup mayonnaise
- 12 oz imitation lobster meat
- 12 oz imitation crab meat

Directions:
1. Spray a 1-quart baking dish with cooking spray and set aside.
2. Insert wire rack in rack position 6. Select bake, set temperature 350 F, timer for 30 minutes. Press start to preheat the oven.
3. In a large bowl, mix together shrimp, green onions, mayonnaise, lobster meat, and crab meat and pour into the baking dish.
4. Sprinkle cheese on top of the shrimp mixture and bake for 25-30 minutes.
5. Serve and enjoy.

Nutritional Value (Amount per Serving):
- Calories 446
- Fat 21.7 g
- Carbohydrates 38.8 g
- Sugar 14.2 g
- Protein 25.5 g
- Cholesterol 134 mg

Crabmeat Casserole

Preparation Time: 10 minutes
Cooking Time: 45 minutes
Serve: 15
Ingredients:
- 8 eggs, lightly beaten
- 1 tsp old bay seasoning
- 4 oz Swiss cheese, chopped
- 1 cup cheddar cheese, shredded
- 1 lb crab meat, chopped
- 1 small eggplant, diced
- 1 red pepper, diced
- 1 green pepper, diced
- 2 cups almond milk
- 1/2 tsp pepper

Directions:
1. Spray a 13*9-inch baking dish with cooking spray and set aside.
2. Insert wire rack in rack position 6. Select bake, set temperature 350 F, timer for 45 minutes. Press start to preheat the oven.

3. Add all ingredients into the mixing bowl and mix well and pour into the baking dish and bake for 45 minutes.
4. Serve and enjoy.

Nutritional Value (Amount per Serving):
- Calories 205
- Fat 15.2 g
- Carbohydrates 5.8 g
- Sugar 2.9 g
- Protein 11.8 g
- Cholesterol 118 mg

Delicious Shrimp Scampi

Preparation Time: 10 minutes
Cooking Time: 12 minutes
Serve: 4

Ingredients:
- 1 lb shrimp, peeled and deveined
- 10 garlic cloves, peeled
- 2 tbsp olive oil
- 1 fresh lemon, cut into wedges
- 1/4 cup parmesan cheese, grated
- 2 tbsp butter, melted

Directions:
1. Line roasting pan with parchment paper and set aside.
2. Insert wire rack in rack position 6. Select bake, set temperature 390 F, timer for 12 minutes. Press start to preheat the oven.
3. Mix together shrimp, lemon wedges, olive oil, and garlic cloves and spread roasting pan.
4. Bake for 12 minutes or until shrimp is opaque.
5. Drizzle with melted butter and sprinkle with parmesan cheese.
6. Serve and enjoy.

Nutritional Value (Amount per Serving):
- Calories 275
- Fat 15.9 g
- Carbohydrates 4.6 g
- Sugar 0.1 g
- Protein 28.2 g
- Cholesterol 258 mg

Dill Chili Salmon

Preparation Time: 10 minutes
Cooking Time: 22 minutes
Serve: 4

Ingredients:
- 2 lbs salmon fillet, skinless and boneless
- 2 lemon juice
- 1 orange juice
- 1 tbsp olive oil
- 1 bunch fresh dill
- 1 chili, sliced
- Pepper
- Salt

Directions:

1. Insert wire rack in rack position 6. Select bake, set temperature 350 F, timer for 22 minutes. Press start to preheat the oven.
2. Place salmon fillet in a baking dish and drizzle with olive oil, lemon juice, and orange juice.
3. Sprinkle with chili and season with pepper and salt.
4. Bake for 22 minutes.
5. Garnish with dill and serve.

Nutritional Value (Amount per Serving):
- Calories 349
- Fat 17.8 g
- Carbohydrates 3.3 g
- Sugar 2.3 g
- Protein 44.6 g
- Cholesterol 100 mg

Lemon Walnut Salmon

Preparation Time: 10 minutes
Cooking Time: 15 minutes
Serve: 4

Ingredients:
- 4 salmon fillets
- 1/4 cup parmesan cheese, grated
- 1/4 cup walnuts
- 1 tsp olive oil
- 1 tbsp lemon rind

Directions:
1. Spray a baking tray with cooking spray and set aside.
2. Insert wire rack in rack position 6. Select bake, set temperature 390 F, timer for 15 minutes. Press start to preheat the oven.
3. Place salmon fillets in the baking dish.
4. Add walnuts into the food processor and process until ground.
5. Mix together walnuts, cheese, oil, and lemon rind and spread on top of salmon fillets.
6. Bake for 15 minutes.
7. Serve and enjoy.

Nutritional Value (Amount per Serving):
- Calories 313
- Fat 18 g
- Carbohydrates 1.3 g
- Sugar 0.2 g
- Protein 38.3 g
- Cholesterol 83 mg

Flavorful Pesto Salmon

Preparation Time: 10 minutes
Cooking Time: 20 minutes
Serve: 2

Ingredients:
- 2 salmon fillets
- 1/4 cup parmesan cheese, grated

For pesto:
- 3 garlic cloves, peeled and chopped
- 1 1/2 cups fresh basil leaves
- 1/4 cup parmesan cheese, grated

- 1/4 cup pine nuts
- 1/4 cup olive oil
- 1/2 tsp pepper
- 1/2 tsp salt

Directions:
1. Insert wire rack in rack position 6. Select bake, set temperature 390 F, timer for 20 minutes. Press start to preheat the oven.
2. Add all pesto ingredients into the blender and blend until smooth.
3. Place salmon fillet on a roasting pan. Spread 2 tablespoons of pesto on top of each salmon fillet. Sprinkle grated cheese on top.
4. Bake for 20 minutes.
5. Serve and enjoy.

Nutritional Value (Amount per Serving):
- Calories 614
- Fat 50.4 g
- Carbohydrates 4.9 g
- Sugar 0.7 g
- Protein 41.4 g
- Cholesterol 87 mg

Herb Baked Salmon

Preparation Time: 10 minutes
Cooking Time: 30 minutes
Serve: 6

Ingredients:
- 2 1/2 lbs large salmon fillet
- 2 cups cherry tomatoes, halved
- 1/2 cup olives pitted
- 2 lemons, sliced
- 1 tsp fresh thyme, chopped
- 1 tsp rosemary, chopped
- 1 tsp oregano, chopped
- 4 tbsp olive oil
- 1/4 cup onion, sliced
- 2 tsp capers
- Pepper
- Salt

Directions:
1. Line roasting pan with parchment paper and set aside.
2. Insert wire rack in rack position 6. Select bake, set temperature 390 F, timer for 30 minutes. Press start to preheat the oven.
3. Place salmon fillets on a roasting pan.
4. Arrange lemon slices and olives, onions, capers, and tomatoes around the salmon. Drizzle with oil and season with pepper and salt.
5. Bake for 30 minutes.
6. Garnish with herbs and serve.

Nutritional Value (Amount per Serving):
- Calories 516
- Fat 36.9 g
- Carbohydrates 6.7 g
- Sugar 2.5 g
- Protein 3.2 g
- Cholesterol 0 mg

Cod with Potatoes & Tomatoes

Preparation Time: 10 minutes
Cooking Time: 25 minutes
Serve: 4

Ingredients:
- 1 lb cod fillet, cut into four pieces
- 4 tbsp olive oil
- 2 cups baby potatoes, diced
- 2 cups cherry tomatoes
- Pepper
- Salt

Directions:
1. Insert wire rack in rack position 6. Select bake, set temperature 390 F, timer for 10 minutes. Press start to preheat the oven.
2. Toss potatoes with half olive oil and place in roasting pan. Bake potatoes for 15 minutes.
3. Remove roasting pan from oven and place cod fillets and cherry tomatoes in the pan.
4. Drizzle with remaining oil and season with pepper and salt.
5. Bake for 10 minutes.
6. Serve and enjoy.

Nutritional Value (Amount per Serving):
- Calories 238
- Fat 15.2 g
- Carbohydrates 5.9 g
- Sugar 2.4 g
- Protein 21.5 g
- Cholesterol 56 mg

Greek Salmon

Preparation Time: 10 minutes
Cooking Time: 20 minutes
Serve: 4

Ingredients:
- 4 salmon fillets
- 2 cups grape tomatoes, halved
- 1 onion, chopped
- 1/2 cup pesto
- 1/2 cup feta cheese, crumbled

Directions:
1. Line roasting pan with parchment paper and set aside.
2. Insert wire rack in rack position 6. Select bake, set temperature 350 F, timer for 20 minutes. Press start to preheat the oven.
3. Place salmon fillet in roasting pan and top with tomatoes, onion, pesto, and cheese.
4. Bake for 20 minutes.
5. Serve and enjoy.

Nutritional Value (Amount per Serving):
- Calories 447
- Fat 28.2 g
- Carbohydrates 8.8 g
- Sugar 6.3 g
- Protein 41.3 g
- Cholesterol 103 mg

Cod with Vegetables

Preparation Time: 10 minutes
Cooking Time: 22 minutes
Serve: 2

Ingredients:
- 1 lb cod fish fillets
- 1/2 tsp oregano
- 1 leek, sliced
- 1 onion, quartered
- 2 tomatoes, halved
- 2 tbsp olive oil
- 1/2 tsp red pepper flakes
- 1/2 cup olives pitted and halved
- 8 asparagus spears
- Pepper
- Salt

Directions:
1. Line roasting pan with parchment paper and set aside.
2. Insert wire rack in rack position 6. Select bake, set temperature 390 F, timer for 22 minutes. Press start to preheat the oven.
3. Arrange fish fillets, olives, tomatoes, onion, leek, and asparagus in roasting pan. Drizzle with olive oil and season with oregano, chili flakes, pepper, and salt.
4. Bake for 22 minutes.
5. Serve and enjoy.

Nutritional Value (Amount per Serving):
- Calories 487
- Fat 19.3 g
- Carbohydrates 22.3 g
- Sugar 9.2 g
- Protein 58.2 g
- Cholesterol 125 mg

Delicious Herb Sardines

Preparation Time: 10 minutes
Cooking Time: 15 minutes
Serve: 4

Ingredients:
- 1 lb sardines, rinsed and pat dry
- 1 1/2 tsp fresh parsley, chopped
- 1 tbsp fresh lime juice
- 1 1/2 tsp mustard
- 2 garlic cloves, minced
- 3 tbsp olive oil
- 1/2 tsp dry onion flakes
- 1/2 tsp paprika
- 1/2 tbsp oregano
- 1/4 tsp sea salt

Directions:
1. Line roasting pan with parchment paper and set aside.
2. Insert wire rack in rack position 6. Select bake, set temperature 390 F, timer for 15 minutes. Press start to preheat the oven.
3. In a large bowl, mix all ingredients except sardines and parsley. Add sardines and coat well.
4. Place sardines in roasting pan and bake for 15 minutes or until cooked through.
5. Garnish with parsley and serve.

Nutritional Value (Amount per Serving):
- Calories 340
- Fat 24 g
- Carbohydrates 2.6 g
- Sugar 0.4 g
- Protein 28.5 g
- Cholesterol 161 mg

Italian Salmon

Preparation Time: 10 minutes
Cooking Time: 30 minutes
Serve: 2

Ingredients:
- 2 salmon filets
- 1/2 cup tomato, diced
- 1/2 cup olives, chopped
- 1 tbsp balsamic vinegar
- 1 tbsp parsley, chopped
- 1/3 cup feta cheese, crumbled
- 1 tbsp olive oil
- Pepper
- Salt

Directions:
1. Line roasting pan with parchment paper and set aside.
2. Insert wire rack in rack position 6. Select bake, set temperature 350 F, timer for 15 minutes. Press start to preheat the oven.
3. Season salmon with pepper and salt.
4. Place salmon in roasting pan and bake for 15 minutes.
5. Meanwhile, mix together tomato, olive oil, vinegar, olives, feta cheese, and parsley.
6. Remove salmon from oven and top with tomato olive mixture.
7. Serve and enjoy.

Nutritional Value (Amount per Serving):
- Calories 607
- Fat 20 g
- Carbohydrates 24.1 g
- Sugar 2.3 g
- Protein 4.3 g
- Cholesterol 22 mg

Flavorful Lemon Fish Fillets

Preparation Time: 10 minutes
Cooking Time: 18 minutes
Serve: 4

Ingredients:
- 1 lb tilapia fillets
- 1/2 tsp dried oregano
- 1 tsp fresh lemon juice
- 2 tsp olive oil
- 1 lemon, sliced

- 1 tsp garlic powder
- 1/2 tsp dried thyme
- 1/2 tsp pepper
- 1 tsp salt

Directions:

1. Line roasting pan with parchment paper and set aside.
2. Insert wire rack in rack position 6. Select bake, set temperature 390 F, timer for 18 minutes. Press start to preheat the oven.
3. Place a fish fillets in roasting pan and brush with lemon juice and olive oil.
4. Mix together garlic powder, thyme, oregano, pepper, and salt and sprinkle over fish fillets. Place lemon slices at the top of the fish fillet.
5. Bake for 15-18 minutes or until cooked through.
6. Serve and enjoy.

Nutritional Value (Amount per Serving):

- Calories 118
- Fat 3.4 g
- Carbohydrates 1.1 g
- Sugar 0.3 g
- Protein 21.3 g
- Cholesterol 55 mg

Fish Fillets with Zucchini

Preparation Time: 10 minutes
Cooking Time: 20 minutes
Serve: 2

Ingredients:

- 8 oz cod fillets
- 1 tbsp olive oil
- 1/2 cup olives
- 1/2 cup cherry tomatoes halved
- 1 bell pepper, sliced
- 1 tbsp balsamic vinegar
- 1 lemon, sliced
- 3 garlic cloves, minced
- Pepper
- Salt

Directions:

1. Insert wire rack in rack position 6. Select bake, set temperature 390 F, timer for 20 minutes. Press start to preheat the oven.
2. Place all vegetables in a baking dish. Season with pepper and salt and drizzle with oil. Bake vegetables for 10 minutes.
3. Season fish fillets with pepper and salt and drizzle with oil.
4. Place fish fillets in the baking dish with cooked vegetables.
5. Arrange lemon slices on top of fish fillets. Drizzle fish fillets and veggies with vinegar.
6. Bake for 10 minutes.
7. Serve and enjoy.

Nutritional Value (Amount per Serving):

- Calories 223
- Fat 11.8 g

- Carbohydrates 9.5 g
- Sugar 3.7 g
- Protein 21.7 g
- Cholesterol 56 mg

Dijon Herb Salmon

Preparation Time: 10 minutes
Cooking Time: 15 minutes
Serve: 4

Ingredients:

- 4 salmon fillets
- 1 tsp dried thyme
- 2 tbsp fresh lemon juice
- 2 tbsp Dijon mustard
- 2 tomatoes, sliced
- 1 small onion, sliced
- 1 tsp dried oregano
- 1 tsp dried rosemary
- Pepper
- Salt

Directions:

1. Spray a baking dish with cooking spray and set aside.
2. Insert wire rack in rack position 6. Select bake, set temperature 390 F, timer for 15 minutes. Press start to preheat the oven.
3. In a bowl, mix together lemon juice, oregano, rosemary, thyme, mustard, pepper, and salt.
4. Add fish fillets and coat well form both sides. Cover and place in the refrigerator for 30 minutes.
5. Arrange sliced tomatoes and onion in the baking dish then place marinated fish fillets on top. Pour remaining marinade over fish fillets.
6. Bake for 15 minutes.
7. Serve and enjoy.

Nutritional Value (Amount per Serving):

- Calories 264
- Fat 11.6 g
- Carbohydrates 5.2 g
- Sugar 2.6 g
- Protein 35.7 g
- Cholesterol 78 mg

Jalapeno Salmon

Preparation Time: 10 minutes
Cooking Time: 30 minutes
Serve: 6

Ingredients:

- 2 lbs salmon fillet, skinless
- 1 lemon, sliced
- 1 orange, sliced
- 1 fennel bulb, sliced
- 3/4 cup olive oil
- 4 dill sprigs
- 1 jalapeno pepper, sliced
- Pepper
- Salt

Directions:

1. Insert wire rack in rack position 6. Select bake, set temperature 325 F, timer for 30 minutes. Press start to preheat the oven.
2. Mix dill, jalapeno, lemon slices, orange slices, fennel in baking dish.
3. Season salmon with pepper and salt and place on top of the dill mixture.
4. Pour oil over salmon and bake for 30 minutes.
5. Serve and enjoy.

Nutritional Value (Amount per Serving):
- Calories 449
- Fat 34.8 g
- Carbohydrates 7.9 g
- Sugar 3 g
- Protein 30.6 g
- Cholesterol 67 mg

Air Fryer Salmon

Preparation Time: 10 minutes
Cooking Time: 8 minutes
Serve: 4

Ingredients:
- 4 salmon fillets
- 1 tbsp honey
- 2 tsp soy sauce
- 1 tsp sesame seeds, toasted
- Pepper
- Salt

Directions:
1. Insert wire rack in rack position 4. Select air fry, set temperature 375 F, timer for 8 minutes. Press start to preheat the oven.
2. Brush salmon with soy sauce and season with pepper and salt.
3. Place salmon on air fryer basket and air fry for 8 minutes.
4. Brush salmon with honey and sprinkle with sesame seeds.
5. Serve and enjoy.

Nutritional Value (Amount per Serving):
- Calories 257
- Fat 11.4 g
- Carbohydrates 4.7 g
- Sugar 4.4 g
- Protein 34.9 g
- Cholesterol 78 mg

Asian Salmon

Preparation Time: 10 minutes
Cooking Time: 10 minutes
Serve: 2

Ingredients:
- 2 salmon fillets, skinless and boneless
- For marinade:
- 2 tbsp scallions, minced
- 1 tbsp ginger, grated
- 2 garlic cloves, minced
- 2 tbsp mirin

- 2 tbsp soy sauce
- 1 tbsp olive oil

Directions:
1. Insert wire rack in rack position 4. Select air fry, set temperature 360 F, timer for 10 minutes. Press start to preheat the oven.
2. Add all marinade ingredients into the zip-lock bag and mix well.
3. Add salmon in a zip-lock bag. The sealed bag shakes well and places it in the refrigerator for 60 minutes.
4. Arrange marinated salmon fillets on the air fryer basket and the air fryer for 10 minutes.
5. Serve and enjoy.

Nutritional Value (Amount per Serving):
- Calories 345
- Fat 18.2 g
- Carbohydrates 11.6 g
- Sugar 4.5 g
- Protein 36.1 g
- Cholesterol 78 mg

Paprika Herb Salmon

Preparation Time: 10 minutes
Cooking Time: 5 minutes
Serve: 2

Ingredients:
- 2 salmon fillets
- 1/4 tsp paprika
- 1 tsp herb de Provence
- 1 tbsp butter, melted
- 2 tbsp olive oil
- Pepper
- Salt

Directions:
1. Insert wire rack in rack position 4. Select air fry, set temperature 390 F, timer for 5 minutes. Press start to preheat the oven.
2. Brush fish fillets with olive oil and sprinkle with paprika, herb de Provence, pepper, and salt.
3. Place fish fillets on air fryer basket and air fry for 5 minutes.
4. Drizzle salmon with butter and serve.

Nutritional Value (Amount per Serving):
- Calories 415
- Fat 31.2 g
- Carbohydrates 0.2 g
- Sugar 0 g
- Protein 35.6 g
- Cholesterol 94 mg

Honey Chili Salmon

Preparation Time: 10 minutes
Cooking Time: 12 minutes
Serve: 3

Ingredients:
- 3 salmon fillets
- 1/2 tsp chili powder
- 1/2 tsp turmeric

- 1 tsp coriander
- 1/4 cup honey
- 1 tbsp red pepper flakes
- Pepper
- Salt

Directions:

1.   Insert wire rack in rack position 4. Select air fry, set temperature 400 F, timer for 12 minutes. Press start to preheat the oven.

2.   Add honey in microwave-safe bowl and microwave until just warm. Add red pepper flakes, chili powder, turmeric, coriander, pepper, and salt in honey and stir well.

3.   Brush salmon fillets with honey and place on an air fryer basket and air fry for 12 minutes.

4.   Serve and enjoy.

Nutritional Value (Amount per Serving):

- Calories 330
- Fat 11.4 g
- Carbohydrates 24.8 g
- Sugar 23.4 g
- Protein 34.9 g
- Cholesterol 78 mg

Easy Salmon Patties

Preparation Time: 10 minutes
Cooking Time: 7 minutes
Serve: 2

Ingredients:

- 8 oz salmon fillet, minced
- 1/4 tsp garlic powder
- 1/4 tsp onion powder
- 1 egg, lightly beaten
- Pepper
- Salt

Directions:

1.   Insert wire rack in rack position 4. Select air fry, set temperature 390 F, timer for 7 minutes. Press start to preheat the oven.

2.   Add all ingredients into the bowl and mix until well combined.

3.   Make small patties from salmon mixture and place on an air fryer basket and air fry for 7 minutes.

4.   Serve and enjoy.

Nutritional Value (Amount per Serving):

- Calories 184
- Fat 9.2 g
- Carbohydrates 0.7 g
- Sugar 0.4 g
- Protein 24.9 g
- Cholesterol 132 mg

Cajun Butter Salmon

Preparation Time: 10 minutes
Cooking Time: 8 minutes
Serve: 4

Ingredients:

- 4 salmon fillets

- 1 tsp Cajun seasoning
- 1/4 cup butter, melted
- Pepper
- Salt

Directions:

1.   Insert wire rack in rack position 4. Select air fry, set temperature 375 F, timer for 8 minutes. Press start to preheat the oven.

2.   Brush salmon fillets with butter and season with Cajun seasoning, pepper, and salt.

3.   Place salmon fillets on an air fryer basket and air fry for 8 minutes.

4.   Serve and enjoy.

Nutritional Value (Amount per Serving):

- Calories 337
- Fat 22.5 g
- Carbohydrates 0 g
- Sugar 0 g
- Protein 34.7 g
- Cholesterol 109 mg

Tuna Patties

Preparation Time: 10 minutes
Cooking Time: 10 minutes
Serve: 10

Ingredients:

- 15 oz can tuna, drained and flaked
- 3 tbsp parmesan cheese, grated
- 1/2 cup breadcrumbs
- 1 tbsp lemon juice
- 2 eggs, lightly beaten
- 1/2 tsp dried herbs
- 1/2 tsp garlic powder
- 2 tbsp onion, minced
- 1 celery stalk, chopped
- Pepper
- Salt

Directions:

1.   Line air fryer basket with parchment paper and set aside.

2.   Insert wire rack in rack position 4. Select air fry, set temperature 360 F, timer for 10 minutes. Press start to preheat the oven.

3.   Add all ingredients into the mixing bowl and mix until well combined.

4.   Make small patties from tuna mixture and place on an air fryer basket and air fry for 10 minutes.

5.   Serve and enjoy.

Nutritional Value (Amount per Serving):

- Calories 91
- Fat 1.9 g
- Carbohydrates 4.4 g
- Sugar 0.6 g
- Protein 13.3 g
- Cholesterol 47 mg

Lemon Pepper Fish Fillets

Preparation Time: 10 minutes
Cooking Time: 10 minutes

Serve: 2

Ingredients:
- 2 tilapia fillets
- 1/2 tsp lemon pepper seasoning
- 1/2 tsp garlic powder
- 1/2 tsp onion powder
- Salt

Directions:
1. Line air fryer basket with parchment paper and set aside.
2. Insert wire rack in rack position 4. Select air fry, set temperature 360 F, timer for 10 minutes. Press start to preheat the oven.
3. Spray fish fillets with cooking spray and place in the air fryer basket. Season chicken with onion powder, lemon pepper seasoning, and salt.
4. Air fry fish fillets for 10 minutes.
5. Serve and enjoy.

Nutritional Value (Amount per Serving):
- Calories 99
- Fat 1.1 g
- Carbohydrates 1.3 g
- Sugar 0.4 g
- Protein 21.3 g
- Cholesterol 55 mg

Delicious Spicy Shrimp

Preparation Time: 10 minutes
Cooking Time: 6 minutes
Serve: 4

Ingredients:
- 1 lb shrimp
- 1/4 tsp red pepper flakes
- 2 garlic cloves, minced
- 2 tsp olive oil
- 1 tbsp parsley, chopped
- 2 tsp fresh lemon juice
- 1 tsp lemon zest, grated
- 1 tsp steak seasoning
- Pepper
- Salt

Directions:
1. Line air fryer basket with parchment paper and set aside.
2. Insert wire rack in rack position 4. Select air fry, set temperature 400 F, timer for 6 minutes. Press start to preheat the oven.

3. Add shrimp and remaining ingredients into the large bowl and toss well.
4. Spread shrimp on an air fryer basket and air fry for 6 minutes.
5. Serve and enjoy.

Nutritional Value (Amount per Serving):
- Calories 159
- Fat 4.3 g
- Carbohydrates 2.5 g
- Sugar 0.1 g
- Protein 26 g
- Cholesterol 239 mg

Easy Shrimp Casserole

Preparation Time: 10 minutes
Cooking Time: 12 minutes
Serve: 4

Ingredients:
- 1 lb shrimp, peeled and deveined
- 1/2 cup breadcrumbs
- 1/4 cup butter, melted
- 2 tbsp wine
- 1 tbsp garlic, minced
- 2 tbsp fresh parsley, chopped
- Pepper
- Salt

Directions:
1. Spray a baking dish with cooking spray and set aside.
2. Insert wire rack in rack position 6. Select bake, set temperature 390 F, timer for 12 minutes. Press start to preheat the oven.
3. Add shrimp into the large bowl. Pour remaining ingredients over shrimp and toss well.
4. Pour shrimp mixture into the baking dish and bake for 12 minutes.
5. Serve and enjoy.

Nutritional Value (Amount per Serving):
- Calories 300
- Fat 14.2 g
- Carbohydrates 12.5 g
- Sugar 1 g
- Protein 28 g
- Cholesterol 269 mg

CHAPTER 7: VEGETABLES

Roasted Butternut Squash

Preparation Time: 10 minutes
Cooking Time: 40 minutes
Serve: 4

Ingredients:
- 3 lbs butternut squash, peeled, seeded, and cut into 1-inch cubes
- 1/2 tsp cinnamon
- 1 1/2 tbsp maple syrup
- 1 1/2 tbsp olive oil
- Pepper
- Salt

Directions:
1. Line roasting pan with parchment paper and set aside.
2. Insert wire rack in rack position 6. Select roast, set temperature 400 F, timer for 40 minutes. Press start to preheat the oven.
3. In a mixing bowl, toss squash cubes with remaining ingredients.
4. Spread squash cubes in a prepared roasting pan.
5. Roast squash cubes for 35-40 minutes.
6. Serve and enjoy.

Nutritional Value (Amount per Serving):
- Calories 219
- Fat 5.6 g
- Carbohydrates 45.1 g
- Sugar 12 g
- Protein 3.4 g
- Cholesterol 0 mg

Oven Roasted Broccoli

Preparation Time: 10 minutes
Cooking Time: 25 minutes
Serve: 4

Ingredients:
- 1 1/2 lbs broccoli florets
- 1 tbsp fresh lemon juice
- 1/4 tsp onion powder
- 1/2 tsp garlic powder
- 2 1/2 tbsp olive oil
- 1/4 tsp pepper
- 1/2 tsp salt

Directions:
1. Line roasting pan with parchment paper and set aside.
2. Insert wire rack in rack position 6. Select bake, set temperature 390 F, timer for 25 minutes. Press start to preheat the oven.
3. In a bowl, toss broccoli with onion powder, garlic powder, olive oil, pepper, and salt.
4. Spread broccoli florets on roasting pan and bake for 25 minutes or until tender.
5. Drizzle lemon juice over broccoli and serve.

Nutritional Value (Amount per Serving):
- Calories 136
- Fat 9.3 g
- Carbohydrates 11.8 g
- Sugar3.1 g
- Protein 4.9 g
- Cholesterol 0 mg

Flavorful Roasted Sweet Potatoes

Preparation Time: 10 minutes
Cooking Time: 40 minutes
Serve: 4

Ingredients:
- 2 large sweet potatoes, cut into 1-inch cubes
- 1/4 tsp onion powder
- 1/2 tsp garlic powder
- 1/2 tsp cumin
- 1/2 tsp chili powder
- 3/4 tsp paprika
- 1 tbsp olive oil
- 1/4 tsp pepper
- 1/2 tsp salt

Directions:
1. Line roasting pan with parchment paper and set aside.
2. Insert wire rack in rack position 6. Select bake, set temperature 390 F, timer for 40 minutes. Press start to preheat the oven.
3. In a mixing bowl, toss sweet potatoes with remaining ingredients until well coated.
4. Spread sweet potatoes on roasting pan and bake for 40 minutes.
5. Serve and enjoy.

Nutritional Value (Amount per Serving):
- Calories 94
- Fat 3.8 g
- Carbohydrates 14.9 g
- Sugar 0.5 g
- Protein 1 g
- Cholesterol 0 mg

Healthy Balsamic Vegetables

Preparation Time: 10 minutes
Cooking Time: 35 minutes
Serve: 4

Ingredients:
- 3 cups Brussels sprouts, cut in half
- 8 oz mushrooms, cut in half
- 1 onion, cut into wedges
- 2 zucchini, cut into 1/2-inch thick half circles
- 2 bell peppers, cut into 2-inch chunks
- 1 tsp thyme
- 2 tbsp balsamic vinegar
- 1/4 cup olive oil
- 1/2 tsp salt

Directions:

1.   Line roasting pan with parchment paper and set aside.
2.   Insert wire rack in rack position 6. Select bake, set temperature 375 F, timer for 35 minutes. Press start to preheat the oven.
3.   Add vegetables into the zip-lock bag. Mix together thyme, vinegar, oil, and salt and pour over vegetables.
4.   Seal zip-lock bag and shake well and place it in the refrigerator for 1 hour.
5.   Spread marinated vegetables on roasting pan and bake for 35 minutes.
6.   Serve and enjoy.

Nutritional Value (Amount per Serving):
- Calories 197
- Fat 13.4 g
- Carbohydrates 18.4 g
- Sugar 8.3 g
- Protein 6.1 g
- Cholesterol 0 mg

Honey Balsamic Roasted Vegetables

Preparation Time: 10 minutes
Cooking Time: 30 minutes
Serve: 3
Ingredients:
- 1 cup sweet potato, cut into chunks
- 1 cup broccoli, cut into chunks
- 1 cup mushrooms, sliced
- 1 cup beet, cut into chunks
- 1 tbsp honey
- 1 tbsp balsamic vinegar
- 1 tbsp olive oil
- Pepper
- Salt

Directions:
1.   Line roasting pan with parchment paper and set aside.
2.   Insert wire rack in rack position 6. Select bake, set temperature 390 F, timer for 25 minutes. Press start to preheat the oven.
3.   In a bowl, toss veggies with oil, pepper, and salt. Spread veggies on roasting pan and bake for 25 minutes.
4.   Once veggies are tender then mix together honey and vinegar and drizzle over vegetables and bake for 5 minutes more.
5.   Serve and enjoy.

Nutritional Value (Amount per Serving):
- Calories 162
- Fat 5.1 g
- Carbohydrates 28 g
- Sugar 15.1 g
- Protein 3.9 g
- Cholesterol 0 mg

Sweet Baked Carrots

Preparation Time: 10 minutes
Cooking Time: 30 minutes

Serve: 4
Ingredients:
- 24 baby carrots
- 6 tbsp butter, melted
- 1/4 cup brown sugar
- 1 tsp cinnamon
- Pepper
- Salt

Directions:
1.   Insert wire rack in rack position 6. Select bake, set temperature 390 F, timer for 30 minutes. Press start to preheat the oven.
2.   Arrange baby carrots in the baking dish. Pour melted butter over baby carrots.
3.   Sprinkle cinnamon, brown sugar, pepper, and salt over baby carrots and bake for 25-30 minutes.
4.   Serve and enjoy.

Nutritional Value (Amount per Serving):
- Calories 210
- Fat 17.4 g
- Carbohydrates 14.3 g
- Sugar 11.7 g
- Protein 0.6 g
- Cholesterol 46 mg

Parmesan Brussels Sprouts

Preparation Time: 10 minutes
Cooking Time: 25 minutes
Serve: 4
Ingredients:
- 16 oz Brussels sprouts, trimmed and cut in half
- 1/4 cup breadcrumbs
- 1/4 cup parmesan cheese, grated
- 3 garlic cloves, minced
- 3 tbsp olive oil
- Pepper
- Salt

Directions:
1.   Line roasting pan with parchment paper and set aside.
2.   Insert wire rack in rack position 6. Select bake, set temperature 390 F, timer for 25 minutes. Press start to preheat the oven.
3.   In a mixing bowl, toss Brussels sprouts with breadcrumbs, cheese, garlic, oil, pepper, and salt until well coated.
4.   Arrange Brussels sprouts on roasting pan and bake for 25 minutes.
5.   Serve and enjoy.

Nutritional Value (Amount per Serving):
- Calories 205
- Fat 13.7 g
- Carbohydrates 16.3 g
- Sugar 2.9 g
- Protein 8.5 g
- Cholesterol 8 mg

Cheesy Broccoli Bake

Preparation Time: 10 minutes
Cooking Time: 25 minutes
Serve: 6

Ingredients:

- 6 cups broccoli florets
- 1/3 cup breadcrumbs
- 1/4 cup mozzarella cheese, shredded
- 3/4 cup cheddar cheese, shredded
- 1 tsp garlic powder
- 2 tbsp milk
- 8 oz cream cheese, softened
- 2 carrots, sliced

Directions:

1. Spray a 2-quart baking dish with cooking spray and set aside.
2. Insert wire rack in rack position 6. Select bake, set temperature 390 F, timer for 25 minutes. Press start to preheat the oven.
3. Cook carrots and broccoli in boiling water for 2 minutes. Drain well and place in mixing bowl.
4. Add mozzarella cheese, cheddar cheese, garlic powder, milk, and cream cheese over broccoli and carrots and mix well.
5. Pour broccoli and carrots mixed into the baking dish and spread well. Sprinkle breadcrumbs on top and cover the dish.
6. Bake for 25 minutes.
7. Serve and enjoy.

Nutritional Value (Amount per Serving):

- Calories 259
- Fat 18.8 g
- Carbohydrates 14.2 g
- Sugar 3.4 g
- Protein 10.5 g
- Cholesterol 57 mg

Balsamic Root Vegetables

Preparation Time: 10 minutes
Cooking Time: 30 minutes
Serve: 4

Ingredients:

- 1 onion, cut into wedges
- 1 rutabaga, peeled and cut into 1-inch chunks
- 1 parsnip, cut into 1-inch chunks
- 3 medium carrots, cut into 1-inch pieces
- 2 tsp Italian seasoning
- 1 tbsp olive oil
- 2 tbsp balsamic vinegar
- Pepper
- Salt

Directions:

1. Line roasting pan with parchment paper and set aside.
2. Insert wire rack in rack position 6. Select bake, set temperature 390 F, timer for 30 minutes. Press start to preheat the oven.
3. In a bowl, toss vegetables with remaining ingredients and spread on roasting pan.
4. Bake vegetables for 25-30 minutes.
5. Serve and enjoy.

Nutritional Value (Amount per Serving):

- Calories 128
- Fat 4.5 g
- Carbohydrates 21.3 g
- Sugar 10.7 g
- Protein 2.3 g
- Cholesterol 2 mg

Delicious Vegetable Casserole

Preparation Time: 10 minutes
Cooking Time: 1 hour 15 minutes
Serve: 12

Ingredients:

- 16 oz frozen broccoli, thawed
- 16 oz frozen cauliflower, thawed
- 8 oz can bean sprouts, drained
- 8 oz can water chestnuts, drained and sliced
- 10.5 oz cream of mushroom soup
- 8 oz mozzarella cheese, grated
- 8 oz cheddar cheese, grated
- 2 eggs, lightly beaten
- 1 onion, diced
- 1 cup mayonnaise
- Pepper
- Salt

Directions:

1. Spray a 9*13-inch baking dish with cooking spray and set aside.
2. Insert wire rack in rack position 6. Select bake, set temperature 350 F, timer for 1 hour 15 minutes. Press start to preheat the oven.
3. In a mixing bowl, mix together mayonnaise, onions, eggs, soup, pepper, and salt.
4. Add broccoli, cauliflower, water chestnuts, and bean sprouts into the baking dish. Pour mayonnaise mixture over vegetable mixture.
5. Sprinkle mozzarella cheese and cheddar cheese on top and bake for 1 hour 15 minutes.
6. Serve and enjoy.

Nutritional Value (Amount per Serving):

- Calories 261
- Fat 17.8 g
- Carbohydrates 13.2 g
- Sugar 4.5 g
- Protein 14 g
- Cholesterol 62 mg

Roasted Frozen Vegetables

Preparation Time: 10 minutes
Cooking Time: 30 minutes
Serve: 3

Ingredients:

- 12 oz mixed frozen vegetables
- 1/2 tsp onion powder
- 1/2 tsp garlic powder

- 2 tbsp olive oil
- 1/2 tsp pepper
- 1/2 tsp salt

Directions:

1. Line roasting pan with parchment paper and set aside.
2. Insert wire rack in rack position 6. Select bake, set temperature 390 F, timer for 30 minutes. Press start to preheat the oven.
3. In a bowl, toss frozen mixed vegetables with remaining ingredients.
4. Spread vegetables on roasting pan and bake for 30 minutes.
5. Serve and enjoy.

Nutritional Value (Amount per Serving):

- Calories 158
- Fat 9.5 g
- Carbohydrates 15.7 g
- Sugar 3.8 g
- Protein 3.4 g
- Cholesterol 0 mg

Delicious Zucchini Bake

Preparation Time: 10 minutes
Cooking Time: 45 minutes
Serve: 6

Ingredients:

- 3 zucchini, grated
- 3 tbsp butter, melted
- 1/2 cup flour
- 1/2 cup mozzarella cheese, shredded
- 1/2 cup feta cheese, crumbled
- 1/2 cup dill, chopped
- 3 eggs, lightly beaten
- Pepper
- Salt

Directions:

1. Spray a 9-inch baking dish with cooking spray and set aside.
2. Insert wire rack in rack position 6. Select bake, set temperature 350 F, timer for 45 minutes. Press start to preheat the oven.
3. In a mixing bowl, mix together zucchini, cheeses, dill, eggs, butter, pepper, flour, and salt.
4. Pour the zucchini mixture into the baking dish and bake for 45 minutes.
5. Serve and enjoy.

Nutritional Value (Amount per Serving):

- Calories 186
- Fat 11.5 g
- Carbohydrates 14.2 g
- Sugar 2.4 g
- Protein 8.4 g
- Cholesterol 109 mg

Brussels Sprouts Casserole

Preparation Time: 10 minutes
Cooking Time: 40 minutes
Serve: 10

Ingredients:

- 2 eggs, lightly beaten
- 1 tsp paprika
- 1 tsp garlic powder
- 1 tsp onion powder
- 1 1/2 cups cheddar cheese, shredded
- 1 cup heavy cream
- 5 bacon slices, cooked and chopped
- 2 tbsp olive oil
- 4 cups Brussels sprouts, halved
- Pepper
- Salt

Directions:

1. Spray 9*13-inch casserole dish with cooking spray and set aside.
2. Insert wire rack in rack position 6. Select bake, set temperature 390 F, timer for 20 minutes. Press start to preheat the oven.
3. In a bowl, toss Brussels sprouts with oil, pepper, and salt and spread on roasting pan and bake for 20 minutes.
4. Remove Brussels sprouts from the oven and set aside.
5. In a large mixing bowl, mix together eggs, paprika, garlic powder, onion powder, cheese, heavy cream, pepper, and salt.
6. Add Brussels sprouts and bacon into the casserole dish. Pour egg mixture over Brussels sprouts and bake for 20 minutes at 320 F.
7. Serve and enjoy.

Nutritional Value (Amount per Serving):

- Calories 215
- Fat 17.9 g
- Carbohydrates 4.5 g
- Sugar 1.1 g
- Protein 10.4 g
- Cholesterol 77 mg

Yummy Cauliflower Bake

Preparation Time: 10 minutes
Cooking Time: 40 minutes
Serve: 8

Ingredients:

- 1 cauliflower head, cut into florets
- 2 cups cheddar cheese, shredded
- 1 cup milk
- 1 1/2 cups Bisquick
- 6 eggs, lightly beaten
- 2 garlic cloves, minced
- 1 tsp oregano
- 3 tbsp butter
- 1 cup onions, chopped

Directions:

1. Spray 9*13-inch casserole dish with cooking spray and set aside.
2. Insert wire rack in rack position 6. Select bake, set temperature 350 F, timer for 40 minutes. Press start to preheat the oven.

3.   Melt butter in a pan over medium heat. Add cauliflower, garlic, oregano, and onion and cook for 5 minutes.
4.   Transfer cauliflower mixture into the casserole dish.
5.   In a bowl, whisk eggs cheese, milk, and Bisquick and pour over cauliflower mixture.
6.   Bake for 40 minutes.
7.   Serve and enjoy.

Nutritional Value (Amount per Serving):
- Calories 322
- Fat 20.9 g
- Carbohydrates 19.1 g
- Sugar 5.7 g
- Protein 14.8 g
- Cholesterol 167 mg

Fluffy Potato Casserole

Preparation Time: 10 minutes
Cooking Time: 60 minutes
Serve: 6
Ingredients:
- 2 eggs
- 3 tbsp butter
- 1 cup sour cream
- 8 oz cream cheese, softened
- 1 cup cheddar cheese, shredded
- 10 potatoes, peeled and halved
- Pepper
- Salt

Directions:
1.   Spray 9*13-inch casserole dish with cooking spray and set aside.
2.   Insert wire rack in rack position 6. Select bake, set temperature 325 F, timer for 50 minutes. Press start to preheat the oven.
3.   Add potatoes in the boiling water and boil for 10 minutes or until tender. Drain well and place in mixing bowl.
4.   Mash the potatoes using masher until smooth. Add remaining ingredients into the mashed potatoes and stir well to combine.
5.   Pour potato mixture into the casserole dish and bake for 50 minutes.
6.   Serve and enjoy.

Nutritional Value (Amount per Serving):
- Calories 607
- Fat 35 g
- Carbohydrates 58.8 g
- Sugar 4.4 g
- Protein 16.6 g
- Cholesterol 148 mg

Simple Baked Zucchini

Preparation Time: 10 minutes
Cooking Time: 40 minutes
Serve: 8
Ingredients:
- 4 cups zucchini, sliced
- 1 1/2 cup milk
- 2 cups cheddar cheese, shredded
- 1 tbsp butter, melted
- 4 eggs, lightly beaten
- 2 cups crushed crackers

Directions:
1.   Spray 9*13-inch casserole dish with cooking spray and set aside.
2.   Insert wire rack in rack position 6. Select bake, set temperature 350 F, timer for 40 minutes. Press start to preheat the oven.
3.   Add sliced zucchini into the casserole dish.
4.   In a bowl, whisk together eggs, butter, milk, and 1 cup cheese and pour over sliced zucchini. Sprinkle with crushed crackers and remaining cheese.
5.   Bake for 40 minutes.
6.   Serve and enjoy.

Nutritional Value (Amount per Serving):
- Calories 251
- Fat 18.8 g
- Carbohydrates 8.7 g
- Sugar 4.1 g
- Protein 12.5 g
- Cholesterol 115 mg

Creamy & Cheesy Brussels Sprout

Preparation Time: 10 minutes
Cooking Time: 30 minutes
Serve: 6
Ingredients:
- 2 lbs Brussels sprouts, cut in half
- 1 cup cheddar cheese, shredded
- 1/4 tsp nutmeg
- 1 tsp Dijon mustard
- 2 cups of milk
- 3 tbsp flour
- 3 tbsp butter
- Pepper
- Salt

Directions:
1.   Spray casserole dish with cooking spray and set aside.
2.   Insert wire rack in rack position 6. Select bake, set temperature 375 F, timer for 30 minutes. Press start to preheat the oven.
3.   Add Brussels sprouts into the boiling water and cook for 8 minutes. Drain well and set aside.
4.   Melt butter in a saucepan over medium heat. Add flour and cook for 1 minute.
5.   Add milk and stir until sauce thickens. Stir in nutmeg, Dijon mustard, pepper, and salt.
6.   Remove saucepan from heat and add 1/2 cup cheddar cheese and stir until cheese is melted. Stir in Brussels sprout.
7.   Pour Brussels sprout mixture into the casserole dish and sprinkle with remaining cheese.
8.   Bake for 30 minutes.
9.   Serve and enjoy.

Nutritional Value (Amount per Serving):

- Calories 248
- Fat 14.3 g
- Carbohydrates 21.1 g
- Sugar 7.1 g
- Protein 13 g
- Cholesterol 42 mg

Smooth & Creamy Cauliflower

Preparation Time: 10 minutes
Cooking Time: 20 minutes
Serve: 4
Ingredients:
- 1 cauliflower head, cut into florets
- 2 tbsp fresh lemon juice
- 1/2 cup cheddar cheese, shredded
- 1/2 cup mayonnaise
- 2 tsp Dijon mustard
- 1/4 cup sour cream

Directions:
1. Insert wire rack in rack position 6. Select bake, set temperature 375 F, timer for 10 minutes. Press start to preheat the oven.
2. Spread cauliflower florets on roasting pan and bake for 10 minutes.
3. In a mixing bowl, stir together cauliflower, lemon juice, cheese, mayonnaise, mustard, and sour cream and pour into the casserole dish.
4. Bake cauliflower mixture for 10 minutes.
5. Serve and enjoy.

Nutritional Value (Amount per Serving):
- Calories 222
- Fat 17.7 g
- Carbohydrates 11.6 g
- Sugar 3.7 g
- Protein 5.7 g
- Cholesterol 29 mg

Flavors Lemon Roasted Potatoes

Preparation Time: 10 minutes
Cooking Time: 60 minutes
Serve: 4
Ingredients:
- 5 potatoes, cut into wedges
- 2 tsp dried oregano
- 3 garlic cloves, minced
- 1/2 cup lemon juice
- 1/3 cup olive oil
- 1 cup of water
- Pepper
- Salt

Directions:
1. Insert wire rack in rack position 6. Select bake, set temperature 325 F, timer for 60 minutes. Press start to preheat the oven.
2. Add potato wedges into the 9*13-inch baking dish.
3. In a bowl, whisk together oregano, garlic, lemon juice, oil, water, pepper, and salt and pour over potatoes.

4. Bake potatoes for 60 minutes.
5. Serve and enjoy.

Nutritional Value (Amount per Serving):
- Calories 341
- Fat 17.4 g
- Carbohydrates 43.7 g
- Sugar 3.8 g
- Protein 4.9 g
- Cholesterol 43.7 mg

Easy Baked Zucchini

Preparation Time: 10 minutes
Cooking Time: 20 minutes
Serve: 2
Ingredients:
- 3 medium zucchinis, cut into chunks
- 1 tsp paprika
- 1 tsp garlic powder
- 2 tbsp olive oil
- Pepper
- Salt

Directions:
1. Line roasting pan with parchment paper and set aside.
2. Insert wire rack in rack position 6. Select bake, set temperature 390 F, timer for 20 minutes. Press start to preheat the oven.
3. In a mixing bowl, toss zucchini chunks with paprika, garlic powder, oil, pepper, and salt.
4. Spread zucchini on roasting pan and bake for 15-20 minutes.
5. Serve and enjoy.

Nutritional Value (Amount per Serving):
- Calories 131
- Fat 14.2 g
- Carbohydrates 2.2 g
- Sugar 0.5 g
- Protein 0.9 g
- Cholesterol 0 mg

Parmesan Zucchini Tomato Bake

Preparation Time: 10 minutes
Cooking Time: 30 minutes
Serve: 6
Ingredients:
- 3 tomatoes, sliced
- 2 yellow squash, sliced
- 2 medium zucchinis, sliced
- 3/4 cup parmesan cheese, shredded
- 1 tbsp olive oil
- Pepper
- Salt

Directions:
1. Spray a 9*13-inch baking dish with cooking spray and set aside.
2. Insert wire rack in rack position 6. Select bake, set temperature 350 F, timer for 30 minutes. Press start to preheat the oven.

3. Arrange sliced tomatoes, squash, and zucchinis alternately in the baking dish. Drizzle with olive oil and season with pepper and salt.
4. Sprinkle parmesan cheese on top of vegetables and bake for 30 minutes.
5. Serve and enjoy.

Nutritional Value (Amount per Serving):
- Calories 80
- Fat 5 g
- Carbohydrates 5.5 g
- Sugar 3.1 g
- Protein 4.9 g
- Cholesterol 8 mg

Creamy Eggplant Gratin

Preparation Time: 10 minutes
Cooking Time: 45 minutes
Serve: 6

Ingredients:
- 2 lbs eggplant, cut into 1/2 inch slices
- 1 tbsp mint, dried
- 1/3 lb feta cheese, crumbled
- 2 tbsp olive oil
- 2 onions, sliced
- 3/4 cup heavy whipping cream
- 6 tbsp cheese, shredded
- 6 tbsp fresh parsley, chopped
- Pepper
- Salt

Directions:
1. Insert wire rack in rack position 6. Select bake, set temperature 390 F, timer for 30 minutes. Press start to preheat the oven.
2. Brush eggplants slices with oil and place in baking dish. Season with salt.
3. Bake eggplant slices until lightly golden brown.
4. Meanwhile, heat little oil in a pan over medium heat.
5. Add onion and sauté until lightly brown.
6. Sprinkle fried onion over baked eggplants then sprinkle parsley and mint.
7. Sprinkle with grated cheese and feta cheese.
8. Pour heavy whipped cream over eggplant and onion layer.
9. Bake for 30 minutes or gratin lightly brown.
10. Serve and enjoy.

Nutritional Value (Amount per Serving):
- Calories 241
- Fat 18.3 g
- Carbohydrates 14.2 g
- Sugar 7.2 g
- Protein 7.7 g
- Cholesterol 50 mg

Roasted Radishes

Preparation Time: 10 minutes
Cooking Time: 30 minutes
Serve: 2

Ingredients:
- 3 cups radish, clean and halved
- 8 black peppercorns, crushed
- 3 tbsp olive oil
- 2 tbsp fresh rosemary, chopped
- 2 tsp sea salt

Directions:
1. Insert wire rack in rack position 6. Select bake, set temperature 390 F, timer for 30 minutes. Press start to preheat the oven.
2. Add radishes, salt, peppercorns, rosemary, and 2 tablespoons of olive oil in a mixing bowl and toss well.
3. Pour radishes mixture on roasting pan and bake for 30 minutes.
4. Heat remaining oil in a pan over medium heat.
5. Add baked radishes in the pan and sauté for 2 minutes.
6. Serve and enjoy.

Nutritional Value (Amount per Serving):
- Calories 220
- Fat 21.7 g
- Carbohydrates 8.3 g
- Sugar 3.2 g
- Protein 1.4 g
- Cholesterol 0 mg

Baked Zucchini Noodles

Preparation Time: 10 minutes
Cooking Time: 35 minutes
Serve: 4

Ingredients:
- 2 medium zucchini, spiralized
- 2 tbsp butter
- 1 tsp fresh thyme, chopped
- 1 small onion, sliced
- 1 cup cheddar cheese, grated
- 2 tsp Worcestershire sauce
- 1/4 cup vegetable broth
- Pepper
- Salt

Directions:
1. Spray a 5*8-inch baking dish with cooking spray and set aside.
2. Insert wire rack in rack position 6. Select bake, set temperature 390 F, timer for 25 minutes. Press start to preheat the oven.
3. Melt butter in a pan over medium heat. Add onion and sauté until softened.
4. Add thyme, Worcestershire sauce, pepper, and salt. Stir for minutes.
5. Add broth in the pan and cook onions for 10 minutes.
6. In a large bowl, mix together zucchini noodles and onion mixture and pour into the baking dish.
7. Top with cheese and bake for 25 minutes.
8. Garnish with thyme and serve.

Nutritional Value (Amount per Serving):
- Calories 193
- Fat 15.4 g
- Carbohydrates 6 g
- Sugar 3.1 g
- Protein 8.8 g
- Cholesterol 45 mg

Squash Casserole

Preparation Time: 10 minutes
Cooking Time: 45 minutes
Serve: 4

Ingredients:
- 4 medium squash, cut into slices
- 1/4 cup parmesan cheese, shredded
- 3/4 stick butter, cut into cubes
- 1 medium onion, sliced
- Pepper
- Salt

Directions:
1. Spray casserole dish with cooking spray and set aside.
2. Insert wire rack in rack position 6. Select bake, set temperature 350 F, timer for 45 minutes. Press start to preheat the oven.
3. Layer squash slices, onion, butter, pepper, and salt in a prepared casserole dish and sprinkle with cheese.
4. Cover dish with foil and bake for 45 minutes.
5. Serve and enjoy.

Nutritional Value (Amount per Serving):
- Calories 212
- Fat 18.8 g
- Carbohydrates 9.4 g
- Sugar 4.6 g
- Protein 4.7 g
- Cholesterol 50 mg

Broccoli Cauliflower Roast

Preparation Time: 10 minutes
Cooking Time: 20 minutes
Serve: 6

Ingredients:
- 4 cups cauliflower florets
- 4 garlic cloves, minced
- 1/3 cup olive oil
- 4 cups broccoli florets
- 2/3 cup parmesan cheese, shredded
- Pepper
- Salt

Directions:
1. Spray a baking tray with cooking spray and set aside.
2. Insert wire rack in rack position 6. Select bake, set temperature 390 F, timer for 20 minutes. Press start to preheat the oven.

3. Add half parmesan cheese, broccoli, cauliflower, garlic, oil, pepper, and salt into the large bowl and toss well.
4. Spread broccoli and cauliflower mixture in a baking dish and bake for 20 minutes.
5. Add remaining cheese. Toss well and serve.

Nutritional Value (Amount per Serving):
- Calories 168
- Fat 13.6 g
- Carbohydrates 8.6 g
- Sugar 2.7 g
- Protein 6.4 g
- Cholesterol 7 mg

Parmesan Green Bean Casserole

Preparation Time: 10 minutes
Cooking Time: 25 minutes
Serve: 4

Ingredients:
- 1 lb green beans, trimmed and cut into pieces
- 2 oz pecans, crushed
- 1 small onion, chopped
- 2 tbsp lemon zest
- 1/4 cup parmesan cheese, shredded
- 1/4 cup olive oil

Directions:
1. Insert wire rack in rack position 6. Select bake, set temperature 390 F, timer for 25 minutes. Press start to preheat the oven.
2. Add all ingredients into the bowl and toss well.
3. Spread green bean mixture into the baking dish and bake for 25 minutes.
4. Serve and enjoy.

Nutritional Value (Amount per Serving):
- Calories 269
- Fat 24.1 g
- Carbohydrates 12.6 g
- Sugar 3 g
- Protein 5.7 g
- Cholesterol 4 mg

Roasted Garlic Cheese Cauliflower

Preparation Time: 10 minutes
Cooking Time: 45 minutes
Serve: 4

Ingredients:
- 1 cauliflower head, cut into florets
- 1 onion, sliced
- 1/2 cup parmesan cheese, shredded
- 3 tbsp extra virgin olive oil
- 2 garlic cloves, chopped
- 1/2 tsp pepper
- 1/2 tsp salt

Directions:
1. Insert wire rack in rack position 6. Select bake, set temperature 390 F, timer for 35 minutes. Press start to preheat the oven.

2. Add all ingredients except parmesan cheese into the mixing bowl and toss well.
3. Spread cauliflower mixture on roasting pan and bake for 35 minutes.
4. Sprinkle cauliflower with cheese and bake for 10 minutes more.
5. Serve and enjoy.

Nutritional Value (Amount per Serving):
- Calories 157
- Fat 13 g
- Carbohydrates 7.2 g
- Sugar 2.8 g
- Protein 5.4 g
- Cholesterol 8 mg

Cheesy Broccoli Casserole

Preparation Time: 10 minutes
Cooking Time: 20 minutes
Serve: 4

Ingredients:
- 2 cups broccoli florets
- 1 cup parmesan cheese, grated
- 1/2 cup sour cream
- 1/2 cup cream

Directions:
1. Spray casserole dish with cooking spray and set aside.
2. Insert wire rack in rack position 6. Select bake, set temperature 350 F, timer for 20 minutes. Press start to preheat the oven.
3. Add broccoli florets into the prepared dish.
4. Pour sour cream and cream over broccoli florets. Stir well.
5. Top with grated cheese and bake for 20 minutes.
6. Serve and enjoy.

Nutritional Value (Amount per Serving):
- Calories 169
- Fat 12.7 g
- Carbohydrates 6 g
- Sugar 1.4 g
- Protein 9.7 g
- Cholesterol 34 mg

Broccoli & Brussels Sprout Roast

Preparation Time: 10 minutes
Cooking Time: 30 minutes
Serve: 6

Ingredients:
- 1 lb broccoli, cut into florets
- 1 lb Brussels sprouts, cut ends
- 1/2 tsp pepper
- 3 tbsp olive oil
- 1/2 onion, chopped
- 1 tsp paprika
- 1 tsp garlic powder
- 3/4 tsp salt

Directions:

1. Insert wire rack in rack position 6. Select bake, set temperature 390 F, timer for 30 minutes. Press start to preheat the oven.
2. Add all ingredients into the mixing bowl and toss well.
3. Spread veggie mixture on a roasting pan and bake for 30 minutes.
4. Serve and enjoy.

Nutritional Value (Amount per Serving):
- Calories 125
- Fat 7.6 g
- Carbohydrates 13.4 g
- Sugar 3.5 g
- Protein 5 g
- Cholesterol 0 mg

Creamy & Cheesy Cauliflower Casserole

Preparation Time: 10 minutes
Cooking Time: 15 minutes
Serve: 6

Ingredients:
- 1 cauliflower head, cut into florets and boil
- 2 oz cream cheese
- 1 cup heavy cream
- 1 tsp garlic powder
- 2 cups cheddar cheese, shredded
- 2 tsp Dijon mustard
- 1/2 tsp pepper
- 1/2 tsp salt

Directions:
1. Spray a 9*9-inch baking dish with cooking spray and set aside.
2. Insert wire rack in rack position 6. Select bake, set temperature 375 F, timer for 15 minutes. Press start to preheat the oven.
3. Add cream in a small saucepan and bring to simmer, stir well.
4. Add mustard and cream cheese and stir until thickens.
5. Remove from heat and add 1 cup shredded cheese and seasoning and stir well.
6. Place boiled cauliflower florets into the baking dish.
7. Pour cream mixture over cauliflower florets and sprinkle with remaining cheese.
8. Bake for 15 minutes.
9. Serve and enjoy.

Nutritional Value (Amount per Serving):
- Calories 268
- Fat 23.3 g
- Carbohydrates 4.2 g
- Sugar 1.4 g
- Protein 11.5 g
- Cholesterol 77 mg

Zucchini Eggplant Casserole

Preparation Time: 10 minutes
Cooking Time: 35 minutes
Serve: 6

Ingredients:
- 3 zucchini, sliced
- 1 medium eggplant, sliced
- 1 tbsp olive oil
- 3 garlic cloves, minced
- 4 tbsp basil, chopped
- 3 oz parmesan cheese, grated
- 1/4 cup parsley, chopped
- 1 cup cherry tomatoes, halved
- 1/4 tsp pepper
- 1/4 tsp salt

Directions:
1. Spray a baking dish with cooking spray and set aside.
2. Insert wire rack in rack position 6. Select bake, set temperature 350 F, timer for 35 minutes. Press start to preheat the oven.
3. Add all ingredients into the large bowl and toss well to combine.
4. Pour eggplant mixture into the baking dish and bake for 35 minutes.
5. Serve and enjoy.

Nutritional Value (Amount per Serving):
- Calories 109
- Fat 5.8 g
- Carbohydrates 10.2 g
- Sugar 4.8 g
- Protein 7 g
- Cholesterol 10 mg

Baked Broccoli

Preparation Time: 10 minutes
Cooking Time: 10 minutes
Serve: 4

Ingredients:
- 1 lb broccoli, cut into florets
- 1/2 cup heavy cream
- 2 garlic cloves, minced
- 1/4 cup parmesan cheese, grated
- 1/2 cup gruyere cheese, shredded
- 1/2 cup mozzarella cheese, shredded
- 1 tbsp butter

Directions:
1. Spray a baking dish with cooking spray and set aside.
2. Insert wire rack in rack position 6. Select bake, set temperature 375 F, timer for 10 minutes. Press start to preheat the oven.
3. Melt butter in a pan over medium heat. Add broccoli and season with pepper and salt.
4. Cook broccoli for 5 minutes or until tender. Add garlic and stir for a minute.
5. Transfer broccoli mixture into the baking dish.

6. Pour heavy cream over broccoli then top with parmesan cheese, gruyere cheese, and mozzarella cheese.
7. Bake for 10 minutes.
8. Serve and enjoy.

Nutritional Value (Amount per Serving):
- Calories 202
- Fat 15 g
- Carbohydrates 8.8 g
- Sugar 2 g
- Protein 10.5 g
- Cholesterol 49 mg

Ranch Broccoli

Preparation Time: 10 minutes
Cooking Time: 30 minutes
Serve: 6

Ingredients:
- 4 cups broccoli florets
- 1/4 cup ranch dressing
- 1/4 cup heavy whipping cream
- 1/2 cup cheddar cheese, shredded
- Pepper
- Salt

Directions:
1. Insert wire rack in rack position 6. Select bake, set temperature 375 F, timer for 30 minutes. Press start to preheat the oven.
2. Add all ingredients into the large bowl and toss until well coated.
3. Spread broccoli in a casserole dish and bake for 30 minutes.
4. Serve and enjoy.

Nutritional Value (Amount per Serving):
- Calories 79
- Fat 5.2 g
- Carbohydrates 4.8 g
- Sugar 1.4 g
- Protein 4.3 g
- Cholesterol 17 mg

Stuffed Peppers

Preparation Time: 10 minutes
Cooking Time: 45 minutes
Serve: 4

Ingredients:
- 4 eggs
- 1 tsp garlic powder
- 1/2 cup parmesan cheese, grated
- 1/2 cup mozzarella cheese, shredded
- 2 bell peppers, sliced in half and remove seeds
- 1/4 cup baby spinach
- 1/4 tsp dried parsley
- 1/2 cup ricotta cheese

Directions:

1.   Insert wire rack in rack position 6. Select bake, set temperature 375 F, timer for 30 minutes. Press start to preheat the oven.
2.   Add cheeses, parsley, garlic powder, and eggs in food processor and process until combined.
3.   Pour egg mixture into each pepper half and top with baby spinach.
4.   Place stuffed peppers on a roasting pan and cover the pan with foil.
5.   Bake for 35-45 minutes.
6.   Serve and enjoy.

Nutritional Value (Amount per Serving):
- Calories 174
- Fat 10 g
- Carbohydrates 7.6 g
- Sugar 3.6 g
- Protein 14.5 g
- Cholesterol 183 mg

Broccoli Cheese Stuffed Peppers

Preparation Time: 10 minutes
Cooking Time: 55 minutes
Serve: 2

Ingredients:
- 4 eggs
- 1/4 cup feta cheese, crumbled
- 1/2 cup broccoli, cooked
- 2 bell peppers, cut in half and remove seeds
- 1/2 cup cheddar cheese, grated
- 1/2 tsp garlic powder
- 1 tsp dried thyme
- 1/4 tsp pepper
- 1/2 tsp salt

Directions:
1.   Insert wire rack in rack position 6. Select bake, set temperature 350 F, timer for 45 minutes. Press start to preheat the oven.
2.   Place bell peppers half in a baking dish. Cut side up.
3.   Stuff broccoli and feta cheese into the peppers.
4.   Beat egg in a bowl with seasoning and pour egg mixture into the pepper cases over feta and broccoli.
5.   Bake for 45-50 minutes. Add grated cheese on top and bake for 10 minutes more.
6.   Serve and enjoy.

Nutritional Value (Amount per Serving):
- Calories 339
- Fat 22.5 g
- Carbohydrates 13.3 g
- Sugar 8.2 g
- Protein 22.8 g
- Cholesterol 374 mg

Creamy Spinach

Preparation Time: 10 minutes
Cooking Time: 20 minutes
Serve: 6

Ingredients:
- 1 lb fresh spinach
- 1 tbsp onion, minced
- 8 oz cream cheese
- 6 oz gouda cheese, shredded
- 1 tsp garlic powder
- Pepper
- Salt

Directions:
1.   Spray an 8*8-inch baking dish with cooking spray and set aside.
2.   Insert wire rack in rack position 6. Select bake, set temperature 390 F, timer for 20 minutes. Press start to preheat the oven.
3.   Spray pan with cooking spray and heat over medium heat. Add spinach and cook until wilted.
4.   Add cream cheese, garlic powder, and onion and stir until cheese is melted.
5.   Remove pan from heat and add Gouda cheese and season with pepper and salt.
6.   Pour spinach mixture into the baking dish and bake for 20 minutes.
7.   Serve and enjoy.

Nutritional Value (Amount per Serving):
- Calories 253
- Fat 21.3 g
- Carbohydrates 4.9 g
- Sugar 1.2 g
- Protein 12.2 g
- Cholesterol 74 mg

Sage Honey Sweet Potatoes

Preparation Time: 10 minutes
Cooking Time: 45 minutes
Serve: 8

Ingredients:
- 4 large sweet potatoes, peel and cut into 1-inch cubes
- 2 tbsp olive oil
- 10 sage leaves
- 1 tsp honey
- 2 tsp vinegar
- 1/4 tsp paprika
- 1/2 tsp sea salt

Directions:
1.   Insert wire rack in rack position 6. Select bake, set temperature 375 F, timer for 35 minutes. Press start to preheat the oven.
2.   Toss sweet potato with olive oil, sage, leaves, and salt in the roasting pan and bake for 35 minutes.
3.   Toss sweet potatoes and bake for 10 minutes more.

4.   Add honey, vinegar, and paprika and toss well.
5.   Serve and enjoy.
Nutritional Value (Amount per Serving):
- Calories 130
- Fat 4 g
- Carbohydrates 23.2 g
- Sugar 1.2 g
- Protein 1.4 g
- Cholesterol 0 mg

Greek Roasted Broccoli

Preparation Time: 10 minutes
Cooking Time: 15 minutes
Serve: 4
Ingredients:
- 4 cups broccoli florets
- 1 tbsp fresh lemon juice
- 1/2 tsp lemon zest
- 2 garlic cloves, minced
- 1 tbsp olive oil
- 2 tsp capers, rinsed
- 1 tsp dried oregano
- 10 olives, pitted and sliced
- 1 cup cherry tomatoes
- 1/4 tsp salt

Directions:
1.   Insert wire rack in rack position 6. Select bake, set temperature 390 F, timer for 15 minutes. Press start to preheat the oven.
2.   In a bowl, toss broccoli, garlic, oil, tomatoes, and salt.
3.   Spread broccoli mixture on roasting pan and bake for 15 minutes.
4.   In a large bowl, mix together lemon juice, capers, oregano, olives, and lemon zest. Add roasted broccoli and tomatoes and stir well.
5.   Serve and enjoy.
Nutritional Value (Amount per Serving):
- Calories 87
- Fat 5.2 g
- Carbohydrates 9.4 g
- Sugar 2.9 g
- Protein 3.3 g
- Cholesterol 0 mg

Balsamic Cauliflower

Preparation Time: 10 minutes
Cooking Time: 25 minutes
Serve: 4
Ingredients:
- 8 cups cauliflower florets
- 1 tsp dried marjoram
- 2 tbsp olive oil
- 1/2 cup parmesan cheese, shredded
- 2 tbsp balsamic vinegar

- Pepper
- Salt

Directions:
1.   Insert wire rack in rack position 6. Select bake, set temperature 390 F, timer for 20 minutes. Press start to preheat the oven.
2.   In a bowl, toss cauliflower, marjoram, oil, pepper, and salt.
3.   Spread cauliflower on roasting pan and bake for 20 minutes.
4.   Toss cauliflower with cheese and vinegar and bake for 5 minutes more.
5.   Serve and enjoy.
Nutritional Value (Amount per Serving):
- Calories 148
- Fat 9.6 g
- Carbohydrates 11.2 g
- Sugar 4.8 g
- Protein 7.6 g
- Cholesterol 8 mg

Spicy Brussels Sprouts

Preparation Time: 10 minutes
Cooking Time: 14 minutes
Serve: 2
Ingredients:
- 1/2 lb Brussels sprouts, trimmed and halved
- 1 tbsp chives, chopped
- 1/4 tsp cayenne
- 1/2 tsp chili powder
- 1/2 tbsp olive oil
- Pepper
- Salt

Directions:
1.   Insert wire rack in rack position 4. Select air fry, set temperature 370 F, timer for 14 minutes. Press start to preheat the oven.
2.   Add all ingredients into the large bowl and toss well.
3.   Spread Brussels sprouts on an air fryer basket and air fry for 14 minutes.
4.   Serve and enjoy.
Nutritional Value (Amount per Serving):
- Calories 82
- Fat 4.1 g
- Carbohydrates 10.9 g
- Sugar 2.6 g
- Protein 4 g
- Cholesterol 0 mg

Italian Potato & Carrot Roast

Preparation Time: 10 minutes
Cooking Time: 40 minutes
Serve: 2
Ingredients:

- 1/2 lb potatoes, cut into 1-inch cubes
- 1/2 onion, diced
- 1/2 tsp Italian seasoning
- 1/4 tsp garlic powder
- 1/2 lb carrots, peeled & cut into chunks
- 1 tbsp olive oil
- Pepper
- Salt

Directions:

1. Insert wire rack in rack position 6. Select roast, set temperature 400 F, timer for 40 minutes. Press start to preheat the oven.
2. In a large bowl, toss carrots, potatoes, garlic powder, Italian seasoning, oil, onion, pepper, and salt.
3. Transfer carrot potato on roasting pan and roast for 40 minutes.
4. Serve and enjoy.

Nutritional Value (Amount per Serving):

- Calories 201
- Fat 7.5 g
- Carbohydrates 32 g
- Sugar 8.2 g
- Protein 3.2 g
- Cholesterol 1 mg

Roasted Asparagus

Preparation Time: 10 minutes
Cooking Time: 15 minutes
Serve: 4

Ingredients:

- 35 asparagus spears, cut the ends
- 1/2 tsp garlic powder
- 1 tbsp olive oil
- Pepper
- Salt

Directions:

1. Insert wire rack in rack position 6. Select roast, set temperature 400 F, timer for 15 minutes. Press start to preheat the oven.
2. Add asparagus into the large bowl. Drizzle with oil.
3. Sprinkle with garlic powder, pepper, and salt. Toss well.
4. Arrange asparagus on roasting pan and roast for 15 minutes.
5. Serve and enjoy.

Nutritional Value (Amount per Serving):

- Calories 73
- Fat 3.8 g
- Carbohydrates 8.4 g
- Sugar 4 g
- Protein 4.7 g
- Cholesterol 0 mg

Roasted Potatoes

Preparation Time: 10 minutes

Cooking Time: 15 minutes
Serve: 4

Ingredients:

- 4 cups baby potatoes, cut into four pieces each
- 1 tbsp garlic, minced
- 2 tsp dried rosemary, minced
- 3 tbsp olive oil
- 1/4 cup fresh parsley, chopped
- 1 tbsp fresh lemon juice
- Pepper
- Salt

Directions:

1. Insert wire rack in rack position 4. Select air fry, set temperature 400 F, timer for 15 minutes. Press start to preheat the oven.
2. In a large bowl, add potatoes, garlic, rosemary, oil, pepper, and salt and toss well.
3. Spread potatoes on an air fryer basket and air fry for 15.
4. Transfer roasted potatoes in a bowl and toss with parsley and lemon juice.
5. Serve and enjoy.

Nutritional Value (Amount per Serving):

- Calories 120
- Fat 10.7 g
- Carbohydrates 6.1 g
- Sugar 0.1 g
- Protein 1.3 g
- Cholesterol 0 mg

Roasted Nut Lemon Cauliflower

Preparation Time: 10 minutes
Cooking Time: 10 minutes
Serve: 2

Ingredients:

- 3 cups cauliflower florets
- 1/2 tsp dried oregano
- 1 1/2 tsp olive oil
- 1 tbsp pine nuts
- 1 tbsp fresh parsley, chopped
- 1/2 tsp fresh lemon juice
- Pepper
- Salt

Directions:

1. Insert wire rack in rack position 4. Select air fry, set temperature 375 F, timer for 10 minutes. Press start to preheat the oven.
2. Toss cauliflower with oil, oregano, pepper, and salt.
3. Transfer cauliflower on an air fryer basket and air fry for 10 minutes.
4. Transfer cauliflower in a bowl and toss with pine nuts, parsley, and lemon juice.
5. Serve and enjoy.

Nutritional Value (Amount per Serving):

- Calories 99
- Fat 6.7 g
- Carbohydrates 8.9 g
- Sugar 3.8 g
- Protein 3.7 g
- Cholesterol 8 mg

Italian Broccoli Roast

Preparation Time: 10 minutes
Cooking Time: 20 minutes
Serve: 6
Ingredients:
- 4 cups broccoli florets
- 1/2 tsp garlic powder
- 1 tsp Italian seasoning
- 3 tbsp olive oil
- 1/2 tsp pepper
- 1 tsp salt

Directions:
1. Insert wire rack in rack position 6. Select bake, set temperature 390 F, timer for 20 minutes. Press start to preheat the oven.
2. Spray a baking tray with cooking spray.
3. Spread broccoli on a baking tray and drizzle with oil and season with garlic powder, Italian seasoning, pepper, and salt.
4. Bake for 20 minutes.
5. Serve and enjoy.

Nutritional Value (Amount per Serving):
- Calories 84
- Fat 7.4 g
- Carbohydrates 4.4 g
- Sugar 1.2 g
- Protein 1.8 g
- Cholesterol 1 mg

Roasted Pepper & Cauliflower

Preparation Time: 10 minutes
Cooking Time: 30 minutes
Serve: 4
Ingredients:
- 1 cauliflower head, cut into florets
- 1/2 cup fresh dill, chopped
- 1/2 onion, sliced
- 1 bell pepper, cut into 1-inch pieces
- 2 tsp olive oil
- 2 tbsp white wine vinegar
- 3 tbsp balsamic vinegar
- Pepper
- Salt

Directions:
1. Insert wire rack in rack position 6. Select bake, set temperature 390 F, timer for 30 minutes. Press start to preheat the oven.

2. Add all ingredients into the zip-lock bag. Seal bag and shake well and place in the refrigerator for 1 hour.
3. Pour marinated cauliflower mixture in the baking dish and bake for 30 minutes.
4. Serve and enjoy.

Nutritional Value (Amount per Serving):
- Calories 72
- Fat 2.8 g
- Carbohydrates 11.2 g
- Sugar 4.3 g
- Protein 3 g
- Cholesterol 0 mg

Parmesan Asparagus

Preparation Time: 10 minutes
Cooking Time: 12 minutes
Serve: 4
Ingredients:
- 1 lb asparagus, wash, trimmed, and cut the ends
- 2 garlic cloves, minced
- 2 tbsp olive oil
- 3 oz parmesan cheese, shaved
- 1 tsp dried oregano
- 1 tbsp dried parsley
- Pepper
- Salt

Directions:
1. Insert wire rack in rack position 6. Select bake, set temperature 390 F, timer for 12 minutes. Press start to preheat the oven.
2. Spray a roasting pan with cooking spray.
3. Arrange asparagus on a roasting pan and drizzle with oil and season with pepper and salt.
4. Sprinkle asparagus with cheese, oregano, parsley, and garlic and bake for 12 minutes.
5. Serve and enjoy.

Nutritional Value (Amount per Serving):
- Calories 155
- Fat 11.8 g
- Carbohydrates 6 g
- Sugar 2.2 g
- Protein 9.5 g
- Cholesterol 15 mg

Cauliflower & Cherry Tomatoes

Preparation Time: 10 minutes
Cooking Time: 20 minutes
Serve: 4
Ingredients:
- 4 cups cauliflower florets
- 3 tbsp olive oil
- 1/2 cup cherry tomatoes, halved
- 2 tbsp fresh parsley, chopped
- 2 garlic cloves, sliced

- 1 tbsp capers, drained
- Pepper
- Salt

Directions:

1. Insert wire rack in rack position 6. Select bake, set temperature 390 F, timer for 20 minutes. Press start to preheat the oven.
2. In a bowl, toss cherry tomatoes, cauliflower, oil, garlic, capers, pepper, and salt and spread on roasting pan.
3. Bake for 20 minutes.
4. Garnish with parsley and serve.

Nutritional Value (Amount per Serving):

- Calories 123
- Fat 10.7 g
- Carbohydrates 6.9 g
- Sugar 3 g
- Protein 2.4 g
- Cholesterol 0 mg

Italian Mushrooms & Cauliflower

Preparation Time: 10 minutes
Cooking Time: 30 minutes
Serve: 6

Ingredients:

- 1 lb mushrooms, cleaned
- 10 garlic cloves, peeled
- 2 cups cherry tomatoes
- 1 tbsp fresh parsley, chopped
- 1 tbsp Italian seasoning
- 2 tbsp olive oil
- 2 cups cauliflower florets
- Pepper
- Salt

Directions:

1. Insert wire rack in rack position 6. Select bake, set temperature 390 F, timer for 30 minutes. Press start to preheat the oven.
2. Add cauliflower, mushrooms, Italian seasoning, olive oil, garlic, cherry tomatoes, pepper, and salt into the large bowl and toss well.
3. Transfer cauliflower mixture on a roasting pan and bake for 25-30 minutes.
4. Garnish with parsley and serve.

Nutritional Value (Amount per Serving):

- Calories 90
- Fat 5.8 g
- Carbohydrates 8.5 g
- Sugar 3.9 g
- Protein 3.9 g
- Cholesterol 2 mg

CHAPTER 8: DEHYDRATED

Dehydrated Pineapple Slices

Preparation Time: 10 minutes
Cooking Time: 14 hours
Serve: 12
Ingredients:
- 1 small pineapple, trim, peel, and cut into 1/8-inch thick slices

Directions:
1. Arrange pineapple slices on the dehydrate basket in a single layer.
2. Insert wire rack in rack position 4. Select DEHYDRATE, set temperature 125 F, timer for 14 hours. Press start.
3. Dehydrate pineapple slices for 14 hours.

Nutritional Value (Amount per Serving):
- Calories 376
- Fat 0.9 g
- Carbohydrates 99.2 g
- Sugar 74.5 g
- Protein 4.1 g
- Cholesterol 0 mg

Dehydrated Mango Slices

Preparation Time: 10 minutes
Cooking Time: 12 hours
Serve: 4
Ingredients:
- 2 mangoes, peel, and cut into 1/4-inch thick slices

Directions:
1. Arrange mango slices on the dehydrate basket in a single layer.
2. Insert wire rack in rack position 4. Select DEHYDRATE, set temperature 135 F, timer for 12 hours. Press start.
3. Dehydrate mango slices for 12 hours.

Nutritional Value (Amount per Serving):
- Calories 101
- Fat 0.6 g
- Carbohydrates 25.2 g
- Sugar 23 g
- Protein 1.4 g
- Cholesterol 0 mg

Dehydrated Green Apple Slices

Preparation Time: 10 minutes
Cooking Time: 8 hours
Serve: 4
Ingredients:
- 2 green apple, cored and cut into 1/8-inch thick slices
- 1 tsp ground cinnamon

Directions:
1. Arrange green apple slices on the dehydrate basket in a single layer. Sprinkle cinnamon on top of apple slices.
2. Insert wire rack in rack position 4. Select DEHYDRATE, set temperature 145 F, timer for 8 hours. Press start.
3. Dehydrate green apple slices for 8 hours.

Nutritional Value (Amount per Serving):
- Calories 59
- Fat 0.2 g
- Carbohydrates 15.9 g
- Sugar 11.6 g
- Protein 0.3 g
- Cholesterol 0 mg

Spicy Almonds

Preparation Time: 10 minutes
Cooking Time: 12 hours
Serve: 4
Ingredients:
- 1 cup almonds, soaked in water for overnight
- 1/2 tbsp olive oil
- 1/2 tsp red chili powder

Directions:
1. Toss almonds with oil and chili powder and spread on dehydrate basket.
2. Insert wire rack in rack position 4. Select DEHYDRATE, set temperature 125 F, timer for 12 hours. Press start.
3. Dehydrate almonds for 12 hours.

Nutritional Value (Amount per Serving):
- Calories 153
- Fat 13.7 g
- Carbohydrates 5.3 g
- Sugar 1 g
- Protein 5.1 g
- Cholesterol 0 mg

Dehydrated Raspberries

Preparation Time: 10 minutes
Cooking Time: 12 hours
Serve: 4
Ingredients:
- 2 cups fresh raspberries, wash and pat dry with a paper towel

Directions:
1. Arrange raspberries on the dehydrate basket in a single layer.
2. Insert wire rack in rack position 4. Select DEHYDRATE, set temperature 135 F, timer for 12 hours. Press start.
3. Dehydrate raspberries for 12 hours.

Nutritional Value (Amount per Serving):
- Calories 32
- Fat 0.4 g
- Carbohydrates 7.3 g
- Sugar 2.7 g
- Protein 0.7 g
- Cholesterol 0 mg

Candied Pecans

Preparation Time: 10 minutes
Cooking Time: 12 hours
Serve: 4
Ingredients:
- 1 cup pecan halves, soaked in water overnight
- 6 tbsp maple syrup
- Pinch of cinnamon

Directions:
1. In a bowl, toss pecan with maple syrup and cinnamon and arrange on the dehydrate basket.
2. Insert wire rack in rack position 4. Select DEHYDRATE, set temperature 105 F, timer for 12 hours. Press start.
3. Dehydrate pecans for 12 hours.

Nutritional Value (Amount per Serving):
- Calories 103
- Fat 2.6 g
- Carbohydrates 20.7 g
- Sugar 18 g
- Protein 0.4 g
- Cholesterol 0 mg

Dehydrated Avocado Slices

Preparation Time: 10 minutes
Cooking Time: 10 hours
Serve: 4
Ingredients:
- 3 avocados, halved, pitted and cut into slices
- 1/4 tsp red chili powder

Directions:
1. Arrange avocado slices on the dehydrate basket in a single layer. Sprinkle chili powder over avocado slices.
2. Insert wire rack in rack position 4. Select DEHYDRATE, set temperature 160 F, timer for 10 hours. Press start.
3. Dehydrate avocado slices for 10 hours.

Nutritional Value (Amount per Serving):
- Calories 308
- Fat 29.4 g
- Carbohydrates 13.1 g
- Sugar 0.8 g
- Protein 2.9 g
- Cholesterol 0 mg

Dehydrated Eggplant Slices

Preparation Time: 10 minutes
Cooking Time: 4 hours
Serve: 4
Ingredients:
- 1 eggplant, cut into 1/4-inch thick slices

Directions:
1. Arrange eggplant slices on the dehydrate basket in a single layer.
2. Insert wire rack in rack position 4. Select DEHYDRATE, set temperature 145 F, timer for 4 hours. Press start.
3. Dehydrate eggplant slices for 4 hours.

Nutritional Value (Amount per Serving):
- Calories 29
- Fat 0.2 g
- Carbohydrates 6.7 g
- Sugar 3.4 g
- Protein 1.1 g
- Cholesterol 0 mg

Dehydrated Zucchini Chips

Preparation Time: 10 minutes
Cooking Time: 8 hours
Serve: 4
Ingredients:
- 2 zucchini, cut into 1/4-inch thick slices
- 1 tsp olive oil
- Pepper
- Salt

Directions:
1. Toss zucchini slices with oil, pepper, and salt and arrange on the dehydrate basket in a single layer.
2. Insert wire rack in rack position 4. Select DEHYDRATE, set temperature 135 F, timer for 8 hours. Press start.
3. Dehydrate zucchini slices for 8 hours.

Nutritional Value (Amount per Serving):
- Calories 26
- Fat 1.4 g
- Carbohydrates 3.3 g
- Sugar 1.7 g
- Protein 1.2 g
- Cholesterol 0 mg

Dehydrated Strawberry Slices

Preparation Time: 10 minutes
Cooking Time: 12 hours
Serve: 4
Ingredients:
- 1 cup strawberries, cut into 1/8-inch thick slices

Directions:
1. Arrange strawberry slices on the dehydrate basket in a single layer.
2. Insert wire rack in rack position 4. Select DEHYDRATE, set temperature 130 F, timer for 12 hours. Press start.
3. Dehydrate strawberry slices for 12 hours.

Nutritional Value (Amount per Serving):
- Calories 12
- Fat 0.1 g
- Carbohydrates 2.8 g
- Sugar 1.8 g
- Protein 0.2 g
- Cholesterol 0 mg

Dehydrated Sweet Potato Slices

Preparation Time: 10 minutes
Cooking Time: 12 hours
Serve: 4
Ingredients:
* 1 large sweet potato, sliced thinly
Directions:
1. Arrange sweet potato slices on the dehydrate basket in a single layer.
2. Insert wire rack in rack position 4. Select DEHYDRATE, set temperature 125 F, timer for 12 hours. Press start.
3. Dehydrate sweet potato slices for 12 hours.
Nutritional Value (Amount per Serving):
* Calories 41
* Fat 0.1 g
* Carbohydrates 9.3 g
* Sugar 2.9 g
* Protein 0.9 g
* Cholesterol 0 mg

Dehydrated Cucumber Chips

Preparation Time: 10 minutes
Cooking Time: 12 hours
Serve: 3
Ingredients:
* 1 cucumber, sliced
* Pepper
* Salt
Directions:
1. Arrange cucumber slices on the dehydrate basket in a single layer. Season with pepper and salt.
2. Insert wire rack in rack position 4. Select DEHYDRATE, set temperature 135 F, timer for 12 hours. Press start.
3. Dehydrate cucumber slices for 12 hours.
Nutritional Value (Amount per Serving):
* Calories 15
* Fat 0.1 g
* Carbohydrates 3.7 g
* Sugar 1.7 g
* Protein 0.7 g
* Cholesterol 0 mg

Dehydrated Broccoli Florets

Preparation Time: 10 minutes
Cooking Time: 12 hours
Serve: 6
Ingredients:
* 1 lb broccoli florets
* Pepper
* Salt
Directions:
1. Arrange broccoli florets on the dehydrate basket in a single layer. Season with pepper and salt.
2. Insert wire rack in rack position 4. Select DEHYDRATE, set temperature 115 F, timer for 12 hours. Press start.
3. Dehydrate broccoli florets for 12 hours.

Nutritional Value (Amount per Serving):
* Calories 26
* Fat 0.3 g
* Carbohydrates 5 g
* Sugar 1.3 g
* Protein 2.1 g
* Cholesterol 0 mg

Dehydrated Zucchini Chips

Preparation Time: 10 minutes
Cooking Time: 6 hours
Serve: 3
Ingredients:
* 1 zucchini, sliced thinly
* 1/4 tsp garlic powder
* 1/4 tsp chili powder
* 1/8 tsp paprika
* Salt
Directions:
1. Toss zucchini slices with garlic powder, chili powder, paprika, and salt.
2. Arrange zucchini slices on the dehydrate basket in a single layer.
3. Insert wire rack in rack position 4. Select DEHYDRATE, set temperature 135 F, timer for 6 hours. Press start.
4. Dehydrate zucchini slices for 6 hours.
Nutritional Value (Amount per Serving):
* Calories 12
* Fat 0.2 g
* Carbohydrates 2.5 g
* Sugar 1.2 g
* Protein 0.9 g
* Cholesterol 0 mg

Dehydrated Beet Slices

Preparation Time: 10 minutes
Cooking Time: 10 hours
Serve: 2
Ingredients:
* 1 beet, sliced thinly
* Salt
Directions:
1. Arrange beet slices on the dehydrate basket in a single layer. Season with salt.
2. Insert wire rack in rack position 4. Select DEHYDRATE, set temperature 135 F, timer for 10 hours. Press start.
3. Dehydrate beet slices for 10 hours.
Nutritional Value (Amount per Serving):
* Calories 22
* Fat 0.1 g
* Carbohydrates 5 g
* Sugar 4 g
* Protein 0.8 g
* Cholesterol 0 mg

Dehydrated Tomato Slices

Preparation Time: 10 minutes

Cooking Time: 12 hours
Serve: 4
Ingredients:
- 4 tomatoes, sliced thinly
- Pepper
- Salt

Directions:
1. Arrange tomato slices on the dehydrate basket in a single layer. Season with pepper and salt.
2. Insert wire rack in rack position 4. Select DEHYDRATE, set temperature 135 F, timer for 12 hours. Press start.
3. Dehydrate tomato slices for 12 hours.

Nutritional Value (Amount per Serving):
- Calories 22
- Fat 0.3 g
- Carbohydrates 4.8 g
- Sugar 3.2 g
- Protein 1.1 g
- Cholesterol 0 mg

Dehydrated Green Beans

Preparation Time: 10 minutes
Cooking Time: 12 hours
Serve: 4
Ingredients:
- 1 lb green beans
- Salt

Directions:
1. Arrange green beans on the dehydrate basket in a single layer. Season with salt.
2. Insert wire rack in rack position 4. Select DEHYDRATE, set temperature 125 F, timer for 12 hours. Press start.
3. Dehydrate green beans for 12 hours.

Nutritional Value (Amount per Serving):
- Calories 35
- Fat 0.1 g
- Carbohydrates 8.1 g
- Sugar 1.6 g
- Protein 2.1 g
- Cholesterol 0 mg

Dehydrated Parsnips Slices

Preparation Time: 10 minutes
Cooking Time: 10 hours
Serve: 3
Ingredients:
- 2 parsnips, peel & thinly sliced
- Salt

Directions:
1. Arrange parsnips slices on the dehydrate basket in a single layer. Season with salt.
2. Insert wire rack in rack position 4. Select DEHYDRATE, set temperature 115 F, timer for 10 hours. Press start.
3. Dehydrate parsnips slices for 10 hours.

Nutritional Value (Amount per Serving):
- Calories 100

- Fat 0.4 g
- Carbohydrates 23.9 g
- Sugar 6.4 g
- Protein 1.6 g
- Cholesterol 0 mg

Dehydrated Carrot Slices

Preparation Time: 10 minutes
Cooking Time: 10 hours
Serve: 4
Ingredients:
- 2 carrots, peel & thinly sliced
- Salt

Directions:
1. Arrange carrot slices on the dehydrate basket in a single layer. Season with salt.
2. Insert wire rack in rack position 4. Select DEHYDRATE, set temperature 115 F, timer for 10 hours. Press start.
3. Dehydrate carrot slices for 10 hours.

Nutritional Value (Amount per Serving):
- Calories 13
- Fat 0 g
- Carbohydrates 3 g
- Sugar 1.5 g
- Protein 0.3 g
- Cholesterol 0 mg

Dehydrated Parmesan Zucchini Chips

Preparation Time: 10 minutes
Cooking Time: 10 hours
Serve: 2
Ingredients:
- 2 zucchini, thinly sliced
- 2 tbsp parmesan cheese, grated
- Salt

Directions:
1. Arrange zucchini slices on the dehydrate basket in a single layer. Season with salt and sprinkle with cheese.
2. Insert wire rack in rack position 4. Select DEHYDRATE, set temperature 135 F, timer for 10 hours. Press start.
3. Dehydrate zucchini slices for 10 hours.

Nutritional Value (Amount per Serving):
- Calories 50
- Fat 1.6 g
- Carbohydrates 6.8 g
- Sugar 3.4 g
- Protein 4.2 g
- Cholesterol 4 mg

Dehydrated Dragon Fruit Slices

Preparation Time: 10 minutes
Cooking Time: 12 hours
Serve: 4
Ingredients:
- 2 dragon fruit, peel & cut into 1/4-inch thick slices

Directions:

1.   Arrange dragon fruit slices on the dehydrate basket in a single layer.
2.   Insert wire rack in rack position 4. Select DEHYDRATE, set temperature 115 F, timer for 12 hours. Press start.
3.   Dehydrate dragon fruit slices for 12 hours.

Nutritional Value (Amount per Serving):

- Calories 23
- Fat 0 g
- Carbohydrates 6 g
- Sugar 6 g
- Protein 0 g
- Cholesterol 0 mg

Dehydrated Orange Slices

Preparation Time: 10 minutes
Cooking Time: 12 hours
Serve: 4

Ingredients:

- 2 oranges, peel & cut into slices

Directions:

1.   Arrange orange slices on the dehydrate basket in a single layer.
2.   Insert wire rack in rack position 4. Select DEHYDRATE, set temperature 135 F, timer for 12 hours. Press start.
3.   Dehydrate orange slices for 12 hours.

Nutritional Value (Amount per Serving):

- Calories 43
- Fat 0.1 g
- Carbohydrates 10.8 g
- Sugar 8.6 g
- Protein 0.9 g
- Cholesterol 0 mg

Dehydrated Kiwi Slices

Preparation Time: 10 minutes
Cooking Time: 12 hours
Serve: 4

Ingredients:

- 2 kiwis, peeled & cut into 1/4-inch thick slices

Directions:

1.   Arrange kiwi fruit slices on the dehydrate basket in a single layer.
2.   Insert wire rack in rack position 4. Select DEHYDRATE, set temperature 135 F, timer for 12 hours. Press start.
3.   Dehydrate kiwi slices for 12 hours.

Nutritional Value (Amount per Serving):

- Calories 23
- Fat 0.2 g
- Carbohydrates 5.6 g
- Sugar 3.4 g
- Protein 0.4 g
- Cholesterol 0 mg

Dehydrated Cinnamon Zucchini Slices

Preparation Time: 10 minutes
Cooking Time: 12 hours
Serve: 4

Ingredients:

- 1 zucchini, sliced thinly
- 1 tsp ground cinnamon

Directions:

1.   Arrange zucchini slices on the dehydrate basket in a single layer. Sprinkle with cinnamon.
2.   Insert wire rack in rack position 4. Select DEHYDRATE, set temperature 135 F, timer for 12 hours. Press start.
3.   Dehydrate zucchini slices for 12 hours.

Nutritional Value (Amount per Serving):

- Calories 9
- Fat 0.1 g
- Carbohydrates 2.1 g
- Sugar 0.9 g
- Protein 0.6 g
- Cholesterol 0 mg

Dehydrated Cinnamon Apple Slices

Preparation Time: 10 minutes
Cooking Time: 8 hours
Serve: 4

Ingredients:

- 2 apples, cut into 1/8-inch thick slices
- 1 tsp ground cinnamon

Directions:

1.   Arrange apple slices on the dehydrate basket in a single layer. Sprinkle cinnamon on apple slices.
2.   Insert wire rack in rack position 4. Select DEHYDRATE, set temperature 135 F, timer for 8 hours. Press start.
3.   Dehydrate apple slices for 8 hours.

Nutritional Value (Amount per Serving):

- Calories 59
- Fat 0.2 g
- Carbohydrates 15.9 g
- Sugar 11.6 g
- Protein 0.3 g
- Cholesterol 0 mg

Dehydrated Spicy Eggplant Slices

Preparation Time: 10 minutes
Cooking Time: 6 hours
Serve: 2

Ingredients:

- 1 medium eggplant, cut into 1/4-inch thick slices
- 2 tsp paprika
- Salt

Directions:

1.   Arrange eggplant slices on the dehydrate basket in a single layer. Season with salt.
2.   Insert wire rack in rack position 4. Select DEHYDRATE, set temperature 140 F, timer for 6 hours. Press start.

3.   Dehydrate eggplant slices for 6 hours.
Nutritional Value (Amount per Serving):
- Calories 63
- Fat 0.7 g
- Carbohydrates 14.6 g
- Sugar 7.1 g
- Protein 2.6 g
- Cholesterol 0 mg

Dehydrated Banana Slices

Preparation Time: 10 minutes
Cooking Time: 6 hours
Serve: 2
Ingredients:
- 2 bananas, peel & cut into 1/8-inch thick slices

Directions:
1.   Arrange banana slices on the dehydrate basket in a single layer.
2.   Insert wire rack in rack position 4. Select DEHYDRATE, set temperature 135 F, timer for 6 hours. Press start.
3.   Dehydrate banana slices for 6 hours.
Nutritional Value (Amount per Serving):
- Calories 105
- Fat 0.4 g
- Carbohydrates 27 g
- Sugar 14.4 g
- Protein 1.3 g
- Cholesterol 0 mg

Dehydrated Chickpeas

Preparation Time: 10 minutes
Cooking Time: 10 hours
Serve: 4
Ingredients:
- 10 oz can chickpeas, drained and rinsed
- Salt

Directions:
1.   Arrange chickpeas on the dehydrate basket in a single layer. Season with salt.
2.   Insert wire rack in rack position 4. Select DEHYDRATE, set temperature 135 F, timer for 10 hours. Press start.
3.   Dehydrate chickpeas for 10 hours.
Nutritional Value (Amount per Serving):
- Calories 84
- Fat 0.8 g
- Carbohydrates 16 g
- Sugar 0 g
- Protein 3.5 g
- Cholesterol 0 mg

Dehydrated Pineapple Chunks

Preparation Time: 10 minutes
Cooking Time: 12 hours
Serve: 2
Ingredients:
- 1 cup pineapple chunks

Directions:
1.   Arrange pineapple chunks on the dehydrate basket in a single layer.
2.   Insert wire rack in rack position 4. Select DEHYDRATE, set temperature 135 F, timer for 12 hours. Press start.
3.   Dehydrate pineapple chunks for 12 hours.
Nutritional Value (Amount per Serving):
- Calories 41
- Fat 0.1 g
- Carbohydrates 10.8 g
- Sugar 8.1 g
- Protein 0.4 g
- Cholesterol 0 mg

Dehydrated Summer Squash Chips

Preparation Time: 10 minutes
Cooking Time: 10 hours
Serve: 2
Ingredients:
- 1 yellow summer squash, sliced thinly
- Pepper
- Salt

Directions:
1.   Arrange squash slices on the dehydrate basket in a single layer. Season with pepper & salt.
2.   Insert wire rack in rack position 4. Select DEHYDRATE, set temperature 115 F, timer for 10 hours. Press start.
3.   Dehydrate squash slices for 10 hours.
Nutritional Value (Amount per Serving):
- Calories 7
- Fat 0 g
- Carbohydrates 1.8 g
- Sugar 0.8 g
- Protein 0.3 g
- Cholesterol 0 mg

Dehydrated Okra

Preparation Time: 10 minutes
Cooking Time: 24 hours
Serve: 2
Ingredients:
- 6 pods okra, slice into rounds

Directions:
1.   Arrange okra slices on the dehydrate basket in a single layer.
2.   Insert wire rack in rack position 4. Select DEHYDRATE, set temperature 130 F, timer for 24 hours. Press start.
3.   Dehydrate okra slices for 24 hours.
Nutritional Value (Amount per Serving):
- Calories 54
- Fat 0.6 g
- Carbohydrates 10.8 g
- Sugar 5.7 g
- Protein 4.5 g
- Cholesterol 0 mg

Dehydrated Lemon Slices

Preparation Time: 10 minutes
Cooking Time: 10 hours
Serve: 4
Ingredients:
- 2 lemons, cut into 1/4-inch thick slices

Directions:
1. Arrange lemon slices on the dehydrate basket in a single layer.
2. Insert wire rack in rack position 4. Select DEHYDRATE, set temperature 125 F, timer for 10 hours. Press start.
3. Dehydrate lemon slices for 10 hours.

Nutritional Value (Amount per Serving):
- Calories 8
- Fat 0.1 g
- Carbohydrates 2.7 g
- Sugar 0.7 g
- Protein 0.3 g
- Cholesterol 0 mg

Dehydrated Pear Slices

Preparation Time: 10 minutes
Cooking Time: 5 hours
Serve: 4
Ingredients:
- 2 pears, cut into 1/4-inch thick slices

Directions:
1. Arrange pear slices on the dehydrate basket in a single layer.
2. Insert wire rack in rack position 4. Select DEHYDRATE, set temperature 160 F, timer for 5 hours. Press start.
3. Dehydrate pear slices for 5 hours.

Nutritional Value (Amount per Serving):
- Calories 60
- Fat 0.2 g
- Carbohydrates 15.9 g
- Sugar 10.2 g
- Protein 0.4 g
- Cholesterol 0 mg

Dehydrated Mushroom Chips

Preparation Time: 10 minutes
Cooking Time: 5 hours
Serve: 4
Ingredients:
- 1 cup mushrooms, clean and cut into 1/8-inch thick slices
- Salt

Directions:
1. Arrange mushroom slices on the dehydrate basket in a single layer. Season with salt.
2. Insert wire rack in rack position 4. Select DEHYDRATE, set temperature 160 F, timer for 5 hours. Press start.
3. Dehydrate mushroom slices for 5 hours.

Nutritional Value (Amount per Serving):
- Calories 4
- Fat 0.1 g
- Carbohydrates 0.6 g
- Sugar 0.3 g
- Protein 0.6 g
- Cholesterol 0 mg

Dehydrated Snap Peas

Preparation Time: 10 minutes
Cooking Time: 8 hours
Serve: 4
Ingredients:
- 2 cups snap peas
- Salt

Directions:
1. Arrange snap peas on the dehydrate basket in a single layer. Season with salt.
2. Insert wire rack in rack position 4. Select DEHYDRATE, set temperature 135 F, timer for 8 hours. Press start.
3. Dehydrate snap peas for 8 hours.

Nutritional Value (Amount per Serving):
- Calories 59
- Fat 0.3 g
- Carbohydrates 10.5 g
- Sugar 4.1 g
- Protein 3.9 g
- Cholesterol 0 mg

Salmon Jerky

Preparation Time: 10 minutes
Cooking Time: 4 hours
Serve: 6
Ingredients:
- 1 1/4 lbs salmon, cut into 1/4-inch slices
- 1 1/2 tbsp fresh lemon juice
- 1 tbsp molasses
- 1/2 cup soy sauce
- 1/2 tsp liquid smoke
- 1 1/4 tsp black pepper

Directions:
1. In a bowl, mix together liquid smoke, black pepper, lemon juice, molasses, and soy sauce.
2. Add sliced salmon into the bowl and mix well. Cover bowl and place in the refrigerator overnight.
3. Remove salmon slices from marinade and arrange on the dehydrate basket in a single layer.
4. Insert wire rack in rack position 4. Select DEHYDRATE, set temperature 145 F, timer for 4 hours. Press start.
5. Dehydrate salmon slices for 4 hours.

Nutritional Value (Amount per Serving):
- Calories 148
- Fat 5.9 g
- Carbohydrates 4.5 g
- Sugar 2.3 g
- Protein 19.7 g
- Cholesterol 42 mg

Chicken Jerky

Preparation Time: 10 minutes
Cooking Time: 7 hours
Serve: 4
Ingredients:
- 1 1/2 lb chicken tenders, boneless, skinless and cut into 1/4 inch strips
- 1/2 tsp garlic powder
- 1 tsp lemon juice
- 1/2 cup soy sauce
- 1/4 tsp ground ginger
- 1/4 tsp black pepper

Directions:
1. Mix all ingredients except chicken into the zip-lock bag. Add chicken and seal bag and place in the refrigerator for 30 minutes.
2. Arrange marinated meat slices on the dehydrate basket in a single layer.
3. Insert wire rack in rack position 4. Select DEHYDRATE, set temperature 145 F, timer for 7 hours. Press start.
4. Dehydrate meat slices for 7 hours.

Nutritional Value (Amount per Serving):
- Calories 342
- Fat 12.6 g
- Carbohydrates 2.9 g
- Sugar 0.7 g
- Protein 51.3 g
- Cholesterol 151 mg

Garlicky Jerky

Preparation Time: 10 minutes
Cooking Time: 4 hours
Serve: 8
Ingredients:
- 3 lbs flank steak, cut into 1/4-inch thick slices
- 1/4 cup coconut amino
- 1 1/2 tbsp garlic powder

Directions:
1. In a bowl, mix together garlic powder and coconut amino. Add meat slices into the bowl and mix until well coated. Cover bowl and place in the refrigerator overnight.
2. Arrange marinated meat slices on the dehydrate basket in a single layer.
3. Insert wire rack in rack position 4. Select DEHYDRATE, set temperature 145 F, timer for 4 hours. Press start.
4. Dehydrate meat slices for 4 hours.

Nutritional Value (Amount per Serving):
- Calories 343

- Fat 14.2 g
- Carbohydrates 2.7 g
- Sugar 0.4 g
- Protein 47.6 g
- Cholesterol 94 mg

Dehydrated Bell Peppers

Preparation Time: 10 minutes
Cooking Time: 24 hours
Serve: 4
Ingredients:
- 4 bell peppers, remove seeds and cut into 1/2-inch chunks

Directions:
1. Arrange bell peppers chunks on the dehydrate basket in a single layer.
2. Insert wire rack in rack position 4. Select DEHYDRATE, set temperature 135 F, timer for 24 hours. Press start.
3. Dehydrate bell pepper chunks for 24 hours.

Nutritional Value (Amount per Serving):
- Calories 38
- Fat 0.3 g
- Carbohydrates 9 g
- Sugar 6 g
- Protein 1.2 g
- Cholesterol 0 mg

Dehydrated Cauliflower Popcorn

Preparation Time: 10 minutes
Cooking Time: 12 hours
Serve: 4
Ingredients:
- 1 cauliflower head, cut into florets
- 2 tsp chili powder
- 1 tbsp olive oil
- Salt

Directions:
1. Toss cauliflower florets with chili powder, oil, and salt and arrange on the dehydrate basket in a single layer.
2. Insert wire rack in rack position 4. Select DEHYDRATE, set temperature 115 F, timer for 12 hours. Press start.
3. Dehydrate cauliflower florets for 12 hours.

Nutritional Value (Amount per Serving):
- Calories 51
- Fat 3.8 g
- Carbohydrates 4.2 g
- Sugar 1.7 g
- Protein 1.5 g
- Cholesterol 0 mg

CHAPTER 9: DESSERTS

Choco Lava Cake

Preparation Time: 10 minutes
Cooking Time: 9 minutes
Serve: 2
Ingredients:
- 1 egg
- 1/2 tsp baking powder
- 2 tbsp water
- 2 tbsp cocoa powder
- 1 tbsp butter, melted
- 1 tbsp flax meal
- 2 tbsp Swerve
- Pinch of salt

Directions:
1. Spray 2 ramekins with cooking spray and set aside.
2. Insert wire rack in rack position 6. Select air fry, set temperature 350 F, timer for 9 minutes. Press start to preheat the oven.
3. In a bowl, whisk together all ingredients until well combined.
4. Pour batter into the prepared ramekins and bake for 9 minutes.
5. Serve and enjoy.

Nutritional Value (Amount per Serving):
- Calories 121
- Fat 11 g
- Carbohydrates 19.9 g
- Sugar 15.3 g
- Protein 4.6 g
- Cholesterol 82 mg

Baked Spiced Apples

Preparation Time: 10 minutes
Cooking Time: 10 minutes
Serve: 6
Ingredients:
- 4 apples, sliced
- 1/2 cup erythritol
- 2 tbsp butter, melted
- 1 tsp apple pie spice

Directions:
1. Insert wire rack in rack position 6. Select bake, set temperature 350 F, timer for 10 minutes. Press start to preheat the oven.
2. Add apple slices in a large bowl and sprinkle with sweetener and apple pie spice. Add melted butter and toss to coat.
3. Transfer apple slices in a baking dish and air fry for 10 minutes.
4. Serve and enjoy.

Nutritional Value (Amount per Serving):
- Calories 73
- Fat 4.6 g
- Carbohydrates 8.2 g
- Sugar 5.4 g

- Protein 0 g
- Cholesterol 0 mg

Cheesecake

Preparation Time: 10minutes
Cooking Time: 10 minutes
Serve: 2
Ingredients:
- 2 eggs
- 16 oz cream cheese, softened
- 2 tbsp sour cream
- 1/2 tsp fresh lemon juice
- 1 tsp vanilla
- 3/4 cup Swerve

Directions:
1. Insert wire rack in rack position 6. Select air fry, set temperature 350 F, timer for 10 minutes. Press start to preheat the oven.
2. Add eggs, lemon juice, vanilla, and sweetener in a large bowl and beat until smooth.
3. Add cream cheese and sour cream and beat until fluffy.
4. Pour batter into the 2 4-inch springform pan and cook for 10 minutes.
5. Place in refrigerator overnight.
6. Serve and enjoy.

Nutritional Value (Amount per Serving):
- Calories 886
- Fat 86 g
- Carbohydrates 97.2 g
- Sugar 91.1 g
- Protein 23.1 g
- Cholesterol 418 mg

Delicious Cream Cheese Muffins

Preparation Time: 10 minutes
Cooking Time: 16 minutes
Serve: 10
Ingredients:
- 2 eggs
- 1 tsp ground cinnamon
- 1/2 tsp vanilla
- 1/2 cup erythritol
- 8 oz cream cheese

Directions:
1. Insert wire rack in rack position 6. Select bake, set temperature 325 F, timer for 16 minutes. Press start to preheat the oven.
2. In a bowl, mix together cream cheese, vanilla, erythritol, and eggs until soft.
3. Pour batter into the silicone muffin molds and sprinkle cinnamon on top.
4. Cook for 16 minutes.
5. Serve and enjoy.

Nutritional Value (Amount per Serving):
- Calories 90
- Fat 8.8 g

- Carbohydrates 13 g
- Sugar 12.2 g
- Protein 2.8 g
- Cholesterol 58 mg

Almond Cinnamon Muffins

Preparation Time: 10 minutes
Cooking Time: 12 minutes
Serve: 20
Ingredients:
- 1/2 cup almond flour
- 1/2 cup coconut oil
- 1/2 cup pumpkin puree
- 1 tbsp cinnamon
- 1 tsp baking powder
- 2 scoops vanilla protein powder
- 1/2 cup almond butter

Directions:
1. Insert wire rack in rack position 6. Select air fry, set temperature 325 F, timer for 12 minutes. Press start to preheat the oven.
2. In a large bowl, mix together all dry ingredients.
3. Add wet ingredients into the dry ingredients and mix until well combined.
4. Pour batter into the silicone muffin molds and cook for 12 minutes.
5. Serve and enjoy.

Nutritional Value (Amount per Serving):
- Calories 80
- Fat 7.1 g
- Carbohydrates 1 g
- Sugar 0.4 g
- Protein 3 g
- Cholesterol 0 mg

Almond Pumpkin Muffins

Preparation Time: 10 minutes
Cooking Time: 20 minutes
Serve: 10
Ingredients:
- 4 large eggs
- 2/3 cup erythritol
- 1 tsp vanilla
- 1/3 cup coconut oil, melted
- 1/2 cup almond flour
- 1/2 cup pumpkin puree
- 1 tbsp pumpkin pie spice
- 1 tbsp baking powder
- 1/2 cup coconut flour
- 1/2 tsp sea salt

Directions:
1. Insert wire rack in rack position 6. Select air fry, set temperature 325 F, timer for 20 minutes. Press start to preheat the oven.
2. In a large bowl, mix together coconut flour, pumpkin pie spice, baking powder, erythritol, almond flour, and sea salt.

3. Stir in eggs, vanilla, coconut oil, and pumpkin puree until well combined.
4. Pour batter into the silicone muffin molds and cook muffins for 20 minutes.
5. Serve and enjoy.

Nutritional Value (Amount per Serving):
- Calories 150
- Fat 13 g
- Carbohydrates 7 g
- Sugar 2 g
- Protein 5 g
- Cholesterol 75 mg

Healthy Blueberry Muffins

Preparation Time: 10 minutes
Cooking Time: 20 minutes
Serve: 12
Ingredients:
- 3 large eggs
- 2 1/2 cups almond flour
- 3/4 cup blueberries
- 1/2 tsp vanilla
- 1/3 cup almond milk
- 1/3 cup coconut oil, melted
- 1 1/2 tsp gluten-free baking powder
- 1/2 cup erythritol

Directions:
1. Insert wire rack in rack position 6. Select air fry, set temperature 325 F, timer for 20 minutes. Press start to preheat the oven.
2. In a large bowl, mix together almond flour, baking powder, erythritol.
3. Stir in the coconut oil, vanilla, eggs, and almond milk.
4. Add blueberries and fold well.
5. Pour batter into the silicone muffin molds and cook muffins for 20 minutes.
6. Serve and enjoy.

Nutritional Value (Amount per Serving):
- Calories 215
- Fat 19 g
- Carbohydrates 5 g
- Sugar 2 g
- Protein 7 g
- Cholesterol 45 mg

Choco Almond Butter Brownie

Preparation Time: 10 minutes
Cooking Time: 16 minutes
Serve: 4
Ingredients:
- 1 cup bananas, overripe
- 1/2 cup almond butter, melted
- 1 scoop protein powder
- 2 tbsp cocoa powder

Directions:
1. Insert wire rack in rack position 6. Select air fry, set temperature 350 F, timer for 16 minutes. Press start to preheat the oven.

2. Spray baking dish with cooking spray.
3. Add all ingredients into the blender and blend until smooth.
4. Pour batter into the prepared baking dish and cook brownie for 16 minutes.
5. Serve and enjoy.

Nutritional Value (Amount per Serving):
- Calories 80
- Fat 2.1 g
- Carbohydrates 11.4 g
- Protein 7 g
- Sugars 5 g
- Cholesterol 15 mg

Vanilla Coconut Pie

Preparation Time: 10 minutes
Cooking Time: 12 minutes
Serve: 6

Ingredients:
- 2 eggs
- 1 1/2 tsp vanilla
- 1/4 cup butter
- 1 1/2 cups coconut milk
- 1/2 cup coconut flour
- 1/2 cup Swerve
- 1 cup shredded coconut

Directions:
1. Spray a 6-inch baking dish with cooking spray and set aside.
2. Insert wire rack in rack position 6. Select bake, set temperature 350 F, timer for 12 minutes. Press start to preheat the oven.
3. Add all ingredients into the large bowl and mix until well combined.
4. Pour batter into the prepared dish and cook for 10-12 minutes.
5. Slice and serve.

Nutritional Value (Amount per Serving):
- Calories 317
- Fat 28.9 g
- Carbohydrates 32.3 g
- Sugar 23.1 g
- Protein 5.1 g
- Cholesterol 75 mg

Moist Chocolate Brownies

Preparation Time: 10 minutes
Cooking Time: 35 minutes
Serve: 9

Ingredients:
- 2 eggs
- 1 tsp baking powder
- 4 tbsp coconut oil, melted
- 2/3 cup unsweetened cocoa powder
- 2 avocados, mashed
- 2 tbsp swerve
- 1/3 cup chocolate chips, melted

Directions:

1. Insert wire rack in rack position 6. Select bake, set temperature 325 F, timer for 35 minutes. Press start to preheat the oven.
2. In a mixing bowl, mix together all dry ingredients.
3. In another bowl, mix together avocado and eggs until well combined.
4. Add dry mixture to the wet along with melted chocolate and oil. Mix well.
5. Pour batter in a baking dish and bake for 35 minutes.
6. Slice and serve.

Nutritional Value (Amount per Serving):
- Calories 207
- Fat 18 g
- Carbohydrates 11 g
- Sugar 3.6 g
- Protein 3.8 g
- Cholesterol 38 mg

Peanut Butter Choco Cookies

Preparation Time: 10 minutes
Cooking Time: 10 minutes
Serve: 24

Ingredients:
- 2 eggs
- 2 tbsp unsweetened cocoa powder
- 1 tsp baking soda
- 2 tsp vanilla
- 1 tbsp butter, melted
- 1 cup peanut butter
- 2/3 cup erythritol
- 1 1/3 cups almond flour

Directions:
1. Line baking sheet with parchment paper and set aside.
2. Insert wire rack in rack position 6. Select bake, set temperature 350 F, timer for 10 minutes. Press start to preheat the oven.
3. Add all ingredients into the mixing bowl and stir to combine.
4. Make 2-inch balls from mixture and place on a baking sheet and gently press down each ball with a fork.
5. Bake for 10 minutes.
6. Serve and enjoy.

Nutritional Value (Amount per Serving):
- Calories 110
- Fat 9 g
- Carbohydrates 9 g
- Sugar 1.3 g
- Protein 4.6 g
- Cholesterol 15 mg

Baked Chocolate Macaroon

Preparation Time: 10 minutes
Cooking Time: 20 minutes
Serve: 20

Ingredients:

- 2 eggs
- 1/3 cup coconut, shredded
- 1/3 cup erythritol
- 1/2 tsp baking powder
- 1 tsp vanilla
- 1/4 cup coconut oil
- 1/4 cup cocoa powder
- 3 tbsp coconut flour
- 1 cup almond flour
- Pinch of salt

Directions:
1. Line baking sheet with parchment paper and set aside.
2. Insert wire rack in rack position 6. Select bake, set temperature 375 F, timer for 30 minutes. Press start to preheat the oven.
3. Add all ingredients into the mixing bowl and mix until well combined.
4. Make small balls from mixture and place on a baking sheet.
5. Bake for 20 minutes.
6. Serve and enjoy.

Nutritional Value (Amount per Serving):
- Calories 80
- Fat 7 g
- Carbohydrates 6.5 g
- Sugar 0.5 g
- Protein 2.3 g
- Cholesterol 16 mg

Choco Almond Cookies

Preparation Time: 10 minutes
Cooking Time: 10 minutes
Serve: 20
Ingredients:
- 2 tbsp chocolate protein powder
- 3 tbsp ground chia
- 1 cup almond flour
- 1 cup sunflower seed butter

Directions:
1. Line baking sheet with parchment paper and set aside.
2. Insert wire rack in rack position 6. Select bake, set temperature 350 F, timer for 10 minutes. Press start to preheat the oven.
3. In a large bowl, add all ingredients and mix until combined.
4. Make small balls from mixture and place on a prepared baking sheet and press lightly down with the back of a fork.
5. Bake for 10 minutes.
6. Serve and enjoy.

Nutritional Value (Amount per Serving):
- Calories 90
- Fat 7 g
- Carbohydrates 4.1 g
- Sugar 0.1 g
- Protein 4.3 g
- Cholesterol 0 mg

Pecan Cookies

Preparation Time: 15 minutes
Cooking Time: 20 minutes
Serve: 15
Ingredients:
- 1 cup pecans
- 2/3 cup Swerve
- 1/3 cup coconut flour
- 1 cup almond flour
- 1/2 cup butter
- 1 tsp vanilla
- 2 tsp gelatin

Directions:
1. Line baking sheet with parchment paper and set aside.
2. Insert wire rack in rack position 6. Select bake, set temperature 350 F, timer for 20 minutes. Press start to preheat the oven.
3. Add butter, vanilla, gelatine, swerve, coconut flour, and almond flour into the food processor and process until crumbs form.
4. Add pecans and process until chopped.
5. Make 15 cookies from mixture and place onto a prepared baking sheet and bake for 20 minutes.
6. Serve and enjoy.

Nutritional Value (Amount per Serving):
- Calories 113
- Fat 11.7 g
- Carbohydrates 1.7 g
- Sugar 0.4 g
- Protein 1.2 g
- Cholesterol 15 mg

Delicious Pumpkin Cookies

Preparation Time: 10 minutes
Cooking Time: 25 minutes
Serve: 25
Ingredients:
- 1 egg
- 1 tsp vanilla
- 1/2 cup butter
- 1/2 cup pumpkin puree
- 2 cups almond flour
- 1 tsp liquid stevia
- 1/2 tsp pumpkin pie spice
- 1/2 tsp baking powder

Directions:
1. Line baking sheet with parchment paper and set aside.
2. Insert wire rack in rack position 6. Select bake, set temperature 320 F, timer for 25 minutes. Press start to preheat the oven.
3. In a large bowl, add all ingredients and mix until well combined.
4. Make 25 cookies from mixture and place onto a prepared baking sheet and bake for 25 minutes.
5. Serve and enjoy.

Nutritional Value (Amount per Serving):
- Calories 46
- Fat 4.6 g
- Carbohydrates 0.9 g
- Sugar 0.3 g
- Protein 0.7 g
- Cholesterol 15 mg

Cinnamon Pumpkin Pie

Preparation Time: 10 minutes
Cooking Time: 30 minutes
Serve: 4
Ingredients:
- 3 eggs
- 1/2 cup cream
- 1/2 cup almond milk
- 1/2 cup pumpkin puree
- 1/2 tsp cinnamon
- 1 tsp vanilla
- 1/4 cup Swerve

Directions:
1. Spray a square baking dish with cooking spray and set aside.
2. Insert wire rack in rack position 6. Select bake, set temperature 350 F, timer for 30 minutes. Press start to preheat the oven.
3. In a large bowl, add all ingredients and whisk until smooth.
4. Pour pie mixture into the prepared dish and bake for 30 minutes.
5. Remove from oven and set aside to cool completely.
6. Place into the refrigerator for 2 hours.
7. Sliced and serve.

Nutritional Value (Amount per Serving):
- Calories 86
- Fat 5.5 g
- Carbohydrates 4.4 g
- Sugar 2 g
- Protein 4.9 g
- Cholesterol 128 mg

Baked Apple Bars

Preparation Time: 10 minutes
Cooking Time: 45 minutes
Serve: 8
Ingredients:
- 1/4 cup dried apples
- 1/4 cup coconut butter, softened
- 1 cup pecans
- 1 cup of water
- 1 tsp vanilla
- 1 1/2 tsp baking powder
- 1 1/2 tsp cinnamon
- 1 tbsp ground flax seed
- 2 tbsp swerve

Directions:
1. Spray 8*8-inch square dish with cooking spray and set aside.

2. Insert wire rack in rack position 6. Select bake, set temperature 350 F, timer for 45 minutes. Press start to preheat the oven.
3. Add all ingredients into the blender and blend until smooth.
4. Pour blended mixture into the prepared dish and bake for 40-45 minutes,
5. Slice and serve.

Nutritional Value (Amount per Serving):
- Calories 160
- Fat 14.8 g
- Carbohydrates 6.3 g
- Sugar 1.8 g
- Protein 2.2 g
- Cholesterol 0 mg

Ricotta Cheese Cake

Preparation Time: 10 minutes
Cooking Time: 55 minutes
Serve: 8
Ingredients:
- 4 eggs
- 1 fresh lemon zest
- 2 tbsp stevia
- 18 oz ricotta
- 1 fresh lemon juice

Directions:
1. Spray cake pan with cooking spray and set aside.
2. Insert wire rack in rack position 6. Select bake, set temperature 350 F, timer for 55 minutes. Press start to preheat the oven.
3. In a large mixing bowl, beat ricotta until smooth.
4. Add egg one by one and whisk well.
5. Add lemon juice, lemon zest, and stevia and mix well.
6. Transfer mixture into the prepared cake pan and bake for 55 minutes.
7. Remove cake from oven and set aside to cool completely.
8. Place cake in the refrigerator for 2 hours.
9. Slices and serve.

Nutritional Value (Amount per Serving):
- Calories 120
- Fat 7.1 g
- Carbohydrates 5 g
- Sugar 1.1 g
- Protein 9.9 g
- Cholesterol 101 mg

Easy Pound Cake

Preparation Time: 10 minutes
Cooking Time: 35 minutes
Serve: 9
Ingredients:
- 5 eggs
- 1 tsp orange extract
- 1 cup Splenda

- 4 oz cream cheese, softened
- 1/2 cup butter, softened
- 1 tsp baking powder
- 7 oz almond flour
- 1 tsp vanilla

Directions:
1. Spray 9-inch cake pan with cooking spray and set aside.
2. Insert wire rack in rack position 6. Select bake, set temperature 350 F, timer for 35 minutes. Press start to preheat the oven.
3. Add all ingredients into the mixing bowl and mix until batter is fluffy.
4. Pour batter into the prepared pan and bake for 35 minutes.
5. Remove cake from oven and set aside to cool completely.
6. Slices and serve.

Nutritional Value (Amount per Serving):
- Calories 287
- Fat 27.2 g
- Carbohydrates 5.2 g
- Sugar 1 g
- Protein 8.5 g
- Cholesterol 132 mg

Moist Almond Choco Muffins

Preparation Time: 10 minutes
Cooking Time: 30 minutes
Serve: 8
Ingredients:
- 2 eggs
- 1/2 cup cocoa powder
- 1 cup ground almonds
- 1/2 cup cream
- 1 tsp vanilla extract
- 4 tbsp Swerve

Directions:
1. Line muffin pan with cupcake liners and set aside.
2. Insert wire rack in rack position 6. Select bake, set temperature 375 F, timer for 30 minutes. Press start to preheat the oven.
3. In a bowl, mix together all dry ingredients.
4. In another bowl, beat together eggs, vanilla, and cream.
5. Pour egg mixture into the dry ingredients and mix well to combine.
6. Pour batter into the prepared muffin pan and bake for 30 minutes.
7. Serve and enjoy.

Nutritional Value (Amount per Serving):
- Calories 86
- Fat 6.9 g
- Carbohydrates 9.7 g
- Protein 4 g
- Sugar 0.8 g
- Cholesterol 35mg

Fluffy Baked Donuts

Preparation Time: 10 minutes
Cooking Time: 15 minutes
Serve: 12
Ingredients:
- 2 eggs
- 1/2 cup buttermilk
- 1/4 cup vegetable oil
- 1 cup all-purpose flour
- 1/2 tsp vanilla
- 1 tsp baking powder
- 3/4 cup sugar
- 1/2 tsp salt

Directions:
1. Insert wire rack in rack position 6. Select bake, set temperature 350 F, timer for 15 minutes. Press start to preheat the oven.
2. Spray donut pan with cooking spray and set aside.
3. In a bowl, mix together oil, vanilla, baking powder, sugar, eggs, buttermilk, and salt until well combined. Stir in flour and mix until smooth.
4. Pour batter into the prepared donut pan and bake for 15 minutes.
5. Serve and enjoy.

Nutritional Value (Amount per Serving):
- Calories 140
- Fat 5.5 g
- Carbohydrates 21.2 g
- Sugar 13.1 g
- Protein 2.3 g
- Cholesterol 28 mg

Eggless Brownies

Preparation Time: 10 minutes
Cooking Time: 40 minutes
Serve: 8
Ingredients:
- 1/4 cup walnuts, chopped
- 1/2 cup butter, melted
- 1/3 cup cocoa powder
- 2 tsp baking powder
- 1 cup of sugar
- 1/2 cup chocolate chips
- 2 tsp vanilla
- 1 tbsp milk
- 3/4 cup yogurt
- 1 cup all-purpose flour
- 1/4 tsp salt

Directions:
1. Spray an 8*8-inch baking dish with cooking spray.
2. Insert wire rack in rack position 6. Select bake, set temperature 350 F, timer for 40 minutes. Press start to preheat the oven.
3. In a large mixing bowl, sift flour, cocoa powder, baking powder, and salt. Mix well and set aside.

4.	In another bowl, add butter, vanilla, milk, and yogurt and whisk until well combined.
5.	Add flour mixture into the butter mixture and mix until just combined. Fold in walnuts and chocolate chips.
6.	Pour batter into the prepared baking dish and bake for 40 minutes.
7.	Slice and serve.

Nutritional Value (Amount per Serving):
- Calories 362
- Fat 17.9 g
- Carbohydrates 48 g
- Sugar 32.4 g
- Protein 5.5 g
- Cholesterol 34 mg

Healthy Banana Brownies

Preparation Time: 10 minutes
Cooking Time: 20 minutes
Serve: 12

Ingredients:
- 1 egg
- 2 medium bananas, mashed
- 4 oz white chocolate
- 1 cup all-purpose flour
- 1 tsp vanilla
- 1/2 cup sugar
- 1/4 cup butter
- 1/4 tsp salt

Directions:
1.	Insert wire rack in rack position 6. Select bake, set temperature 350 F, timer for 20 minutes. Press start to preheat the oven.
2.	Add white chocolate and butter in microwave-safe bowl and microwave for 30 seconds. Stir until melted.
3.	Stir in sugar. Add mashed bananas, eggs, vanilla, and salt and mix until combined.
4.	Add flour and stir to combine.
5.	Pour batter into the square baking dish and bake for 20 minutes.
6.	Serve and enjoy.

Nutritional Value (Amount per Serving):
- Calories 178
- Fat 7.4 g
- Carbohydrates 26.4 g
- Sugar 16.4 g
- Protein 2.3 g
- Cholesterol 26 mg

Simple Choco Cookies

Preparation Time: 10 minutes
Cooking Time: 8 minutes
Serve: 30

Ingredients:
- 3 egg whites
- 1 3/4 cup confectioner sugar
- 1 1/2 tsp vanilla extract
- 3/4 cup cocoa powder, unsweetened

Directions:
1.	Spray a baking sheet with cooking spray and set aside.
2.	Insert wire rack in rack position 6. Select bake, set temperature 350 F, timer for 8 minutes. Press start to preheat the oven.
3.	In a mixing bowl, whip egg whites until fluffy soft peaks. Slowly add in cocoa, sugar, and vanilla.
4.	Drop teaspoonful onto a baking sheet into 30 small cookies.
5.	Bake for 8 minutes.
6.	Serve and enjoy.

Nutritional Value (Amount per Serving):
- Calories 132
- Fat 1.1 g
- Carbohydrates 30.9 g
- Sugar 0.3 g
- Protein 2.8 g
- Cholesterol 0 mg

Simple Butter Cake

Preparation Time: 10 minutes
Cooking Time: 30 minutes
Serve: 8

Ingredients:
- 1 egg, beaten
- 3/4 cup sugar
- 1/2 cup butter, softened
- 1 cup all-purpose flour
- 1/2 tsp vanilla

Directions:
1.	Insert wire rack in rack position 6. Select bake, set temperature 350 F, timer for 30 minutes. Press start to preheat the oven.
2.	In a mixing bowl, mix together sugar and butter.
3.	Add egg, flour, and vanilla and mix until combined.
4.	Pour batter into an 8*8-inch square baking pan and bake for 30 minutes.
5.	Slice and serve.

Nutritional Value (Amount per Serving):
- Calories 211
- Fat 10.9 g
- Carbohydrates 27.4 g
- Sugar 16.8 g
- Protein 2.2 g
- Cholesterol 45 mg

Chocolate Chip Cookies

Preparation Time: 10 minutes
Cooking Time: 10 minutes
Serve: 30

Ingredients:
- 1 egg
- 12 oz chocolate chips
- 1 tsp vanilla
- 1 cup butter, softened

- 2 cups self-rising flour
- 1/2 cup brown sugar
- 2/3 cup sugar

Directions:
1. Spray cookie sheet with cooking spray and set aside.
2. Insert wire rack in rack position 6. Select bake, set temperature 375 F, timer for 10 minutes. Press start to preheat the oven.
3. Add butter, vanilla, and egg in a large mixing bowl and beat until combined.
4. Add brown sugar and sugar and beat until creamy.
5. Add flour and mix until just combined. Fold in chocolate chips.
6. Scoop out cookie dough balls onto a prepared cookie sheet.
7. Bake for 10 minutes.
8. Serve and enjoy.

Nutritional Value (Amount per Serving):
- Calories 174
- Fat 9.7 g
- Carbohydrates 19.9 g
- Sugar 12.7 g
- Protein 2 g
- Cholesterol 24 mg

Almond Butter Brownies

Preparation Time: 10 minutes
Cooking Time: 20 minutes
Serve: 4

Ingredients:
- 1 scoop protein powder
- 2 tbsp cocoa powder
- 1/2 cup almond butter, melted
- 1 cup bananas, overripe

Directions:
1. Spray brownie pan with cooking spray.
2. Insert wire rack in rack position 6. Select bake, set temperature 350 F, timer for 20 minutes. Press start to preheat the oven.
3. Add all ingredients into the blender and blend until smooth.
4. Pour batter into the prepared pan and bake for 20 minutes.
5. Serve and enjoy.

Nutritional Value (Amount per Serving):
- Calories 82
- Fat 2.1 g
- Carbohydrates 11.4 g
- Protein 6.9 g
- Sugars 5 g
- Cholesterol 16 mg

Almond Madeleine's

Preparation Time: 10 minutes
Cooking Time: 8 minutes
Serve: 4

Ingredients:

- 4 tbsp coconut oil
- 2 cups almond flour
- 1 tsp vanilla extract
- 4 tbsp maple syrup

Directions:
1. Insert wire rack in rack position 6. Select bake, set temperature 350 F, timer for 8 minutes. Press start to preheat the oven.
2. In a mixing bowl, combine together all ingredients until formed soft dough.
3. Add the dough in Madeline mold and bake for 8 minutes.
4. Serve and enjoy.

Nutritional Value (Amount per Serving):
- Calories 508
- Fat 40.2 g
- Carbohydrates 25.6 g
- Protein 12 g
- Sugars 12 g
- Cholesterol 0 mg

Oatmeal Cookies

Preparation Time: 10 minutes
Cooking Time: 10 minutes
Serve: 20

Ingredients:
- 3/4 cup almonds, sliced
- 1/2 cup grass-fed butter, melted
- 1 egg
- 1 1/2 cups rolled oats
- 1/2 cup Truvia
- 1 tsp vanilla

Directions:
1. Line baking sheet with parchment paper.
2. Insert wire rack in rack position 6. Select bake, set temperature 350 F, timer for 10 minutes. Press start to preheat the oven.
3. In a bowl, whisk together egg, Truvia, vanilla, and butter until smooth.
4. Add almonds and oatmeal and mix well.
5. Drop mixture onto a prepared baking sheet and using spatula flatten each cookie.
6. Bake for 10 minutes.
7. Serve and enjoy.

Nutritional Value (Amount per Serving):
- Calories 67
- Fat 4.6 g
- Carbohydrates 6.8 g
- Protein 1.8 g
- Sugars 2.1 g
- Cholesterol 14 mg

Amaretti Biscuits

Preparation Time: 10 minutes
Cooking Time: 15 minutes
Serve: 20

Ingredients:
- 2 egg whites
- 1 1/2 cups almond flour

- 1 tsp almond extract
- 3 tbsp Swerve

Directions:

1. Line baking sheet with parchment paper.
2. Insert wire rack in rack position 6. Select bake, set temperature 325 F, timer for 15 minutes. Press start to preheat the oven.
3. In a bowl, add egg whites and beat until stiff peaks form.
4. Combine swerve and almond flour together and add in beaten eggs. Add extract and mix well.
5. Spoon out batter onto prepared baking sheet and shape round biscuits.
6. Bake for 15 minutes.
7. Serve and enjoy.

Nutritional Value (Amount per Serving):

- Calories 53
- Fat 4 g
- Carbohydrates 2.2 g
- Protein 2.2 g
- Sugars 0.1g
- Cholesterol 0 mg

Apple Almond Cake

Preparation Time: 10 minutes
Cooking Time: 40 minutes
Serve: 6

Ingredients:

- 3 organic eggs
- 4 tbsp almonds, sliced
- 1/4 cup no sugar fruit butter
- 4 tbsp grass-fed butter, melted
- 1/2 cup Splenda
- 1 1/2 tsp baking powder
- 1/4 cup all-purpose flour
- 1 cup almond flour
- Pinch of salt

Directions:

1. Spray round cake pan with cooking spray and set aside.
2. Insert wire rack in rack position 6. Select bake, set temperature 350 F, timer for 20 minutes. Press start to preheat the oven.
3. In a small bowl, combine together almond flour, salt, baking powder, and flour.
4. In another bowl, add eggs and beat until light yellow.
5. Add Splenda, sugar fruit butter, and melted butter and blend until smooth.
6. Add almond flour mixture and blend until well combined.
7. Pour batter into the prepared cake pan and spread evenly.
8. Sprinkle sliced almonds over the top of cake batter.
9. Bake for 20 minutes.
10. Serve and enjoy.

Nutritional Value (Amount per Serving):

- Calories 320

- Fat 16.8 g
- Carbohydrates 30.6 g
- Protein 8.2 g
- Sugars 20.5 g
- Cholesterol 92 mg

Baked Almond Donuts

Preparation Time: 10 minutes
Cooking Time: 15 minutes
Serve: 8

Ingredients:

- 2 eggs
- 1 1/2 tsp vanilla extract
- 3 tbsp maple syrup
- 1 cup almond flour
- 1/4 tsp baking soda

Directions:

1. Spray donut pan with cooking spray and set aside.
2. Insert wire rack in rack position 6. Select bake, set temperature 320 F, timer for 15 minutes. Press start to preheat the oven.
3. In a large bowl, add all ingredients and mix well until smooth.
4. Pour batter into the greased donut pan and bake for 15 minutes.
5. Serve and enjoy.

Nutritional Value (Amount per Serving):

- Calories 122
- Fat 7.8 g
- Carbohydrates 8.2 g
- Protein 4.4 g
- Sugars 4.6 g
- Cholesterol 41 mg

Vanilla Butter Cake

Preparation Time: 10 minutes
Cooking Time: 30 minutes
Serve: 8

Ingredients:

- 1 egg, beaten
- 1/2 cup butter, softened
- 1 cup all-purpose flour
- 1/2 tsp vanilla extract
- 3/4 cup sugar

Directions:

1. Insert wire rack in rack position 6. Select bake, set temperature 350 F, timer for 30 minutes. Press start to preheat the oven.
2. In a mixing bowl, mix together sugar and butter.
3. Add egg, flour, and vanilla and mix until combined.
4. Pour batter into an 8*8-inch square baking pan and bake for 30 minutes.
5. Slice and serve.

Nutritional Value (Amount per Serving):

- Calories 211
- Fat 10.9 g

- Carbohydrates 27.4 g
- Sugar 16.8 g
- Protein 2.2 g
- Cholesterol 45 mg

Sweet Cinnamon Cookies

Preparation Time: 10 minutes
Cooking Time: 8 minutes
Serve: 35
Ingredients:
- 1 large egg
- 1 tsp vanilla
- 1/2 cup powdered sugar
- 1/2 cup brown sugar
- 1/2 cup oil
- 1/2 cup butter, softened
- 2 1/4 cups flour
- 1/4 tsp salt
- 1/2 tsp cream of tarter
- 1/2 tsp baking soda
- 1/2 tbsp ground cinnamon

Directions:
1. Insert wire rack in rack position 6. Select bake, set temperature 350 F, timer for 8 minutes. Press start to preheat the oven.
2. In mixing bowl, beat together sugar, butter, and oil until smooth and creamy.
3. Add vanilla and egg and beat until combine.
4. Sift together flour, cinnamon, salt, cream of tartar and baking soda. Add slowly in the egg mixture and mix well until combine.
5. Using cookie scoop drop dough into a baking tray and bake for 8 minutes.
6. Serve and enjoy.

Nutritional Value (Amount per Serving):
- Calories 95
- Fat 5.8 g
- Carbohydrates 9.7 g
- Protein 1.0 g
- Sugar 3.6 g
- Cholesterol 12 mg

Vanilla Peanut Butter Cookies

Preparation Time: 10 minutes
Cooking Time: 10 minutes
Serve: 60
Ingredients:
- 2 large eggs
- 2 tsp baking soda
- 1/2 tsp salt
- 1 cup peanut butter
- 1 cup brown sugar
- 1 cup of sugar
- 3 cups flour
- 1 cup vegetable shortening
- 1 1/2 tsp vanilla extract

Directions:

1. Insert wire rack in rack position 6. Select bake, set temperature 350 F, timer for 10 minutes. Press start to preheat the oven.
2. In mixing bowl, beat together shortening, brown sugar and sugar until creamy.
3. Add eggs, flour, vanilla extract, baking soda, salt, and peanut butter. Mix well until combine.
4. Make 1-inch balls from dough then roll balls in sugar and place onto a baking tray. Using the back of the spoon slightly flatten balls.
5. Bake for 10 minutes.
6. Serve and enjoy.

Nutritional Value (Amount per Serving):
- Calories 72
- Fat 2.4 g
- Carbohydrates 11.3 g
- Protein 1.9 g
- Sugar 6.1 g
- Cholesterol 6 mg

Easy Brown Sugar Cookies

Preparation Time: 10 minutes
Cooking Time: 8 minutes
Serve: 40
Ingredients:
- 1 large egg
- 1 cup sour milk
- 1 tsp baking soda
- 1/2 cup butter, softened
- 1 1/2 cup brown sugar
- 2 1/2 cups flour
- 1/4 tsp salt
- 1 tsp baking powder

Directions:
1. Insert wire rack in rack position 6. Select bake, set temperature 375 F, timer for 30 minutes. Press start to preheat the oven.
2. In mixing bowl, beat together butter, sugar, and egg until creamy.
3. Sift together flour, baking powder, and salt. Add baking soda into the milk and stir well.
4. Add milk and dry ingredients alternately into the egg mixture. Mix well.
5. Drop teaspoonfuls batter onto a baking tray and bake for 8 minutes.
6. Serve and enjoy.

Nutritional Value (Amount per Serving):
- Calories 71
- Fat 2.5 g
- Carbohydrates 11.4 g
- Protein 1.0 g
- Sugar 5.3 g
- Cholesterol 11 mg

Healthy Banana Cake

Preparation Time: 10 minutes
Cooking Time: 40 minutes
Serve: 8
Ingredients:

- 2 large eggs, beaten
- 1 1/2 cup sugar, granulated
- 1 tsp vanilla extract
- 1/2 cup butter
- 1 cup milk
- 2 cups all-purpose flour
- 2 bananas, mashed
- 1 tsp baking soda
- 1 tsp baking powder

Directions:

1.   Grease baking dish with butter and set aside.
2.   Insert wire rack in rack position 6. Select bake, set temperature 350 F, timer for 40 minutes. Press start to preheat the oven.
3.   In a mixing bowl, beat together sugar and butter until creamy. Add beaten eggs and mix well.
4.   Add milk, vanilla extract, baking soda, baking powder, flour, and mashed bananas into the mixture and beat for 2 minutes. Mix well.
5.   Pour batter into the prepared baking dish and bake for 40 minutes.
6.   Serve and enjoy.

Nutritional Value (Amount per Serving):

- Calories 334
- Fat 11.0 g
- Carbohydrates 56.0 g
- Protein 5.0 g
- Sugar 34.2 g
- Cholesterol 64 mg

Chocolate Chip Cake

Preparation Time: 10 minutes
Cooking Time: 45 minutes
Serve: 10

Ingredients:

- 2 eggs
- 1 3/4 cups flour
- 1 cup vegetable shortening
- 2 tbsp cocoa powder, unsweetened
- 1 tsp salt
- 1 tsp baking soda
- 3/4 cup chocolate chips
- 1 cup boiling water
- 1 tsp vanilla extract
- 1 cup of sugar

Directions:

1.   Grease baking dish with butter and set aside.
2.   Insert wire rack in rack position 6. Select bake, set temperature 350 F, timer for 45 minutes. Press start to preheat the oven.
3.   In mixing bowl, combine together flour, cocoa powder, salt, and baking soda. Set aside.
4.   In another bowl, beat together sugar and shortening until creamy.
5.   Add egg and vanilla and beat for 2 minutes.
6.   Add flour mixture into the shortening mixture and fold well.

7.   Pour boiling water into the batter and mix until combine.
8.   Add chocolate chips into the batter and fold well.
9.   Pour batter into the prepared baking dish and bake for 45 minutes.
10.   Slices and serve.

Nutritional Value (Amount per Serving):

- Calories 238
- Fat 5.0 g
- Carbohydrates 44.9 g
- Protein 4.5 g
- Sugar 26.7 g
- Cholesterol 36 mg

Easy Oatmeal Cake

Preparation Time: 10 minutes
Cooking Time: 40 minutes
Serve: 8

Ingredients:

- 2 large eggs
- 1 cup powdered sugar
- 1 cup brown sugar
- 1/2 cup margarine
- 1 1/2 cups flour
- 1 tsp vanilla extract
- 1 1/2 tsp baking soda
- 1 tsp ground cinnamon
- 1 1/2 cups warm water
- 1 cup quick oats
- 1 tsp salt

Directions:

1.   Grease baking dish with butter and set aside.
2.   Insert wire rack in rack position 6. Select bake, set temperature 350 F, timer for 40 minutes. Press start to preheat the oven.
3.   Mix together quick oats and warm water. Set aside.
4.   In a mixing bowl, beat together sugar, brown sugar and margarine until creamy.
5.   Add eggs, salt, cinnamon, baking soda, vanilla, and flour mix until combine.
6.   Add oats and water mixture into the batter and fold well.
7.   Pour batter into the prepared baking dish and bake for 40 minutes.
8.   Slice and serve.

Nutritional Value (Amount per Serving):

- Calories 373
- Fat 13.5 g
- Carbohydrates 58.1 g
- Protein 5.5 g
- Sugar 32.6 g
- Cholesterol 47 mg

Delicious Amish Cake

Preparation Time: 10 minutes
Cooking Time: 25 minutes

Serve: 6

Ingredients:

- 1 large egg
- 1/2 tsp salt
- 1 1/4 cups flour
- 3 tbsp butter, melted
- 1/2 cup milk
- 2 tsp baking powder
- 1/2 cup sugar
- For nut topping:
- 1 tbsp butter
- 4 tbsp nuts, chopped
- 4 tbsp brown sugar
- 2 tsp ground cinnamon
- 1 tbsp flour

Directions:

1. Grease baking dish with butter and set aside.
2. Insert wire rack in rack position 6. Select bake, set temperature 375 F, timer for 25 minutes. Press start to preheat the oven.
3. For the topping: In a small bowl, mix together cinnamon, flour, nuts, and brown sugar. Add butter and mix until coarse crumbs. Set aside.
4. In a large bowl, mix together flour, salt, baking powder, and sugar.
5. In a separate bowl whisk together melted butter, egg, and milk. Pour into the flour mixture and stir well until combine.
6. Pour batter into the prepared baking dish.
7. Sprinkle nut topping on top of cake batter and bake for 25 minutes.
8. Slice and serve.

Nutritional Value (Amount per Serving):

- Calories 312
- Fat 12.2 g
- Carbohydrates 47.3 g
- Protein 5.7 g
- Sugar 23.8 g
- Cholesterol 53 mg

CHAPTER 10: 30-DAY MEAL PLAN

Day 1
Breakfast-Basil Tomato Frittata
Lunch-Crispy Chicken Thighs
Dinner-Basil Pepper Beef

Day 2
Breakfast-Italian Breakfast Frittata
Lunch-Classic Greek Chicken
Dinner-Italian Beef Roast

Day 3
Breakfast-Healthy Baked Omelet
Lunch-Crispy & Tasty Chicken Breast
Dinner-Meatballs

Day 4
Breakfast-Easy Egg Casserole
Lunch-Broccoli Bacon Ranch Chicken
Dinner-Mediterranean Beef

Day 5
Breakfast-Flavor Packed Breakfast Casserole
Lunch-Jerk Chicken Legs
Dinner-Balsamic Braised Beef

Day 6
Breakfast-Vegetable Sausage Egg Bake
Lunch-Creamy Cheese Chicken
Dinner-Baked Lamb Patties

Day 7
Breakfast-Ham Egg Brunch Bake
Lunch-Protein Packed Baked Chicken Breasts
Dinner-Meatballs

Day 8
Breakfast-Cheese Broccoli Bake
Lunch-Flavors Balsamic Chicken
Dinner-Olive Feta Beef

Day 9
Breakfast-Cheese Ham Omelet
Lunch-Simple & Delicious Chicken Thighs
Dinner-Olives Artichokes Beef

Day 10
Breakfast-Sweet Potato Frittata
Lunch-Tender & Flaky Chili Lime Salmon
Dinner-Baked Beef Casserole

Day 11
Breakfast-Squash Oat Muffins
Lunch-Sweet & Spicy Salmon
Dinner-Roasted Sirloin Steak

Day 12
Breakfast-Hash brown Casserole

Lunch-Maple Dijon Salmon
Dinner-Garlic Rosemary Pork Chops

Day 13
Breakfast-Mexican Breakfast Frittata
Lunch-Lemon Butter Cod
Dinner-Slow Cook Pork with Couscous

Day 14
Breakfast-Perfect Brunch Baked Eggs
Lunch-Spicy Tilapia Fish Fillets
Dinner-Artichoke Olive Pork Chops

Day 15
Breakfast-Green Chile Cheese Egg Casserole
Lunch-Buttery Baked Scallops
Dinner-Spicy Shredded Pork

Day 16
Breakfast-Kale Zucchini Bake
Lunch-Baked Basa Fish Fillets
Dinner-Pork Stew

Day 17
Breakfast-Cheesy Breakfast Casserole
Lunch-Easy Lemon Pepper Tilapia
Dinner-Italian Pork Chops

Day 18
Breakfast-Easy Hash Brown Breakfast Bake
Lunch-Garlicky Shrimp
Dinner-Cheese Stuff Pork Chops

Day 19
Breakfast-Mexican Chiles Breakfast Bake
Lunch-Crispy & Cheesy Parmesan Chicken
Dinner-Herb Pork Roast

Day 20
Breakfast-Delicious Amish Baked Oatmeal
Lunch-Baked Chicken & Potatoes
Dinner-Perfect Steak

Day 21
Breakfast-Chewy Breakfast Brownies
Lunch-Delicious Honey Mustard Sauce Chicken
Dinner-Meatballs

Day 22
Breakfast-Peach Banana Baked Oatmeal
Lunch-BBQ Chicken Wings
Dinner-Simple Beef Roast

Day 23
Breakfast-Healthy Poppy seed Baked Oatmeal
Lunch-Perfect Baked Chicken Breasts
Dinner-Broccoli & Beef

Day 24
Breakfast-Healthy Berry Baked Oatmeal
Lunch-Perfect Baked Shrimp
Dinner-Simple Sirloin Steak
Day 25
Breakfast-Apple Oatmeal Bars
Lunch-Cheesy Scallop Gratin
Dinner-Flavors Kebab
Day 26
Breakfast-Walnut Banana Bread
Lunch-Dill Mustard Fish Fillets
Dinner-Meatballs
Day 27
Breakfast-Cinnamon Zucchini Bread

Lunch-Baked Crab Cakes
Dinner-Spiced Steak
Day 28
Breakfast-Italian Breakfast Bread
Lunch-Healthy Salmon Patties
Dinner-Burger Patties
Day 29
Breakfast-Coconut Zucchini Bread
Lunch-Baked Catfish Fillets
Dinner- Simple Sirloin Steak
Day 30
Breakfast-Protein Banana Bread
Lunch-Tasty Parmesan Baked Shrimp
Dinner- Italian Pork Chops

APPENDIX : RECIPES INDEX

Chili Chickpeas 77
Chinese Chicken Wings 45
Choco Almond Butter Brownie 126
Choco Almond Cookies 128
Choco Lava Cake 125
Chocolate Chip Cake 135
Chocolate Chip Cookies 131
Cinnamon Pumpkin Pie 129
Cinnamon Zucchini Bread 19
Classic Greek Chicken 30
Coconut Zucchini Bread 20
Coconut Zucchini Muffins 25
Cod Sticks 81
Cod with Potatoes & Tomatoes 96
Cod with Vegetables 97
Country Style Baked Pork Chops 68
Crab Croquettes 83
Crabmeat Casserole 94
Cream Cheese Muffins 29
Creamy & Cheesy Brussels Sprout 106
Creamy & Cheesy Cauliflower Casserole 110
Creamy Cheese Chicken 31
Creamy Eggplant Gratin 108
Creamy Pork Chops 70
Creamy Spinach 112
Creamy Spinach Mushroom Quiche 26
Creamy Spinach Quiche 24
Creole Pork Chops 59
Creole Pork Chops 70
Crispy & Cheesy Parmesan Chicken 33
Crispy & Tasty Chicken Breast 30
Crispy Broccoli Florets 82
Crispy Chicken Thighs 30
Crispy Chicken Wings 86
Crispy Crusted Pork Chops 65
Crispy Crusted Salmon Patties 92
Crispy Potato Wedges 72
Crispy Tofu 76
Crustleass Cheese Egg Quiche 24
Cuban Pork 61

D

Dehydrated Avocado Slices 118
Dehydrated Banana Slices 122
Dehydrated Beet Slices 119
Dehydrated Bell Peppers 124
Dehydrated Broccoli Florets 119
Dehydrated Carrot Slices 120
Dehydrated Cauliflower Popcorn 124
Dehydrated Chickpeas 122
Dehydrated Cinnamon Apple Slices 121
Dehydrated Cinnamon Zucchini Slices 121
Dehydrated Cucumber Chips 119
Dehydrated Dragon Fruit Slices 120
Dehydrated Eggplant Slices 118

Dehydrated Green Apple Slices 117
Dehydrated Green Beans 120
Dehydrated Kiwi Slices 121
Dehydrated Lemon Slices 123
Dehydrated Mango Slices 117
Dehydrated Mushroom Chips 123
Dehydrated Okra 122
Dehydrated Orange Slices 121
Dehydrated Parmesan Zucchini Chips 120
Dehydrated Parsnips Slices 120
Dehydrated Pear Slices 123
Dehydrated Pineapple Chunks 122
Dehydrated Pineapple Slices 117
Dehydrated Raspberries 117
Dehydrated Snap Peas 123
Dehydrated Spicy Eggplant Slices 121
Dehydrated Strawberry Slices 118
Dehydrated Summer Squash Chips 122
Dehydrated Sweet Potato Slices 119
Dehydrated Tomato Slices 119
Dehydrated Zucchini Chips 118
Dehydrated Zucchini Chips 119
Delicious Amish Baked Oatmeal 17
Delicious Amish Cake 135
Delicious Burger Patties 70
Delicious Cream Cheese Muffins 125
Delicious Crisp Okra 78
Delicious Curried Chicken 34
Delicious Dijon Salmon 93
Delicious Herb Sardines 97
Delicious Honey Mustard Sauce Chicken 33
Delicious Mexican Chicken Lasagna 40
Delicious Pork Carnitas 62
Delicious Pork Patties 67
Delicious Pumpkin Cookies 128
Delicious Seafood Bake 93
Delicious Shrimp Scampi 95
Delicious Spicy Shrimp 101
Delicious Vegetable Casserole 104
Delicious Zucchini Bake 105
Dijon Herb Salmon 98
Dijon Zucchini Gratin 28
Dill Chili Salmon 95
Dill Mustard Fish Fillets 90

E

Easy Baked Zucchini 107
Easy Brown Sugar Cookies 134
Easy Buffalo Chicken Dip 72
Easy Cheese Pie 29
Easy Egg Casserole 12
Easy Hash Brown Breakfast Bake 17
Easy Kale Muffins 21
Easy Lemon Pepper Tilapia 90
Easy Oatmeal Cake 135

Printed in the USA
CPSIA information can be obtained
at www.ICGtesting.com
LVHW070736241223
767241LV00008B/825